DANGEROUS SPIRIT OF LIBERTY

Dangerous Spirit of Liberty

The Politics of Slaves and Rebels in Early America and the West Indies, 1688–1748

Justin James Pope

University of Missouri Press
Columbia

University of Missouri Press, Columbia, Missouri 65211
Printed and bound in the United States of America
 First printing, 2025.

Library of Congress Cataloging-in-Publication Data

Names: Pope, Justin, 1977- author.
Title: Dangerous spirit of liberty : the politics of slaves and rebels in early America and the West Indies, 1688-1748 / by Justin Pope.
Identifiers: LCCN 2024028322 (print) | LCCN 2024028323 (ebook) | ISBN 9780826223197 (hardcover) | ISBN 9780826275080 (ebook)
Subjects: LCSH: Slave rebellions--Atlantic Ocean Region--History--18th century. | Enslaved persons--Political activity--Atlantic Ocean Region--History--18th century. | Human rights--Atlantic Ocean Region--History--18th century. | Antislavery movements--Atlantic Ocean Region--History--18th century.
Classification: LCC HT1031 .P67 2024 (print) | LCC HT1031 (ebook) | DDC
326.097/09033--dc23/eng/20240802
LC record available at https://lccn.loc.gov/2024028322
LC ebook record available at https://lccn.loc.gov/2024028323

∞™ This paper meets the requirements of the
American National Standard for Permanence of Paper
for Printed Library Materials, Z39.48, 1984.

Typeface: Jenson and Celestia Antiqua

For Alanna Krolikowski and Theodore Pope

With gratitude and great hope for the future

CONTENTS

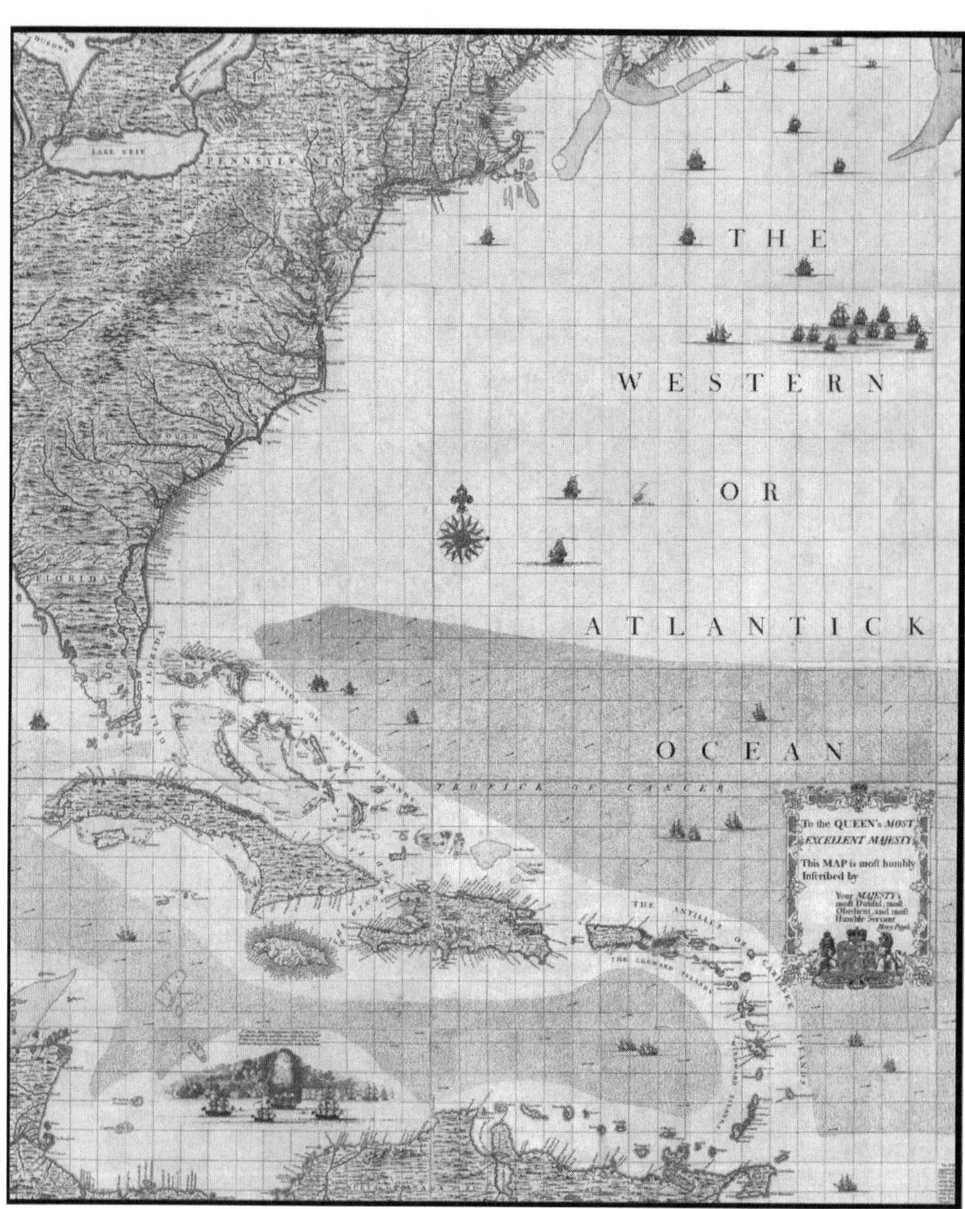

Figure 1. Henry Popple, *A Map of the British Empire in America with the French and Spanish Settlements Adjacent Thereto* (London, 1733). Courtesy David Rumsey Map Collection, David Rumsey Map Center, Stanford Libraries, Stanford University, Stanford, California

DANGEROUS SPIRIT OF LIBERTY

INTRODUCTION

The Dance

3 October 1736
Antigua, British West Indies

> "Se wo were fi na wosankofa a yenkyi." [It is not wrong to go back to that which you have forgotten.]
>
> —Twi proverb

THE PEOPLE WHO FEARED THE man called Court said he was "ambitious" and "very proud." They said he was dangerous.[1]

Court's ambition was on full display after the cane harvest in 1736. He announced a great dance and procession, and his people walked long distances across the British island of Antigua to see it. Even some of the baccara, the whites, joined the nearly two thousand Black people who gathered to watch the slave claim his throne.[2]

Court dressed like the Big Men he remembered from his childhood. He assembled his "royal habit" in his room in his master's house. He put aside his Englishman's coat. He wrapped cloth around his torso and between his legs and back around his middle, throwing the end over his left shoulder.[3] He kept his right shoulder bare.[4] He took up his cap. It was "made of green silk, embroidered with Gold," a nightcap worn by rich baccara to cover their heads at bedtime. Court pushed three feathers into the top and put it on. The men who feared him would remember the cap. It was "proper to the kings of his country," they said.[5]

Court took his seat in the pasture, in "royal habit," beneath a canopy painted with a pigeon, and the leading enslaved men of Antigua took their places behind him.[6] That was his greatest achievement—to bring the leaders of the many factions of slaves to sit behind him for all to see.

Tomboy was the most powerful. He was Court's rival, a man born into slavery in the Americas, a skilled carpenter whose work was so fine, his apprentices so admired, that baccara masters pleaded with him to train their slaves in his craft.[7] People said Tomboy had earned enough money to buy his freedom whenever he wished.

Gift held Court's cutlass. He was an enslaved carpenter owned by John Hawe. On that October day, Gift painted his face white like an Eguafo man preparing to meet his ancestors.[8] And there were others: Hercules, Quamina, Quashi, men who could bring followers with them. They all sat behind Court before the crowd.

He rose at the call of drums—barefoot, stepping to the beat and a clanging cowbell.[9] Court slid his left arm through the straps of a wicker shield, called an *ikyem*. He grasped a spear with his right.[10]

Court leapt toward the crowd, stabbing the air, his feet shuffling across the dry earth.

"Takyi!" the Big Men shouted.[11]

That was his second achievement—to bring the crowd of two thousand to join him in the pasture. They stood assembled in the shape of a crescent, or the horns of a bull, with Court and his canopy in the center.[12]

The baccara enslaved most of the people in the crowd. The British had created a brutal diversity, taking men, women, and children from at least sixty-seven West African ports, along a coastline that stretched more than four thousand miles, and carrying them across the western ocean to Antigua.[13] The survivors of the passage spoke at least twenty languages and perhaps hundreds more (we cannot be certain).[14] Most were strangers to British America and to each other. They were not one people but many.

The drums beat the rhythm. The bell banged in time.

Court had brought the Creoles together too: Black men and women who had never seen Africa. They were born into slavery, as would be their children and their children's children. The baccara had bought and sold them as well, so that some few had been born as far away as New England or Brazil. "[There are] as many nations . . . among them, as there are landscapes, cities and places in America," wrote Danish planter J. L. Carstens in 1740.[15]

They had come to see something mysterious—incredible even: an American slave elevated through the rites of Africa. Court had promised a ceremony and called them to him . . . and they had come.

"Takyi!" they chanted.

The drums beat the rhythm. The bell banged in time.

Court leapt forward and back, his spear rent the air, striking his invisible foe.

They lived at a time of growing unrest. It had been a little over two years since sailors had brought word of a rebellion to the north.[16] Enslaved Africans had captured the Danish colony of St. John, fighting off armies of Dutch and English and French. The rebels had beaten back the baccara for nine months. St. John had become an African country, a Black country, for a time.

"Takyi!" the people shouted.

The drums beat the rhythm. The bell banged in time.

Court rocked back suddenly and raised his shield in "defensive motions," as if fending off blows from an unseen enemy.[17]

Those were days of great suffering for the slaves of the Leeward Islands. In 1736, there was too little rain and not enough to drink. The cane withered in the sun. The poorest baccara wandered St. John's Town with empty bowls begging for water.[18] That July, the governor declared a day of fasting and prayer to "deprecate God's anger" against the Britons. The prayers did not bring rain. "The like instance of dry weather," Josiah Martin wrote that year, "has not been known in ye memory of the oldest men here."[19]

The drought brought on the "Blast," an aphid insect disease that infested the crops. The baccara sent the people into the fields to save the cane. Enslaved men, women, and children pinched insects off stalks and wiped tar from leaves. When those efforts failed, the masters ordered the smoke. Men lit bonfires on the windward edge of the crop, pumping billows to blow fumes over the field and drive away the insects.[20] When the billows failed too, the baccara set the cane on fire, sending columns of smoke high into the air like a signal spreading an alarm across the land.

If the cane failed, hunger was sure to follow. The plantations did not produce enough food to feed the people. Planters purchased provisions with sugar. A failed crop could mean starvation for the enslaved.

It was in those desperate days that the fever came. It burned through the people in the night. It stole away the children.[21]

"Takyi!" the people cried.

Court stumbled suddenly, feigned exhaustion as if he could dance no more. He swung his arms high into the air and dropped his shield and fell backward . . . into the arms of the Big Men who waited behind his stool. They caught Court and held him and lowered him to his seat for all to see.[22]

"Takyi!" the people shouted.

The drums called again.

He rose from his seat, undaunted. He took the cutlass from Gift and swung the blade; back and forth he swung the blade. He moved faster to the beat, "whirling his Body round about," "dancing and leaping" from one end of the crowd to the other.[23]

Court danced toward Tomboy, his rival, the leader of the American-born slaves. Court raised the cutlass high and swung the blade down—stopping at the tip of Tomboy's nose.[24]

"I will not be afraid of any danger or Hard-ship in Defence of [the] people," Court shouted for all to hear.[25]

"Takyi! Takyi! Takyi! Kokuroo [Great] Takyi!" the Big Men cried.[26]

Court set out to organize the slaves of Antigua during a time of widespread unrest in the Americas. There were more slave insurrections and conspiracy trials in North America and the West Indies in the 1730s and 1740s than in any period before the American Revolution. African-born slaves rose in rebellion and captured the Danish Island of St. John (1733), and Maroons waged a successful war in Jamaica (1728–1740), events that became news in the wider Atlantic world. There were purported rebellions or accusations of slave conspiracies in the Leeward Islands, Jamaica, the Bahamas, Bermuda, South Carolina, Virginia, Maryland, East Jersey, and New York. The governor of Jamaica warned the ministers of the British Empire that slaves were spreading a "dangerous Spirit of Liberty" throughout the British plantations. His concerns were echoed by European colonists on the northern mainland. By the early 1740s, word of rebellion had taken hold in communities from the Leeward Islands to the harbors of New York City.

This book is a history of this slave unrest. It explains many of the slave conspiracies and insurrections of the 1730s and 1740s not as isolated events in the histories of specific colonies but rather as political movements that transcended the boundaries of provinces and empires. Most historians have assumed slaves confined their unrest to

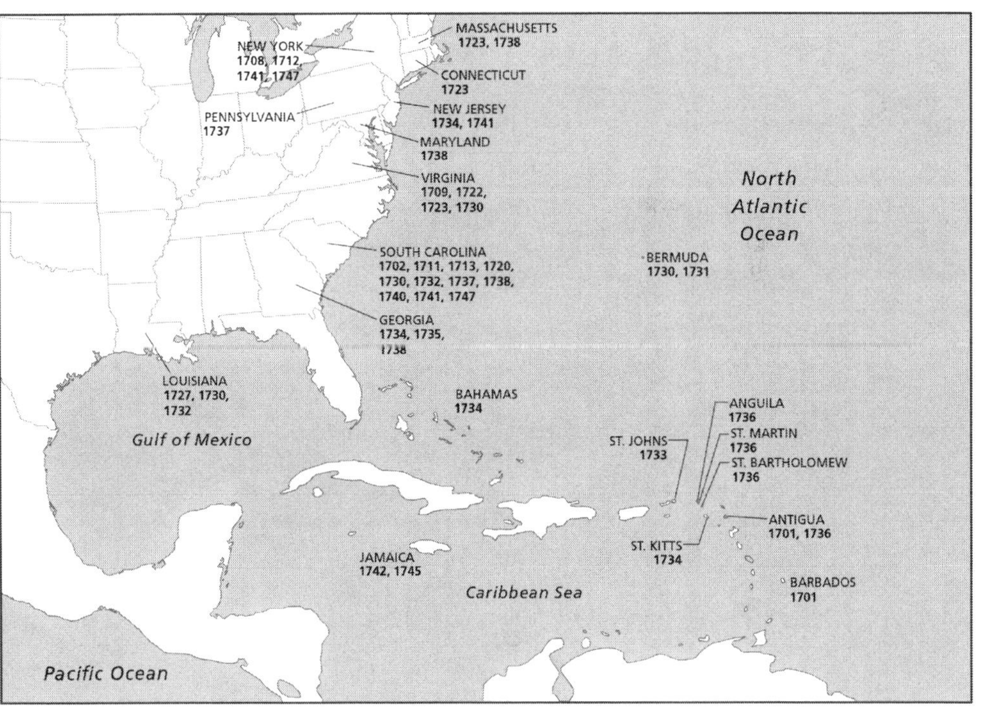

Map 1. Slave insurrections and slave conspiracies in the Atlantic world as reported in British correspondence and newspapers, 1701–1750

small locales in the first half of the eighteenth century.[27] In fact, slaves shared news across provinces to great effect. They carried rumors of emancipation—and stories of rebels rising—across rivers and seas. It was in the second quarter of the eighteenth century that many enslaved Black people began to express a common plight against their bondage, a belief they could organize to challenge the colonists who held them in chains.

There were enslaved people who sought to invent a politics of their own in the early eighteenth century. By a politics of slaves, I mean the ways in which enslaved people acted together to govern themselves: how they chose their leadership, how they sought to organize, how they created their social movements and institutions. Their politics were remarkable for the time. They were informed by memories of Africa, more than Europe, its rites and customs adapted to return dignity to the lives of a people in bondage.

There were historical forces that bore an outsized influence on the emerging politics of slaves in the first half of the eighteenth century. The first was the expansion of the British Atlantic slave trade. In the late seventeenth century, planters intensified plantation production and pushed westward, bringing new ground in the West Indies and the North American mainland under cultivation. European colonists clamored for laborers—slave laborers—to harvest crops and work in the increasingly crowded harbors along the edges of the Atlantic. To profit from the growing demand, British merchants more than tripled the number of slave-carrying ships that crossed the ocean from western Africa to the Americas.[28] In their holds, these deep-water vessels carried more people than ever before, increasing fourfold the number of slaves disembarked on the mainland between 1710 and 1740.[29] This forced migration increased the proportions of Black slaves in every British American colony except New Hampshire. As colonial authorities would later write of Court, with such large populations, a leader of slaves "might at once make proof of his Numbers."[30]

Enslaved communication and news-sharing also influenced the emerging politics of slaves in the early eighteenth century. Colonial

American populations became increasingly dependent on European manufactured goods and luxury trade items in the early eighteenth century. British merchant shipping responded to this demand, increasing from nearly 500 ships a year in 1700 to 1,500 annually by 1730.[31] This expansion of commerce created a system of public news-sharing throughout British North America and the West Indies. In the provinces, the number of newspapers grew from one press in 1719 (*Boston News-Letter*) to sixteen presses in nine British colonies by 1736. Historians have discovered great significance in this commerce, arguing that advances in communication helped to forge new empires and create a burgeoning Atlantic world.[32] This historical process also fostered the dissemination of rumor and rebellion among provinces and across oceans, reaching a fevered pitch by the mid-1730s.

Black slaves were participants in this commercial empire even as they were excluded from its prosperity and liberties. Slaves sailed aboard ships and worked in harbors and ports, though their participation varied across colonies and over time. Planters in Virginia and the Carolinas refused to allow slaves to work aboard deep-water vessels, for example, while slaveholders in Bermuda and the West Indies relied heavily on enslaved sailors by the 1730s. As slaves crisscrossed the boundaries of provinces and empires, Black communities became more aware of the actions of slaves in neighboring lands.

Wars and rumors of war provided sensational news for slaves to share. The kingdom of Spain threatened war against the British Empire throughout the 1730s, their magistrates resentful of British merchants who carried on illegal trade with the plantations of New Spain. In 1733, the British settled the new colony of Georgia on lands long claimed by the Spanish Empire. To undermine British expansion, the king of Spain issued proclamations emancipating British slaves who escaped to Spanish provinces in Florida and Puerto Rico. Enslaved British sailors shared these proclamations as far south as Barbados and as far north as Boston, Massachusetts. Rebels in South Carolina in 1739 made Spanish Florida their destination for freedom. And for every rebel at Stono River, there were many more who met in meetings across the plantations of the South Carolina Lowcountry, sharing stories of emancipation in Spanish lands.

These tumultuous forces created the conditions for a new politics of slaves, but people of African ancestry set this politics in motion. It took on many forms across North America and the West Indies. The body politic of the slaves, their specific African or American-born identity, had a tremendous influence on their politics. A rumor of emancipation inspired Black slaves to gather in large meetings across five counties in Virginia in 1730. Their politics emerged from a majority American-born slave population and an African population so diverse no nation or culture could gain sway over the rest. Far to the south, in the Danish Virgin Islands, the Akwamu revolt represented a vision nearly opposite to that of the Chesapeake. The Akwamu sought to resurrect their African kingdom in America. Most slaves in this time sought out a politics somewhere in between the Akwamu and the Chesapeake. As the First Jamaican Maroon War raged across Jamaica, and the British and Spanish Empires moved toward war, slave communities recognized an opportunity to invent a politics of their own.

Court experienced these historical forces in his own life. His loss of community in West Africa, his passage into slavery, and his attempt to unite the slaves of his colony were all influenced by this tumultuous age. Of the enslaved leaders who emerged from the British provinces in his time, his life is one of the best documented. His struggle to unite Antigua provides the narrative arc to this political history of slaves in the 1730s.

Historiographical Contribution

The book seeks to contribute to a new political history of slaves in early America and the Caribbean. When Bernard Bailyn sought to understand the origins of American political culture in his influential *The Origin of American Politics* (1968), he never considered the politics of slaves in his study.[33] Like Bailyn, few American scholars have looked deep into the political culture of early America's enslaved people to understand the origins of American political history. But by forgetting an era when Africans and American-born slaves sought to create a politics of their own, we have seriously misread our past and missed moments of American political invention that rivaled the novelty of the revolutionaries in Philadelphia in 1776.

For the most part, historians have examined the influence of slave resistance on the broader politics of European colonial empires. Slaves who joined white servants in Bacon's Rebellion (1676) or rioted alongside Irish servants in St. Christopher (1689) threatened the balance of power in English America.[34] In *Slave Law and the Politics of Resistance in the Atlantic World* (2018), Edward Rugemer argues that slave resistance had an important influence on the colonial assemblies of Jamaica and South Carolina, which responded to rebel slaves with draconian laws.[35] Historians of the American and French Revolutions have long noted the myriad ways in which enslaved Black people petitioned Massachusetts assemblies for freedom, volunteered to fight in wars, and shared reports of rebellion across empires. And if there is a consensus in these many histories, it is that the rebels of Saint-Domingue brought new meaning to these revolutions by challenging white revolutionaries to live up to their beliefs in the "rights of man" and the principle that "all men are created equal."[36] Less understood is the long history of slaves trying to govern themselves.

There is a scholarship that examines the interior politics of slaves. Historians have discovered in the records of specific slave revolts a hidden politics within eighteenth-century slave communities. In *Blood on the River* (2020), Marjolene Kars uncovers a complicated "politics of rebellion" among the thousands of slaves who navigated the Dutch Berbice slave rebellion of 1763. She finds deep disagreements among Black participants over the meaning of freedom and autonomy as they tried to survive the revolt. Vincent Brown recovers similar tensions among slave rebels in his study of Tacky's Revolt in 1760 Jamaica. As Brown explains, to understand rebels who waged a slave war, historians must examine "why so many other black people stood against them or stood to the side."[37] Both Kars and Brown use evidence produced by white officials to gain insight into the political perspectives of enslaved people. Their work has influenced my own, as I have mined the evidence from slave revolts to better understand the politics of slaves. My approach differs, however, in that I understand rebels to be factions within a broader political community. Revolts were rare, and for every slave who warred against planters in the 1730s, there were hundreds more who met in open meetings, elected leaders, participated in protests, or ran away.[38] Revolts were part of a larger struggle for autonomy and community in the 1730s.

This book has benefited the most from a generation of scholarship on the experience of African peoples in the Americas. Slaveholders in the early eighteenth century often ascribed certain tendencies to what they called "nations" of Africans. Even though slaves gathered on one ship might originate from scores of different kingdoms stretching more than a thousand miles into the interior of Africa, planters insisted they could discern specific characteristics that we would today call ethnicities, or shared traits within an identifiable group. Historian of ethnic group formation, or ethnogenesis, have traced the slave cultures of West Africa across the Atlantic into the Americas.[39] They have found that shared language and religious practices and political symbols allowed peoples violently severed from their homelands to create a new ethnic group identity in the Americas. I have leaned heavily on this vast literature, even as I have found ethnicity was surprisingly ineffective for organizing slaves in the 1730s. Black slave populations were too diverse (even Jamaica's large Akan speaking population made up only 30% of the Africans on the island in 1730). As Court understood in 1736 (and as the Akwamu rebels discovered in their rebellion), any successful leader of slaves had to transcend ethnicity and origin in the second quarter of the eighteenth century.

The politics of slaves has its own history. There were at least three distinct periods over the course of the seventeenth and eighteenth centuries. In the early years of European colonization of the Americas, Black slaves sought to assimilate into the political culture of white colonists. In the 1650s, they labored and lived alongside American Indians and white servants in colonies as diverse as Santo Domingo, Barbados, Virginia, and Massachusetts. Most colonies permitted slaveholders to manumit their bondsmen in the middle of the seventeenth century, and this remained the hope for many slaves. For the vast majority who were never freed, they influenced colonial politics through resistance—protests, running away, or revolt—but their smaller numbers and dispersed populations prevented a significant political culture of their own. In this first period, the politics of slaves was that of an oppressed minority seeking some influence on the people who held them in bondage.

In the second period of this history, Black slaves invented an interior politics of their own. This new form of governance emerged first in the West Indies in the late seventeenth century. European slave merchants carried hundreds of thousands of Africans to meet the demand of sugar planters, whose slaveries created Black majorities across the islands. In this version of a New World, enslaved Africans made up most of the body politic. In Barbados in 1675, one report told of a purported conspiracy to be led by a man from the Gold Coast named Cuffee, who was to be crowned king.[40] On Antigua in 1687, an overseer described slaves on a plantation electing a "governor" and carrying the man on their shoulders.[41] By the opening of the eighteenth century, a similar process was well underway on the American mainland.

The third period of this history was a politics born of the Age of Revolution. Enslaved Black people appropriated the revolutionary ideals of liberty and the rights of man to challenge European empires and their slaveholding regimes. These generations fought in the revolutionary wars, petitioned rebel assemblies to live up to their expressed ideals, and embraced a nascent abolitionist movement that took hold on both sides of the Atlantic Ocean. Slaves became political actors on the world stage, influencing the political upheavals of the Old and New Worlds. With this book, I have sought to examine the middle period of this political history.

Methodology

The records from slave conspiracy trials are the most problematic evidence in this study. Historians have struggled to interpret the critical records from these trials, expressing concern that colonial courts used coercion and torture to force slaves to confess to accusations of plotting.[42] As Jason Sharples has argued, many white colonists developed a trope or story of slave conspiracy and coerced slaves to confess to slaveholder's assumptions.[43] The "violence committed on enslaved bodies pervades the archive," argues Marisa J. Fuentes, and systems of power obscure or distort the voices of the enslaved.[44] The trial records from Antigua (1736) and New York City (1741), for example, contain fascinating transcriptions of slave testimony, but one cannot accept their confessions as accurate knowing that slaves were promised a violent death if they did not confirm the accusations of white authorities.

While I treat coerced confessions with skepticism, I have found a diverse body of evidence in the archives of early America. Not all records are the same. The Arbuthnot Report of 1736, Justice of the Peace Robert Arbuthnot's initial report of his investigation to the Antigua governor in council, records coerced interviews with slaves that produced no confessions at all. The historical record from this period contains significant evidence of slaves electing leaders, holding public meetings, protesting in public, and sometimes acting in overt rebellions. I have even sought to read "against the grain" of trial transcripts, ignoring confessions of plotting but noting references in slave testimony to events in neighboring provinces. This book concludes that in the second quarter of the eighteenth century, white colonial authorities sought to intimidate slave populations with conspiracy trials and brutal executions as a reaction against an increasingly restive Black political culture.

The book begins *in medias res* in 1736 with Court's African ennobling ceremony establishing his authority over slaves on the island of Antigua. The chapters that follow seek to explain the historical origins of this restive politics of slaves. Moving back in time to 1690s Atlantic Africa, the narrative follows a chronological story of an expansive Atlantic slave trade that produced larger Black communities across eastern North America by the 1730s. These enslaved Black populations increasingly labored in an Atlantic commerce that helped colonists and slaves share news. By the 1730s, enslaved people were aware of their numbers and responsive to rumors of emancipation and rebellion circulating across the Atlantic. The last chapters chronologically tell the story of the 1730s unrest, climaxing with Court's attempt to organize the island of Antigua in 1736 within the broader history of slave unrest in this period.

Court's strategy was twofold: among the American-born slaves of the towns, he embraced the political practices of British America. For the slaves born on the Gold Coast of Africa, he looked back to his homeland. Slaves in many parts of early America did the same. This is a history of their struggle in that time.

CHAPTER ONE

The Investigation

11 October 1736
St. John's, Antigua

FOR EIGHT DAYS, THE PEOPLE of Antigua spoke of Court's dance in the pasture. Some people called it a play; others, a coronation. Court had been crowned king of the slaves, they said. And for eight days, there was no public alarm and no recorded concern from the white British government of the island.

It was Robert Arbuthnot who first warned of an imminent slave rebellion. He feared a plot, he said, and as justice of the peace for the town of St. John's, initiated an investigation that led him across town, interviewing Antiguans both slave and free. Arbuthnot began his investigation on Monday, 11 October 1736. Four days later, Arbuthnot stood before the Colonial Council of Antigua and announced the slaves "were forming a Design of some attempt or other to throw of their Yoke, which appeared to him to be a thing of full of Danger considering their Superiority of Numbers and our Over Great Security."[1] The governor, Captain General William Mathew, appointed a panel of judges, sometimes called commissioners—one of whom was Arbuthnot—to form a commission to interrogate slaves and exhort confessions.

For nearly three hundred years, Arbuthnot's conclusions have served as historical fact. Within weeks of his announcement, Arbuthnot and the commissioners had come to believe "the Slaves had formed and resolved to execute a Plot, whereby all the white Inhabitants of this Island were to be murdered, and a new form of Government to be established by the Slaves among themselves."[2] British newspapers reported Arbuthnot's conclusions and spread the story of the conspiracy across the empire. Antigua's governor reported the plot as fact to the secretary of state, the Duke of Newcastle.[3] The commissioners produced a report on the trials and interrogations and published it as a broadside in Ireland. Printers on both sides of the Atlantic reprinted excerpts of the *Genuine Narrative of the Intended Conspiracy of the Negroes at Antigua*. Within only a few months, Arbuthnot's warning had become a truth shared across the Atlantic world.

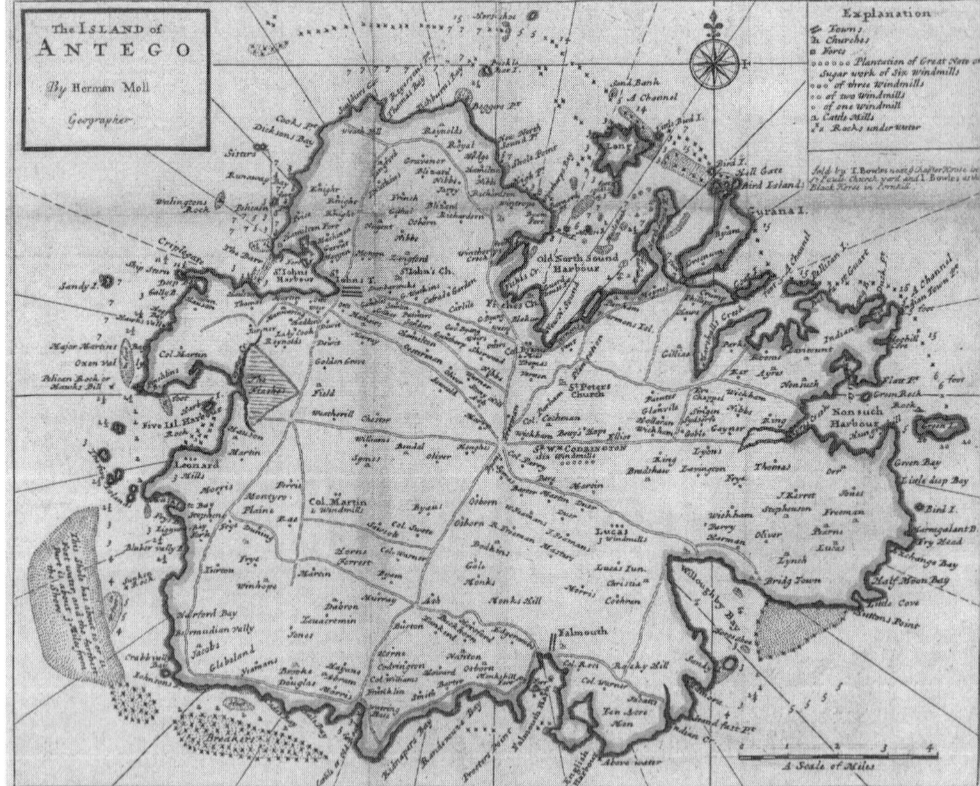

Figure 2. Herman Moll, *The Island of Antego*, [1736?]. Courtesy David Rumsey Map Collection, David Rumsey Map Center, Stanford Libraries, Stanford University, Stanford, California

Historians have long relied on this evidence to understand the intentions of Antigua's slaves. They have viewed the conspiracy as an act of resistance against colonial slavery. Relying on the evidence produced by the commissioners, most accepted that Court had planned a violent rebellion in which he sought to murder white inhabitants and overthrow the government. They concluded that Court and his accomplices were rebels willing to risk their lives and wage war for their liberty.[4]

Historians have more recently found good reason to challenge this traditional interpretation of the plot. Most evidence emerged from the efforts of the judges who tried the slaves. British officials refused to listen to slaves who denied accusations of plotting. The judges used coercion to force slaves to confess, promising brutal execution if anyone refused to admit guilt.[5] In a few cases, the judges used torture.[6] Like the witch trials in Massachusetts, the officials required slaves to confirm the court's suspicions to save their lives. Slave confessions produced through so many forms of coercion are not reliable. Perhaps there was no plot at all.

But there is a great deal of evidence that should not be dismissed. Arbuthnot's initial report to the council, the "Arbuthnot Report," is the most important concerning the intentions of the slaves. He conducted his first interviews before he was certain of a plot. He did not force slaves to confess to a conspiracy. None did. His witnesses related what they had seen in the previous weeks, without certainty concerning his intentions. The council's clerk recorded his account into the minutes, copied the minutes into a giant ledger, and mailed that ledger to England. It survives today in a box on a shelf in the British National Archives. Arbuthnot's report to the colonial council is the best surviving record of what white and Black people said to each other in the eight days after Court's dance in the pasture.

Arbuthnot discovered a moment of remarkable political invention in early America—and misunderstood it. His fear of the enslaved people—his recognition of the brutal oppression of slaves on the island—led him to conclude that Court was plotting a massacre. Arbuthnot made a terrible mistake.

It is possible to retell this history by approaching the evidence from the investigation at the beginning of the trial, to reconstruct how Arbuthnot misconstrued the intentions of the enslaved population. He encountered an enslaved population in the process of forming a body politic, a people flush with the excitement of choosing a leader and discovering a new community of their own. They would have their own militia, like the free white men who paraded across the colony in dress and arms, and their own leaders. Most of all, they would have a king.

Arbuthnot's investigation began with a knock on his door.

Thomas Kerby was at the height of his power as he stood at the entryway of Arbuthnot's home on the morning of Monday, 11 October. He was Speaker of the Assembly of Antigua, the highest-ranking elected official in the province, and wealthy. Kerby had been born into his estates on the island; orphaned as a child, he inherited from his father land and slaves. He was middle-aged, a gentleman who had never worked with his hands.

Kerby and Arbuthnot were men of near equal rank, but not quite. Kerby would have kept his hat on his head. He would have spoken first, offered Arbuthnot a single nod, and affected an air of being unhurried, even if he was rushed. Arbuthnot would have returned the greeting with a deep nod of his own and an inquiry as to how he might be of service.[7] Eighteenth-century Britons marked their "place"—their rank and status—with specific movements and language. They called it manners.

The constables had arrested Black men over the weekend, Kerby explained. He planned to try them in his home. He "Desir'd [Arbuthnot] to go to his House, and Sit with Mr. Jenings upon Tryal of some Slaves inform'd against for Gaming."[8]

Kerby's house sat just off the corner of Long and Market Streets in St. John's Town, two blocks east of the harbor.[9] The building has not survived, but its layout, with a front room and back room, probably looked a great deal like the home of Jededdiah Hutchinson, who described his house on the neighboring island of St. Christopher in his petition to the English government in 1706: "a dwelling house in Towne of 36 foot Long 18 foot wide of 2 rooms one boarded underfoot the other Brikt of Mastick Ironwood."[10] Through the entryway Arbuthnot entered a small English hall: a vaulted ceiling with exposed timbers, plastered walls, and windows without glass.[11]

The trial took place in the front room. Kerby had summoned Walther Jennings, the other justice of the peace, to assist Arbuthnot in the trial. The people pressed together. Johnny, a Black man owned by a Mrs. Merceir, stood with the slaves charged with gambling.[12] White Britons, unnamed in the record, stood ready to accuse or just watch. People rarely bathed in the early eighteenth century. The throng of unwashed bodies must have smelled in the midday heat.

Johnny had no lawyer to defend him against these accusations. The slaves could look only to their owners to plead their case, or if their masters did not attend the examination, they could beg Arbuthnot and Jennings for mercy. If the justices showed them no mercy, they could expect to be paraded about town and lashed by a constable with a whip.

Arbuthnot and Jennings ordered the examination to begin and called the first witnesses. There was no jury. By law, Arbuthnot and Jennings decided guilt or innocence and the punishment of slaves.[13] In 1702, the Antiguan assembly's "Act for the Better Government of Slaves, and Free Negroes" required two justices of the peace to "give Sentence as the Crime deserveth" for noncapital slave offenses.[14] There was not even a clerk to record testimony. Arbuthnot's limited memory provided the only record of the trial.

Gambling was a petty crime to charge a slave. British men gambled all over America. Rich men, poor men, sailors and craftsmen, planters and slaves, and American Indians—they gambled. London in the 1730s was notorious for bear-baiting and cockfights and for parlors filled with men gaming. Virginia was already known for horse racing. Gentlemen played cards into the night across British America. Planters bet their land and possessions and future crops and even the people they owned, smoking tobacco and sipping madeira until their teeth turned the color of blood. In 1723, the Antigua Assembly discouraged rampant gambling by fining any gambler three times the amount of his winnings.[15] By all accounts, Antiguan men continued to gamble.

Black men gambled too, shooting dice on Saturday evenings and Sundays. They met in Morgan's pasture and Otto's fields and wherever they could find a spot of their own away from the eyes of baccara.[16]

There was one man in the room that Arbuthnot could not afford to ignore. Thomas Kerby presided over the entire affair. It was the custom in the British American provinces for great men—men of rank and property—to host trials in their homes. Kerby possessed much of what Arbuthnot did not have. Kerby led a faction of powerful planters, men whose authority resided in the land they owned and the people they owned. He owned plantations and many slaves and had a family too. His son, Hamilton, sixteen years old in 1736, probably sat beside his father during the trial. His wife and three daughters might have watched the proceedings or worked nearby.

Kerby's big house in the center of town was a testament to his rank, as was his ability to summon Arbuthnot. Few men could order two justices of the peace to their home in the province. When Kerby "desir'd" Arbuthnot and Jennings to hold a trial, the two men went.

Arbuthnot's attention focused suddenly on the examination: what had the witness just said?

The witness (whose name Arbuthnot would not remember) was providing an account of Johnny's wayward behavior: "And Mrs. Browne overheard said Johnny, belonging to Mr. Merceir, Say something to another Slave about a List of Officers and Soldiers."[17]

What "List of Officers and Soldiers?" Arbuthnot asked.

A Mrs. Browne had said she had overheard Johnny talking about a list of officers and soldiers, slaves. . . .

Arbuthnot stopped the examination. He ordered Mrs. Browne sent for at once. The court waited. She appeared at the door and entered the front room where she was greeted by a small crowd waiting for her testimony.

"Yes," she said, she had heard Johnny discussing a list of slave officers.

Arbuthnot recounted her testimony in his report: "That One Night about three weeks ago She Overheard the said Johnny speaking to another Slave, unknown, to her about some slaves who had Received Publick Correction in the Town that Day," she said.

"'Johnny had said,"'Hey Day. They have been Punishing Our Officers & Soldiers.' To which the other Slave said 'I was to have been punished If I had not out of the way' and then Asked the said Johnny 'If the Noise of it was over' Johnny made Answer 'Yes it was but said he they have whipped One Negro but he was not in Our List.'"

"Not in Our List. . . ."

Arbuthnot took Johnny into the back room. He told the slave he "should not only be forgiven but Rewarded if he wou'd Explain those words by given an Account of the Meaning of that List, and what Slaves were Mentioned in it."

Johnny "Denyed Obstinately that he Ever said the words or that he Knew or heard of any List, or of any Slaves being Officers or Soldiers," Arbuthnot remembered.

Arbuthnot sent Johnny back and called on the other slaves, bringing each one to the back room to question them. Each slave "being Examined apart in the Same manner, Denyed they knew or ever heard anything of the Matter."[18]

It was Mrs. Browne's testimony against the slaves. She swore they had spoken of their officers and soldiers. The accused men denied it. They refused, to a man, any knowledge of such a list. Frustrated, Arbuthnot convicted them of gambling. He ordered their "Public Correction about the Town."[19]

But as soon as he had ordered their floggings, Arbuthnot turned to the master of the house. He felt he had to communicate his sentiments "freely and Publickly on this Occasion to Mr. Kerby."

"The Island appeared to him to be in the Utmost Danger from the Slaves," Arbuthnot said.

He proposed they issue a "Search Warrant immediately to Search all Negro Houses not only in the Town, but the Plantations contiguous to it." They would look for "Gunns Cutlasses Powder, Shott &c. and

Every thing Else of a Suspicious Nature and so Apprehend any Slaves on whom any of those things should be found." Jenings agreed.[20]

The two justices of the peace summoned the constables. They gave "Directions to the Constables to Execute the Warrant with the Utmost Dispatch and Secrecy." To encourage each constable "to do their Duty upon this Occasion," Arbuthnot promised to do "all that lay in his Power that they should be paid by the Public for their Extraordinary Trouble."[21]

Carrying their warrants, the constables set out to ransack the homes of slaves in search of weapons and any other items of "Suspicious nature."

Faster than the constables, the people of St. John's Town began to spread the word. They spoke of a trial in the home of the Speaker of the Assembly. They whispered Arbuthnot's warning of a "Danger to the island," a secret army hidden within the Black population of British Antigua. As night fell across the town, the baccara worried over what might lay in wait for them in the dark.

British colonists could easily imagine a rebellion of slaves. Stories of servile conspiracy—the secret plan of a group of oppressed people to obtain their liberty by force—emerged throughout the Americas in places where colonists oppressed subaltern peoples.[22] Europeans justified the subjection of Indians and people of African ancestry by imposing distinctions of race and religion but feared these groups might hold secret councils to coordinate rebellion.[23] Because "plotting" took place away from colonists' view, officials relied on informants who could reveal the clandestine conversations of servants or slaves.[24] A witness's first warning of an impending insurrection could send an entire European colonial community into a panic. These events, called conspiracy scares, emerged from the colonists' exploitation of subaltern peoples and their fear of a secret plan for revolt.

Conspiracy scares unfolded in remarkably similar ways across colonies and over time. Colonists responded to the first warning of an imminent rebellion with public alarm and coercive trials, only ending the episode with an execution to intimidate the subaltern population.[25] In Virginia in 1710, a Black slave named Will warned his owner of a purported conspiracy of both African and Indian slaves to rise in rebellion across eight Tidewater counties.[26] The planters raised the alarm and sheriffs arrested the men and women accused by the informant. British officials interrogated and coerced confessions from the enslaved prisoners, producing an account of the conspiracy tainted by the methods of the court.[27] At the end of the trial, British magistrates ordered the convicted conspirators "drawn and quartered," displaying their torn body parts across the counties to intimidate the slave population.[28] Episodes like that of Virginia had become a terrifying feature of British colonial American life in the decades before the Antigua conspiracy. Britons believed they had foiled plots in the West Indies and Atlantic islands and on the mainland colonies of South Carolina, Virginia, Maryland, and East Jersey.[29]

Arbuthnot was a stranger to slave conspiracy. He was an outsider, part of a great migration of Scottish-born men who sought to profit in the British American colonies after the Act of Union in 1707. Scottish merchants and professionals set up extensive networks across the British West Indies and the colonial south.

But he was an ambitious man. He appears in the Antigua record for the first time in 1731, volunteering to serve in the militia.[30] By 1733, the governor had appointed him justice of the peace for St. John's. There is no record that he owned a plantation or any property outside of the town. He was seeking to become an agent for the Royal African Company in 1736, looking to enter the lucrative slave trade. The investigation was an opportunity for Arbuthnot to prove himself to his benefactors.

The roosters crowed before dawn on Tuesday. In St. John's Town, the smell of cooking fires from the outdoor kitchens mixed with the salt air. As the sun rose in the east, Black women and children passed through the wide lanes carrying clay vessels of water on their heads. The distant banging of mallets signaled that the coopers had begun hammering the hogshead barrels near the wharf.

As Arbuthnot had ordered, the constable, a Mr. Murphy, punished Johnny before the town of St. John's. For the crime of gambling, Arbuthnot had ordered Johnny struck with "100 lashes" and paraded through the port town. Constables used "the cat" when punishing slaves in Antigua, a whip of nine tails. Each strike of "the cat" made nine thin slashes on the skin: nine thin slashes, one hundred times.[31]

Murphy pushed Johnny down the streets, striking him with the whip and calling out his crime of gaming. Women paused in their many labors to watch—their hanging of clothes or carrying water or sweeping or tending to infants or cooking in the outdoor kitchens to stand and watch Murphy whip Johnny. Children halted their play to see the constable strike the Black man with the whip. By the end of the punishment, the constable had lacerated Johnny's back.

When the punishment was over, another slave called out to Johnny. He noted that Johnny had not flinched "nor shed a tear."

"It was true it was a severe whipping," Johnny shouted back, "but he matter'd it no more than a moskito."[32]

Mr. Murphy reported Johnny's words to Arbuthnot on Tuesday afternoon. Arbuthnot wrote Johnny's response down as evidence against him. It was "further Proof of the Insolence of the Slaves and how much they despised Common Punishments," he said.[33]

It was also proof that Johnny was proud. He had refused to let anyone see his tears.

Henry James appeared first at Arbuthnot's door. He was eager to share gossip from last night ("amongst other discourses," Arbuthnot noted). James said he had been told by a Mr. Philip Darby that Jack, Darby's slave, had lost his temper at the constable's search.[34]

James had heard it all secondhand. His account wandered through a bewildering path of hearsay: he had been told by Darby that Darby's sister, a Mrs. Duglas, had been talking to Darby's slave Jack. . . . It was a lot for anyone to follow.

Jack had lost his temper, according to James, and complained to Darby's sister about constables searching the homes of slaves. Arbuthnot recorded James' account of the conversation:

"What do the Baccararas mean by Punishing the Slaves," Jack had said to Duglas. "Do they think Negros Can live upon a Bit and Six herrings a Week[?]"

"Mrs. Duglas, Sister to Mr. Darby, gently Repremanded him for Speaking in this Manner and told him that 'perhaps he would be taken up by and by.'"

"What," said he, "can they Do to me [?] they can only whip me."

"'Yes,' said She, 'they can Do worse.'"

"'What, they can only hang or burn me what Signifies it[?] I can but Die.'"

"She having it Seems heard that Court/Mr. Kerby's Principal Slave had been Croned King at a Play said in Banter to him 'What Court is King, and you are to be one of his Officers?'"

"'Yes,' said he, 'Court is King and I am to be one of his Generals.'"[35]

That Tuesday morning, Arbuthnot might have dismissed James's account of the conversation as gossip and hearsay. He might have accepted Jack's anger as the "Clamorous and impolitick" complaints of a man upset with the hard plight and hunger of the island's slaves. But for Arbuthnot, Jack's outburst was confirmation that slaves had taken the title of officers. Jack had said he would be a "general," James explained. And Jack had said "Court is King."

Out of respect, Arbuthnot first waited upon Thomas Kerby. Arbuthnot said later that he had never heard of Court, Kerby's "Principal Slave," nor was he aware of Court's "play" in the pasture. Arbuthnot told Kerby that a slave had called Court the "King."[36] Arbuthnot was on his way to investigate, to interview Mrs. Duglas and Jack, and asked if Kerby would join him. Kerby agreed to go.

They set out together across St. John's Town. It was a frontier village in 1736, housing 1,500 souls at the end of a narrow harbor on the northwestern coast of the island. The king's engineers had laid out the town as a grid of streets extending east from the water in 1702. They built a fort at the harbor's mouth in 1706, creating a harbor protected from enemy ships.

The town would have had all the sights and smells and sounds of English colonial America in the early eighteenth century. West Indian houses had outdoor kitchens with clay or brick ovens. The smell of cooking fires hung heavy in the air. The English brought pigs wherever they lived, and a sow and her brood might have rutted through the waste as the men made their way down the street. There was surely the ubiquitous rooster waiting until the last moment to hurry out from under foot.

St. John's Town was a lively port in October, but it was the silence that would have most surprised a visitor from our own time. Even in town, a person would have often found themself walking in quiet.

Kerby and Arbuthnot called upon Duglas at her home.

She could not have expected to see the Speaker of the Assembly and the justice of the peace at her door. She had shared Jack's complaints with her brother, not the gossipy Mr. James, and certainly not Arbuthnot.

She confirmed to the justice that Jack had complained about the "Baccararas" and "owned everything, except what related to Court." Arbuthnot did not believe Duglas. He "imagined she had a Reserve," he said, a polite way of saying he thought she was lying to him.[37]

Arbuthnot said he wished to speak to Jack.

He had "gone aboard ship," Duglas said, as Jack was an enslaved sailor.

Arbuthnot told her to send for the slave. When Jack came to her home, Duglas was to send him on to the justice's house. As a parting shot, Arbuthnot also told Duglas that he would speak to her brother, Mr. Darby, about how she had first reported the conversation. Arbuthnot would know the truth.

As they walked back through town, Arbuthnot asked Kerby about Court, the Speaker's "Principal Slave." Arbuthnot was "quite a Stranger to [Court] and his Character."

He had owned Court "near Thirty Years," Kerby said. "[Court] was his head Slave, and had always behaved with great Fidelity and honesty."

"He seemed to think him incapable of a Bad Design," the Justice remembered.[38]

Arbuthnot asked Kerby if he could meet Court. Kerby said he would arrange it.

The constables began arriving at Arbuthnot's door that Tuesday afternoon. Each had a story about suspicious activities of slaves. James Hanson waited on Arbuthnot with a report of a slave who had threatened him.

The law required constables to break up meetings of slaves. In 1723, the elected assembly "authorized and required" constables to disperse "any Number of Negroes assembled in a tumultuous Manner." Constables were to make "three Proclamations, requiring such Negroes to separate, and disperse, and to retire to their Homes." If the crowd refused, "upon Contempt of the said Proclamation, or the Negroes not dispersing," the constable was to "seize one or more of such Slaves, and carry him before a Magistrate." The law allowed the constable to fire on slaves and kill them if they continued to resist his order.[39]

There had been an unusually large gathering of Black people last Sunday night, Hanson explained. He "had Endeavoured to Disperse a great Multitude of Slaves, and gave One of them a flash with his Whip," he told Arbuthnot.

"God Damn your Blood, I know you and I will come up with You," the Black man had shouted at Hanson. It startled the constable: a slave had cursed and threatened him. It was scary enough and rare enough to be shared with the justice of the peace.

The constables spoke of another meeting too, one beyond the gathering last Sunday. There were rumors of assemblies of slaves late in the night. There were rumors of mysterious horns sounding in the dark.

"Mr. Morgan, the constable, could give a particular Account of that Matter," the constables told the justice.[40]

Morgan had to be summoned by Arbuthnot. He had not appeared at the justice's door like the other men. Arbuthnot ordered Morgan to appear at his home and when the constable arrived, deposed him:

"On Tuesday the 5th of October about one a Clock in the morning," Morgan began, there had been a sound. It startled him awake. He heard the sound again in the dark. "The blowing of a conch shell near [my] house," Morgan explained. He lived "at the upper end of town where there are few inhabitants," near Cross Street in the northeastern corner of St. John's Town. Cross Street ran north out of town, becoming the old High Road (Friar's Hill Road today) that goes to Pope's Head and the northern coast.

Morgan listened in the dark. He rose from bed and "Softly Open'd his Window and by the light of the Moon very plainly saw in the Cross

Road by Wavell Smith's House Upwards of One hundred Negro Men / so far as he could guess / some armed with Cutlasses brandishing them about and some few with Guns."[41]

Morgan watched the armed slaves in the moonlight. They "Discharged two of their Gunns" and swung their cutlasses and blew the conch shell, mustering their forces in the night.

It occurred to the constable that he should shout at them, chastise the slaves for gathering against the law. But Morgan was struck with fear. He "was afraid to speak to them or Call out to them to Separate."

After a quarter of an hour, "they all March'd Down towards the Country Pond and Otto's Pasture making hurra's and a great Noise as they went along."[42] They traveled south on a route that closely parallels Independence Avenue today.

Morgan said he was not the only witness. It had not been a figment of his imagination. He had "Since seen Several People that lived towards Otto's Pasture who told him they heard the blowing of a Conk shell that night."

As if to prove he was no coward, Morgan explained to Arbuthnot that he had recovered his bravery three nights later, the previous Friday, when he was alerted to another assembly of slaves. Morgan had attacked the meeting, ordered the slaves dispersed, and stung one Black man who loitered with the bull whip. "Damn you Boy!" the Black man had shouted. "It's your turn now, but it will be myne soon, bye and bye."[43]

Arbuthnot scratched out Morgan's report on the page. He wrote out the quote, "It's your turn now, but it will be myne soon, bye and bye."

The enslaved sailor Jack appeared at Arbuthnot's door a short time later. He was accompanied by the white St. John merchant Ambrose Lynch, who had come to speak for Jack and attest to his good character. They had chosen a bad moment to meet with the justice of the peace.

Arbuthnot "immediately took the said Slave Aside and Asked him about the Words." Had Jack complained about the treatment of the slaves? Had Jack said "Court was King" and that he would be his general?

"He Denyed them at first," Arbuthnot remembered, "but after much sifting he Owned he said that he was to be One of Courts Generals."

Arbuthnot asked "[What] he ment by this Expression?" and offered Jack a "Reward for his Discovering the Whole Truth."

"He made great Professions of his Innocence and said he only spoke these words in Jest, and that he had no sort of Ill Meaning in Saying Them." Arbuthnot pressed him. Jack said, "He knew of no Design of Court or any other Negros going forwards, and if he Did he certainly would Discover."

Arbuthnot "broke off" and said he would send Jack to jail.

Lynch, the merchant, tried to intervene. He "gave a very good character of the said Slave, Saying he had lived with him many Years and always behaved faithfully and well." Lynch "Desired [Jack] might not be committed."

"There was all the Reason in the World to Suspect a Conspiracy of the Slaves," Arbuthnot told Lynch. "This fellow was Concerned in it." Arbuthnot ordered Jack to jail.

The constables James Hanson and a Mr. Bolan knocked on Arbuthnot's door. "They had made use of the Search Warrant on Kerbys Court," they said. They had searched the slave's room, "where they found a Purse which they thought had more than One hundred Pistoles in it, and an Exceeding fine Wrought Drum," which "they cut to pieces." They had also "heard that he had some Arms, but that Mr. Milney Clerk to Mr. Kerby and likewise Court himself prevented their Searching any further by telling them that Mr. Kerby himself and made a Search there the Night before."

Arbuthnot focused his mind on Court: the king of the slaves. Kerby had said Court "had always behaved with great Fidelity and honesty." Kerby said he was "incapable of a Bad Design." But as Arbuthnot asked "people" about Kerby's manservant, they said he had a "very bad Character," that "[Court] was a Dark Designing Ambitious Insolent Fellow." People said Court "upon some Occasions he had threatned Young Mr. Gamble that if it was not for the Difference of Colour he would tear his Hearts blood Out—That his Master had too good an Opinion of him was in great Measure blind to his Faults," Arbuthnot noted in his report. "That [Kerby] allowed him to Carry on Trade and many other and greater Indulgences than were allowed to any Slave in the Island."

"Court had a greater Ascendance and Influence Over the Slaves of this Island than any other Slave whatsoever," Arbuthnot reported to the council, "particularly Over those of his Own Country, the Coromantees who all pay him great Homage and Respect & stood in great awe of him."

Arbuthnot decided that he would seek out this king of the slaves, this man called Court, and learn his intentions for British Antigua.[44]

CHAPTER TWO

A Memory of Africa

20 March 1696
Eguafo Kingdom, Gold Coast, West Africa

HE LIVED IN ANTIGUA AS a man. He lived in Africa as a boy, in the lands the Europeans called the Gold Coast. Court was born into a time and place in which common men became leaders and kingdoms collapsed suddenly under the weight of armies from the north. He was just a little boy when slave merchants took him from Africa, no older than ten years old. His memories of his homeland were the impressions of a child. To try to understand the political experience he carried to America—"to look over his shoulder" at the past—is to reconstruct the late seventeenth-century Gold Coast through the eyes of a little boy.

His memories offered lessons for a man seeking to invent a politics for slaves in the new world. Court remembered the rituals required to elevate a man's status among southern Gold Coast peoples.[1] He was common-born in his homeland, of no royal lineage, and a slave in Antigua.[2] He performed the rites of the shield dance to be ennobled and made fit to lead. At his ceremony, Court assigned the most revered enslaved men of St. John's specific roles to recreate the leadership of a southern Gold Coast state. He gave them offices and symbols of a kingdom.[3] Black witnesses later reported that Court sought out an old Gold Coast spiritual leader to teach him the proper movements in preparation for the dance, an elder to explain a political culture Court had witnessed, though perhaps not understood, as a boy.[4]

There were other lessons to remember from his childhood. He knew he would have to overcome the violent divisions among Africans. Enemies had surrounded the boundaries of Court's homeland when he was a child. Rumors of invaders and the threat of being taken away would have been part of his childhood. Court, like most of the enslaved African-born population, had been harmed by neighboring peoples through his passage into slavery. His attempt to build a new kingdom, through his ennobling ceremony and the rituals of state, was an effort to overcome the violence among peoples, to unite strangers in the New World.

Court lost more than his freedom when slavers took him from his home. He lost his family, his father and mother, and her ancestral clan. He lost his mother's ancestors, whom his people believed slept beneath the earth and watched over him. He was severed from his village, who shared with him a lineage back to the ancient ones. Robert Arbuthnot's interrogations and the commissioners' trial records do not adequately convey the sense of loss experienced by Court as a child. Like the hundreds of thousands of Gold Coast peoples held in bondage across the Americas in the seventeenth and eighteenth centuries, Court's attempt to rebuild a political community began with a memory of Africa. He would have to look back, remember, and carry what was useful into the New World.

No one knows for certain where Court was born. He did not share the name of his homeland with the people of Antigua, or at least no one bothered to write it down. The clues to his birthplace are hidden in a baccara's words recorded by a clerk in a giant ledger shipped to England.[5] The paper comes apart in your hand when you turn the page.

Court was about forty-five years old in 1736.[6] His white master, Thomas Kerby, told Arbuthnot he purchased Court "near 30 years ago" and that Court had been brought to Antigua "when he was about ten."[7] If Court was forty-five in 1736, he was born around 1691, carried to British Antigua as a ten-year-old boy about 1701, and purchased by Kerby between 1706 and 1707. His childhood in Africa spanned the last years of the seventeenth century, one of the most tumultuous in West African history.

The commissioners wrote that Court was a "Coromantee," a slave "born on the Gold Coast of Africa."[8] The British used the term "Coromantee" to refer to peoples who spoke a similar language and shared customs that today are called Akan.[9] European slave ships took Akan peoples from a coastline extending roughly 250 miles from the Tano River in the west to the Volta River in the east, a region that stretched northward across at least forty-eight separate kingdoms and polities (and probably many more) to the Volta River Basin.[10] The British named them all after the coastal village Kormantse where the English built their first small fort in 1638.[11] Akanni merchants living hundreds of miles to the north sold men, women, and children from village to village and across kingdoms on a slow journey that could take months and sometimes years before captives gazed for the first time on ships anchored at sea.[12] Despite the diversity of peoples in the towns of the forest and grass, the English called them all Coromantee and imagined their shared "country."[13]

The weight of evidence suggests Court was from Eguafo, a small kingdom located in what is today the central coast of Ghana. The best clue is the name shouted by the crowd at the height of Court's ceremony: "Tackey." The Antigua Council reported the assembly shouted "Tackey, Tackey, Tackey, Coquo Tackey!" translated by an enslaved interpreter as "King, King, King, Great King." But "Tackey" does not mean "king."[14]

Takyi is a surname in the Akan languages, a name one earned or gave to oneself for personal achievement. A man might earn the name Ankoanna, "does not sleep without fighting," or Bediako, "came to engage in wars."[15] A person could assume many names over the course of their life. "The Number [of names] given to some men amounts to twenty," the Dutch merchant Willem Bosman noted of this Gold Coast practice in the 1690s.[16] "Takyi" means the "supporter of causes/initiatives/campaigns" or "the one who gives support from behind."[17] When Court sought to organize the slaves of Antigua in 1736, he renamed himself Takyi, "the supporter of campaigns" (when the Fante-born Tacky led a revolt across Jamaica in 1760, he did the same).[18] While the meaning of the name makes sense for Court, it does not explain why the enslaved interpreter translated "Tackey" as "king," rather than as a surname. Nor does it explain why across Antigua, the slaves toasted Court as "King Tacky" in the months before his dance.[19]

Court may have adopted the name of King Abe Takyi, the king of Eguafo in the 1690s. King Takyi (whom the English called "Great Tagee") warred fiercely against the Dutch and their allies when Court was a boy. There were at least five people named Takyi in Eguafo's ruling family in those years.[20] Amo Takyi led the king's armies.[21] Takyi Ankan, the king's nephew, launched a civil war against his uncle in 1696. Outside of Eguafo, I have not found another reference to the name Tacky in European records from the seventeenth-century Gold Coast.[22]

There was good reason for Court to associate himself with the famous ruler. As historian James H. Sweet observes of West Africans enslaved in Brazil, "In some instances, the perceived power of the group was tied directly to the memory of historically important political figures [in West Africa]." Enslaved spiritual leaders would invoke the famous dead to tap into "potent memories of political power and redemption in the [African] homeland."[23] By calling himself "King Takyi," Court took on the mantle of a famous African ruler. And this best explains the misunderstanding between the Antigua commissioners and their interpreter: the slaves shouted the king's *name*, "Great Takyi," rather than "Great King."[24]

There are other clues that suggest Court's birthplace in Eguafo. His shield dance in Antigua closely resembled a shield ceremony witnessed by Bosman, who was stationed at the Eguafo coastal town of Little Komenda in the mid-1690s (called Ackey-Tackey by the Eguafo).[25] There is also evidence Court used a proto-Fante dialect, the language of Eguafo and its coastal neighbors to the east. In Antigua, Court spoke of a person he remembered from Africa: "Quamina Jumper." Quamina (Kwamina) is a Fante name for a boy born on Saturday (as opposed to Kwame in Twi).[26] There is evidence the Fante day name Kwamina was in common use on the Eguafo Coast in the 1680s and 1690s.[27]

Eguafo seems like a good guess for Court's homeland. But it is only a guess. Court's likely homeland encompasses a range of possibilities from most probable—Court was born in Eguafo, adopted the name of "Great Tagee," performed a dance documented by a Dutch observer who lived on Eguafo's coast, spoke the mfantse dialect, and so on—to slightly less probable—Court was from a different kingdom on the Gold Coast, such as Denkyira, which was conquered by the Asante in 1701—to the improbable—he was not born in Africa at all. Without more evidence, we cannot be sure of his birthplace.

Nevertheless, Eguafo's documented past can teach us a great deal about the experience of a child in the late seventeenth-century Gold Coast. Eguafo was a small kingdom centrally located on the southern Atlantic Coast, between the Pra River Basin and the Sweet River, in what is today the nation of Ghana. The kingdom controlled one of the critical routes of trade between European forts on the coast and the large inland kingdoms to the north. In 1694, Eguafo's rulers began a civil war that quickly drew in neighboring kingdoms and European companies, setting in motion a vast conflict remembered as the Komenda Wars (1694–1700).[28] Europeans produced an extensive record of this conflict, one that allows for a rare window into the struggles of a West African people seeking to survive a desperate war in the late seventeenth century. It was a war that produced many casualties and many captives, a war whose combatants might have enslaved Court when he was ten years old.

Court's childhood experience was structured by the family, the village, and the forest. A male child born in the southern Gold Coast in the late seventeenth century was made to understand that he shared kinship with his mother's extended family and with her matriclan, called the *abusua*.[29] The Akan people passed their lineage through the line of the mother and grandmother. His village was composed of many matriclans, all responsible to each other and sharing a common origin with the ancient ones, the first of their people.[30] Their many villages and towns were united in the *oman*, the kingdom, led by an *ohene* (king), *caboceers* (headmen), and men who guarded the community. Beyond the bounds of the villages and shared fields was the forest, a place of spirits and animals, a place of strangers who threatened to bring ruin and steal children away.

Court might have remembered children's stories on feast days. These were nighttime gatherings in which elders shared fables about their people's origins with little boys and girls. European merchants wrote of storytelling in the Gold Coast towns in the late seventeenth and early eighteenth centuries. "[They] assemble in moonlight," wrote Ludewig Romer, a Danish merchant, "sitting out of doors, fifty in a circle, while the old people tell the young about this Nanni."[31] As the children listened, the storyteller recounted tales about Ananse Kokuroko, the Great Spider, and her creation of the first people. In the mid-eighteenth-century version related by the Dane, the universal spirit ordered Ananse to weave a cloth. From the spider's cloth the spirit made human beings. When she finished weaving, Ananse Kokuroko expected the people to thank her for her toil. But they abandoned her. So, from the last thread, the great spider wove her own person. He took her name, her famous name, calling himself Ananse ("Nanni"), the trickster.[32]

"When the Negroes tell this story about Nanni, they act it all out," Romer continued. "If Nanni walked from one place to another, they also take a few steps. If [Nanni] struck someone, the storyteller grabs hold of one of the party and strikes him. If Nanni ate something that tasted good, if he wept, laughed, danced, limped, and so on, the storyteller does the same."[33] The elders shared these fables across towns and kingdoms, each story offering a lesson to be long remembered. Children taken up and sold across the sea would continue to tell stories of "Nanni," the trickster who outsmarted the powerful and cruel.

While stories of Ananse were common, most southern Gold Coast peoples believed they had descended from distinctive ancient ones, separate from their neighbors and rivals. Their first people had fallen from the sky or climbed out of the earth. The Asebu kingdom, east of Eguafo, said their first ancestors had emerged from the sea. The Fetu and Agona said their people had come from the rivers or the bushes.[34] The Eguafo, in stories first documented in the early nineteenth century maintained an oral tradition that their ancient ancestors had fallen from heaven in a brass pan, called Ayewa Kese, and began to plant and weed near where they landed. These stories shared a common theme: their ancestors were the first inhabitants of the land. In Ghana today the Eguafo chieftaincy is considered an *oman panyin* (elder state) because the Eguafo are seen as one of the oldest kingdoms on the Gold Coast.[35]

Eguafo stories also related their origins to the Dompɔw, the sacred grove on the hill above the principal town. Many southern Gold Coast peoples identified certain patches of woods as dwelling places of ancestors and spirits. Archaeologist Gerard Chouin argues these sacred groves appear to have developed at the site of abandoned settlements or old cemeteries.[36] Eguafo's Dompɔw was first occupied more than a thousand years ago as a defensive hilltop settlement. In the late 1600s, the Eguafo might have only just begun to regard the Dompɔw as sacred. Archaeologist Samuel Spiers, in his excavations, found evidence that the hilltop had been abandoned sometime in the sixteenth or seventeenth century. When Court was a child, Eguafomon, the capital town, had spread along the hillside and across the valley.[37]

The children understood that their ancestors watched over them. Ancestors lived in the grove or in the soft forest earth or even in the floors of their homes. Willem Bosman, writing in 1704, explained that Gold Coast peoples believed in a "future state" where the dead lived "in the same character as here, and makes use of all the Offering of his Friends and Relations."[38] In 1881, two centuries after Court's childhood, the missionary J. G. Christaller sought to explain the location of ancestors in his Twi dictionary. "It is said," he wrote, "the realm of the dead is below (in the earth); some say: it is above (in heaven); about this there is no surety. Where one is taken to, when one dies, there his spirit is; when you die and they take you to the spirits grove, then your spirit is in the grove."[39] You could summon your ancestors in prayer and ask them for help. You might send them gifts of food and drink to comfort them in the afterlife.

When the storyteller finished, the children made their way home across the familiar paths of the village. They sang songs and passed men and women sitting in the night air. Beyond the thatched houses was the hilltop forest. The starlit sky wheeled above, unencumbered by the artificial light of later centuries. The children returned from storytelling to the homes of their mothers to sleep and dream.

He awoke in a kingdom composed of villages and a great town built on the side of the mountain. The Eguafo called their capital Eguafomon (Eguafo state), though the Europeans called it Komenda, a name they used for both the largest town and the entire kingdom. Eguafomon lay seven miles inland, a town of perhaps four hundred houses and two thousand people in the late seventeenth century.[40] Smaller villages stretched across the valley at key points along paths that led south to the coast and Little Komenda, a fishing village grown to encompass a population of 1,500 people after two centuries of Atlantic trade. "The country is densely populated," noted the French trader Jean Barbot after his visit to the Eguafo Coast in 1678. "It is warlike, and the king can put 20,000 men in the field when necessary."[41]

Court did not share his memories of his mother, but she would have been at the center of his memories of his childhood. A child "usually lives with [his mother] and is brought up by her till it is eight or ten," wrote Barbot.[42] Court's mornings were organized around helping her labor, as she carried water and pounded millet or maize with two hands, all while carrying his infant brothers and sisters "tied to her back, from morning to night, without leaving them, no matter what she does."[43] T. E. Kyei in his autobiography of growing up in the rural Gold Coast of the early twentieth century noted that his first memory was of waving flies away from his infant brother while his mother tended her crops.[44]

There were moments only Court would have remembered: perhaps the look of his mother at first light when she went to fetch water. She would have crouched down, back straight, and placed the circular cloth on her head and then the vessel. She stood straight up, no need to steady the weight with her hands, balancing the vessel as she made her way to the waterside with Court in tow.

He had understood his place in his mother's lineage since before memory, all the way back to his outdooring ceremony, the moment when a newborn child was first introduced to his people. His mother's clan had waited eight days after his birth before they met him, to make sure the infant would survive, to be certain the spiritual being of the child would not try to return to the afterlife. His mother and father were kept at home during this period of danger, while a priest administered rituals to encourage the child to stay.[45] In a region of high infant mortality, the Akan peoples of the southern Gold Coast developed the ceremony to protect the community from loss. (As late as 1931, British surveys of mothers in Gold Coast rural villages found that 40 percent of children did not survive to adulthood.)[46] On the eighth day, the child was brought forth to relatives and the village, washed, and given gifts and a name, marking his social existence and place among his family.[47]

Court's birth contributed to the wealth and status of his family. "As we are told," wrote the Antigua commissioners, "Court was of a considerable Family in his own Country, but not as was commonly thought of Royal-Blood."[48] A "considerable" family in the Gold Coast measured their wealth in subordinate people, both children and slaves. Children provided work for the household and in the fields, and were expected to provide for their relatives as they aged.[49] A man's "wealth consists only of his children and slaves," wrote Romer in 1760. "If none of his ancestors is buried [in his house], he would sell his hut for a few rixalder [a Danish currency equivalent to six English shillings]." His "children and slaves are really his wealth, his power, his protection."[50] In the seventeenth and eighteenth centuries, a maternal uncle had the right to pawn his children, to offer them up as collateral to pay his debt, perhaps the simplest example of the right of ownership of a child.[51]

Court's "considerable family" would have lived in a polygamous compound, his father marrying multiple wives who each maintained their own house, the father moving among houses on specific days of the week.[52] Their houses were thatched, rectangular, and arranged in a square with doorways facing out to a courtyard. Kitchens were outside.[53] These compounds ran up alongside one another. Farmland, assigned for cultivation by headmen, stretched to the edge of the forest.

If the seventeenth-century Gold Coast child belonged to a family and town, the forest represented the world outside those bounds. Parents taught their children to fear the forest. Children grew up learning folktales and sharing beliefs about humanlike animals that crossed over between the realm of the spiritual and physical, called familiars. These spiritual beings assisted witches. In one study in the British Gold Coast colony of the 1950s, ethnologists asked children to draw their fears on a piece of paper. The British ethnologists were surprised to see Gold Coast children from both urban and rural communities drawing animals, especially birds like hawks and other fowl, as representations of their fears. One ethnologist noted that Gold Coast children were as likely to believe that animals were the familiars of witches as American children were to believe in Santa Claus and flying reindeer.[54] While no similar studies exist for the late seventeenth century, Akan children were raised with folktales of spirit animals, suggesting their belief system would have nurtured similar fears.[55]

There were greater dangers beyond the forest. The child born into the Gold Coast of the late seventeenth century lived within a confined geography, bounded by neighboring kingdoms that were often hostile. Eguafo's northern boundary in the 1690s probably lay no more than twenty miles inland from the coast.[56] Outside those northern bounds, and to the east and west, any subject of Eguafo might be captured by foreign people, ransomed, or sold to European ships waiting at sea. Beyond the villages was great danger for any child.

At the end of his day, as the little boy lay down on his mat to sleep, his connection to the Eguafo town was clear. He knew he shared an origin to the first people, that he had descended from the sky above or from the sacred grove. He knew that his ancestors slept in the earth, even beneath his mat, listening for his prayers. By the soft sounds of his family sleeping in the dark, he knew he was safe. The little boy could close his eyes assured that the living and the dead watched over him.

Court did not try to recreate the ancestral villages of his youth in Antigua. There is no evidence he sought out matriclans or even prayed to the spirits of his ancestors. Perhaps he did not think it was possible.

He was separated by an ocean from his birthplace, and after all, kinship could not easily be invented among strangers. The slaves of Antigua were descended from different homelands and different ancestors.

He sought instead to use political customs of the Gold Coast to unite the slaves of the province. He chose a ceremony from his youth: the shield dance, an ennobling ceremony in which political leaders elevated a common-born man to the status of an *abirempon,* a Big Man, an ennobled rich person. Wealthy and influential men could ask permission from the *ohene* or *caboceer* to perform the dance, to feast and fete the people as proof of their status. If the elders gave permission, the commoner announced to "all Relations and Acquaintances that they may come and make merry with them for Several Days together."[57] These were elaborate events easily remembered by a Gold Coast child.

A commoner purchased the right to be ennobled. He brought livestock—sheep, goats, and cows—palm wine, and any other liquors that might please the men and women of the town. "These with their wives and slaves appear with as much Pomp and Splendor as is possible," Bosman wrote in 1704, "borrowing Gold and Coral of their Friends to make the greater show." The feast began with horns. "To acquire a Reputation and great Name amongst their Fellow-Citizens, [they] buy seven small Elephants' Teeth, which they make into Blowing horns, upon which they cause their People to learn in the manner of the Land, to play, to blow, all sorts of Tunes," wrote Bosman.[58]

To a little boy, such a feast must have been a grand thing. Wealthy men swayed on litters above the crowd, slaves bearing their weight. Bell-beaters banged on cowbells and drummers led the way followed by retainers bearing muskets. Behind them all walked the wealthy men's wives and children and more slaves.[59] Ennobling celebrations embraced the pageantry of the *oman,* its officers and symbols, and encouraged the political leadership to display their status. There was the umbrella and the sword, the *braffo* (general) and the warriors. The town elders looked on as rich men paraded their new wealth. The public officials stood barefoot beneath the canopies. Their divine authority was sanctioned by their connection to the ancestors in the earth and the *oman*.[60] Despite the audacity of the parade, they made sure to share the harvest with the ancestors at the new year.

Figure 3. "A Nobleman, Trader and Interpreter," plate no. 2 in Pieter de Marees, *Description and Historical Account of the Gold Kingdom of Guinea* (Amsterdam, 1602). In this early seventeenth-century engraving, the figure on the left is meant to represent an *abirempon,* or Big Man, on the Gold Coast. Courtesy KB, National Library of the Netherlands, Amsterdam

The *abirempon* enjoyed great privileges for their ennoblement. As historian Ray A. Kea explains, a noble on the Gold Coast secured the right to buy and sell slaves and trade goods. He could carry symbols of authority, such as umbrellas, shields, drums, and "horse tails," and he could participate in governance with other town leaders.[61]

The Atlantic trade with Europeans—a trade in gold and slaves and European goods—created new forms of wealth among the common classes of people, challenging the older hereditary political order of nobility.[62] The expansion in this trade was a source of profound social disruption to the Eguafo. They had been led by hereditary leaders, men who sat on leading family stools created by divine sanction. These nobles presided over courts and had the divine right to call men to battle.

The *abirempon* purchased their family stools and demonstrated their status by surrounding themselves with slaves and their own people.[63] The differences between old authority and new power were apparent for all to see in Eguafomon. Bosman wrote of the Gold Coast in the 1690s that "only the richest man is the most honored, without the least regard to nobility." Although the title of king or captain might descend from the matrilineal line, by 1700 "so much regard is had to his riches in slaves and money, that he who is plentifully stored with these, is often preferred to the Right Heir."[64]

Commoners used the feasts to achieve that elevation. They used the shields to earn the right to lead their people. Bosman explained that the shield ceremony represented a pledge to defend the *oman:* "A Negro thus far advanced in honor, usually makes himself master of first one and another shield." He "is obliged to lye the first night with all his family in battle array in the open air; intimating that he will not be afraid of any danger or Hard-ship in Defence of his People." The ennobled man spent the next eight days "in shooting and martial exercises." The shield, called an *eykem,* was an important symbol of martial honor.[65]

Court would perform the same dance forty years later. He would organize the slaves of Antigua into a community of militia and have them perform "shooting and martial" exercises in the night. The ceremony was not an act of war, as the commissioners of Antigua claimed. To dance with spear and shield was a symbolic act accompanied by an oath. The ennobled man took on the obligation to protect his people through his new rank. The spear and shield were sacred objects assigned for a peaceful performance.

But in the world that Court knew on the 1690s Gold Coast, a time and place in which warfare among neighboring peoples was a fact of life, the *abirempon* oath to protect his people meant more than a simple gesture. Any nobleman, high born or common, rich or poor, could expect to have his promise to defend his people tested in combat. In a kingdom at war, the shield ceremony was preparation for real violence.

Court's childhood coincided with a series of internecine conflicts remembered as the Komenda Wars. The Eguafo kingdom (known as Komenda to Europeans) descended into civil war in 1694, its feuding rulers inviting neighboring African and European powers into the violence. If Court was born in 1691 in Eguafo, his childhood memories would have been troubled by these wars. He would have remembered regular episodes of rumored invasions. He would have seen wounds and death. He would have viewed many neighboring peoples as a near constant threat, capable of tearing him away from his village and family at any time. In Antigua, as a man, Court probably took the name of Eguafo's famous leader King Abe Takyi, whose victories over the Dutch and his African rivals in the Komenda Wars were well known on the southern Gold Coast of Court's youth.

The famed King Abe Takyi rose to power sometime around 1688.[66] Bosman, who knew him only by reputation, said Takyi "excelled" all of his contemporaries in "valour and conduct."[67] As late as 1687, he was known to the English as "Tagee, a rebel," the cousin of the Eguafo king. "Tagee" ruled several villages and consistently feuded with his family. The English noted that when Takyi attempted to trade with the Dutch in his home village, the king promptly captured the Dutch envoy and executed him.[68] In May 1688, Abe Takyi allied with the Dutch and rebelled against his king, a war that ended with his royal cousin's death.[69] Takyi took the Eguafo stool and the title of "Eguafohene," or Eguafo king.

Throughout the rest of his reign, King Takyi sought to preserve the autonomy of Eguafo by pitting his kingdom's powerful enemies against each other. His first act was to invite the English to build a new fort on the Eguafo Coast. It was a daring move. The Dutch had joined his rebellion because his predecessor had invited the French to build a fort near the same spot.[70] The Dutch ruled the walled town of Elmina in the center of the Eguafo Coast and a second fort to the west, at the village of Little Komenda. They paid tribute to the Eguafohene even as they jealously forbade any other European companies from building a fort on the shore. Takyi invited the English to weaken the Dutch monopoly on his southern border.

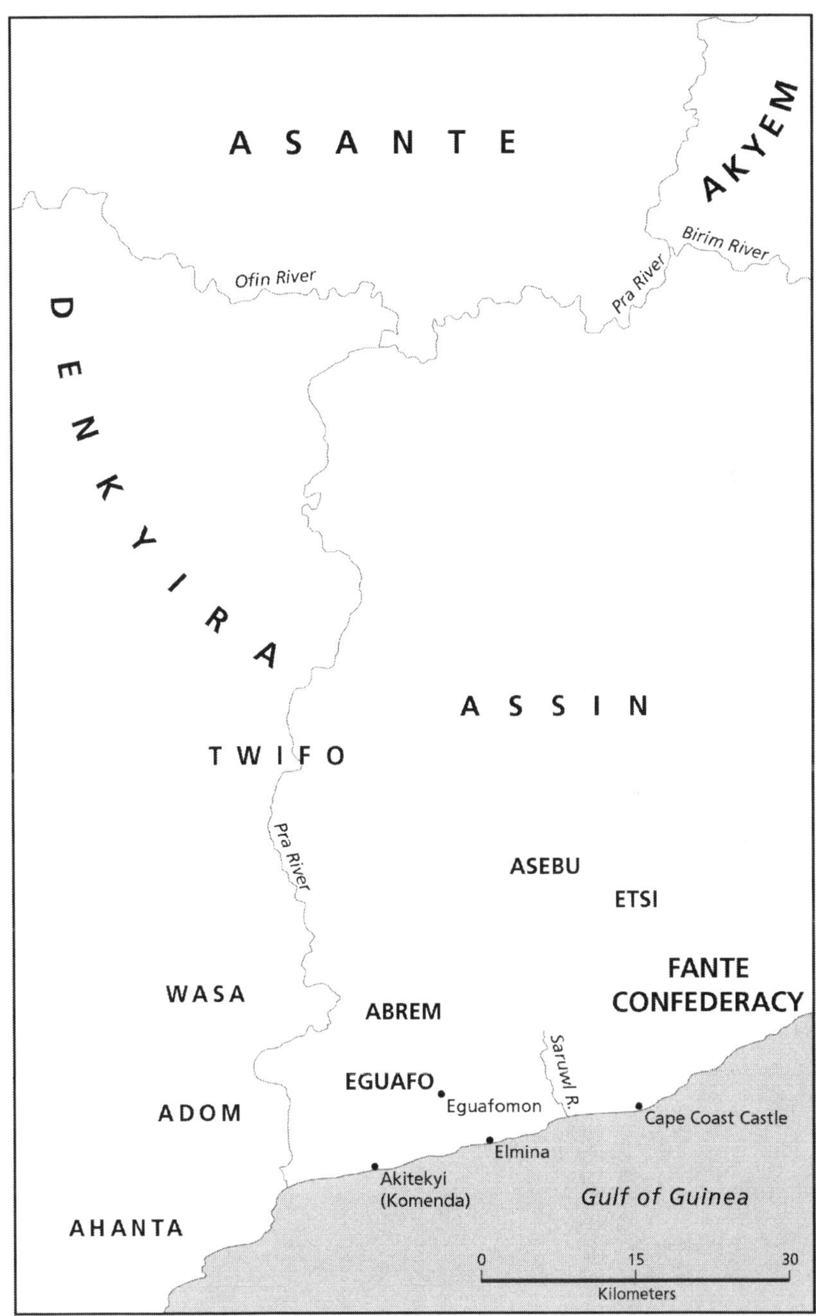

Map 2. Eguafo and neighboring kingdoms, c. 1700

Eguafo's most dangerous enemies resided in the north, where the populous forest kingdom of Denkyira cast its shadow over the smaller polities of Adom and its allies Twifo, Assin, Wasa, and Cabess Terra. Denkyira demanded tribute from its neighbors, including the Asante kingdom, which lay deep in the interior beyond the Ofrin River.[71] Eguafo's location on the routes between the coast and Denkyira allowed Takyi to control access to the Atlantic. The Eguafo taxed all merchants, caravans of Akanni traders who traversed the northern kingdoms, and European companies crowded along the southern shore.[72] They aggressively guarded their borders. Denkyira and the northern kingdoms resented Eguafo's control of Atlantic commerce.

Like most southern Gold Coast states in the seventeenth and eighteenth centuries, Eguafo was organized politically into an *oman,* or kingdom. In 1704, Bosman wrote that Gold Coast polities were either "monarchies" or "commonwealths," and by this he meant they were ruled either by a king or by an oligarchy of headmen.[73] In Eguafo, the Eguafohene ruled over subchiefs, called *caboceers,* who governed towns or villages and their surrounding farmland and paid tribute to the *ohene.*[74] They were supported in their governance by *abirempon,* who participated in councils and enjoyed privileges of status and trade. The *caboceers* held court and administered justice. The *caboceers* also served in council as a check on the king's power. The Eguafohene could not negotiate treaties or wage war without their tacit support.[75]

By the 1690s, King Takyi and the Eguafo *caboceers* had become reliant on the control and taxation of the coastal trade. The Eguafohene redistributed the taxes taken from merchants and the tribute paid by Europeans to his subchiefs. Eguafo produced neither gold nor slaves, the two commodities demanded by the European monopolies. The inland forest kingdoms, like Denkyira, Asante, and Akyem, produced the commodities desired by the strangers on the coast.[76] The Eguafohene's control of the trade became a singular source of wealth for its leaders and one that invited jealousy. In 1695, these jealousies threatened to destroy Eguafo from without and within.

The war began with the construction of the English Royal African Company's fort. On 20 November 1694, the English established their new settlement for trade at Little Komenda on the Eguafo Coast. Takyi had invited their presence for several years, but the Dutch had long warned the English of violence if they trespassed there. On 6 December, the Dutch cannoneers at Fort Vredenburgh, in Little Komenda, opened fire on the English party. When the local *caboceer* at Little Komenda asked why the Dutch had fired on his invited English guests, the Dutch shouted, "The English should not live here." At their headquarters in Elmina, the Dutch sent out envoys to neighboring nations, inviting an alliance against Eguafo.[77]

King Takyi learned in January 1695 that the powerful Denkyira and Twifo, Eguafo's close neighbors to the north, were negotiating a war alliance with the Dutch. Twifo, a tributary of Denkyira, complained openly to the Dutch of being denied access to the "Komenda trade." In the south, Takyi discovered that young Willem Bosman, the Dutch trader placed in command of Fort Vredenburgh, had attempted to assassinate the *caboceer* of Little Komenda during a meeting on the beach.[78] The Dutch fort and the southern villages were in open war. Enemies gathered to the north and south. It must have seemed as if the walls were closing in on Takyi.

King Takyi surprised his African and Dutch enemies. He assembled allies, members of the Fante Confederacy to the east, armed with guns and powder from the English Royal African Company stationed at Cape Coast Castle. On 28 April, King Takyi and his younger brother Takyi Kuma led an army against Twifo and the Dutch. There is no detailed account of the battle. We know only that King Takyi decisively defeated his enemies and drove them into the Dutch fortresses on the coast.[79]

King Takyi's victory was short lived. "We should never have been able to make any fresh attempt," wrote Bosman, writing from the Dutch perspective, "if the enemies themselves had not seasonably placed an opportunity into our hands by their intestine divisions."[80] Sometime in 1695, after the defeat of Twifo and the Dutch, King Takyi's brother Takyi

Kuma (Takyi Junior) rose in rebellion. The causes of the dispute are not clear, but like Takyi before him, Takyi Kuma, whom the English called "Little Tagee," sought to seize the title of *ohene* for himself.[81] Whatever the first reasons for the quarrel, any attempt to gain power in Eguafo required control of the Atlantic trade and the stool of the king.

Takyi Kuma built a powerful new alliance. He launched a true civil war, bringing villages across Eguafo to his side. The southern villages near Little Komenda proved especially supportive of his cause. "A great many people are revolted from [King Takyi]," wrote the English factor Thomas Wilson. They "went to Little Tagee both from this town and all the adjacent [towns]."[82] Takyi drew in warriors from the kingdom of Adom and Akani soldiers from the north. He allied with the Dutch.[83] On 21 January 1696, a fleet of Dutch canoes from Elima blocked the Eguafo port of Little Komenda. "Little Tagee is to fight Great Taggee," wrote Wilson to Cape Coast Castle.[84]

Court would have been five years old as the men of his Eguafo village prepared for war. Perhaps he would have remembered the moment: the men gathered in a great crowd in the village center. The priests smeared white clay, called *hyire,* on the bodies and faces of warriors because it was believed to purify a person and prepare them for communication between the living and the dead.[85] The warriors strung charms around their neck for protection, the priest calling on the spirits and ancestors to protect the townsmen. They carried muskets. Their leaders wore ceremonial swords, "shaped like a sort of chopping knives," whose purpose was mostly to sever heads from dead bodies at the end of battle.[86] If Court saw any of it, even as a little boy, the scene of painted warriors marching forth singing songs to their ancestors and their king would not easily have been forgotten.

Where King Takyi met Takyi Kuma in battle is not known. Bosman provided an account of the fighting, writing in the first person as if he might have engaged in the battle himself. Fighting on the Gold Coast began with musketeers running "stooping and listening that bullets may fly over their heads. Others creep toward the enemy, and being come close, let fly at them." The *caboceers* followed with their warriors, each "commander hath his men close together in a sort of crowd in the midst of which he is to be found." The battle between the two Takyis was "so warm on both sides, that Victory was long dubious," Bosman wrote, "till at last it seemed to encline on our side so far that our Army fell greedily to plunder." As Takyi Kuma's armies began plundering baggage (and perhaps the dead), "Great Tagee," who had "hitherto kept himself out of the Fight and laid us this Bait: he unexpectedly Marched towards us with fresh Forces, who had their Musquets turned the wrong way in order to deceive us." Takyi Panin's soldiers flipped their weapons, fired into the ranks of Takyi Kuma and the Dutch, and charged. Bosman's army broke "and obliged every Body to save his Life as well as he could."[87]

If Court lived in a village loyal to King Takyi, he heard the public rejoicing of the news as the first warriors returned. The Dutch sued for peace, and Takyi Kuma, who survived the battle, retreated to their protection. For King Takyi, the battle reaffirmed his rule over the Eguafo Coast, creating new competition between the English and Dutch. On 24 September 1696, King Takyi allowed Kuma to return home to Eguafo.[88]

From the perspective of a child living in the southern Gold Coast in the late 1690s, King Takyi must have seemed triumphant: the conqueror of rival armies, vanquisher of his usurping brother, victor over the white people by the sea.

In 1736, when Court sought to unite the slaves of Antigua, King Abe Takyi provided a model for a successful Gold Coast ruler. He was an *ohene* who had united his people against foreign African neighbors and the Dutch. For those "Coromantees" who might share stories of King Takyi, there was a powerful association of victory in war and defiance in the name of "King Takyi."

But perhaps there was a greater lesson for Court from his memory of childhood conflict. The Gold Coast of the 1690s had been a homeland subsumed in war. To unite the many African peoples of Antigua, he would have to transcend the boundaries of homelands. Court's campaign in Antigua would bear all the semblance of a man seeking to bring disparate peoples together, Africans and American creoles, under his leadership as King Takyi.

Court sought to bring what was useful from Africa into the Americas. He performed the ennobling dance. He sought to rebuild the *oman* from his youth. He was just a child when slavers took him from his home. He would have to construct from the memories of his Gold Coast youth a new vision for a New World.

CHAPTER THREE

Passages into Slavery

November 1698
Eguafo Kingdom

IT WAS NOT POLITE TO speak of a king's death on the seventeenth-century Gold Coast. You did not say a "king has died" but rather "a great tree has fallen."[1] A king's death was a calamity for his people. Speaking of such a loss invited misfortune. You might celebrate the life of a king, just as you celebrate the life of all great ancestors. T. E. Kyei, writing of his Asante youth in the early twentieth-century Gold Coast, remembered that whenever his grandmother mentioned a matrilineal relative, she would raise herself "slightly up" from her stool and say, "So-and-so, I rise in his/her honour."[2] Kyei's grandmother lauded her ancestors. But she did not speak of their deaths.

Court would have been seven years old when the English murdered King Takyi. The Eguafohene had demanded his customs from the Royal African Company (RAC) for trading on his coast in 1698. When the English would not pay, Takyi sought a new treaty with the Dutch at Elmina castle. The RAC, in retaliation, courted the king's brother Takyi Kuma, "Little Tagee," and offered him a secret alliance.[3] In early November, RAC officials invited King Takyi to Cape Coast Castle to "come make merry with them." They murdered the Eguafohene inside their walls, in a "manner esteemed barbarous by all Europeans," Willem Bosman wrote.[4]

News of Takyi's death sparked outrage across the Gold Coast. Fifty miles to the east, a *caboceer* of Winneba confronted an English trader, saying the "English had killed Great Taggee."[5] The French slave trader Jean Barbot, arriving on the western edge of the Gold Coast five months later, recorded local rumors of the English murdering "a Black King."[6] Even if Court did not grow up in Eguafo (we cannot know for sure), he might have heard of King Takyi, the Eguafohene who defeated his rivals in war.

King Abe Takyi, "great Tagee," sought to harness the global marketplace and protect his kingdom's boundaries against enemies resentful of his control over the Atlantic trade. He saw in his own life the numbers of European ships growing on his shore. He saw the inland kingdoms, which sold gold and increasingly slaves, expand in power as they clamored for European goods. As Karl Marx noted long ago, "Men make their own history, but they do not make it just as they please; they do not make it under circumstances chosen by themselves, but under circumstances directly encountered."[7] Takyi sought to control the rising transatlantic trade. In the end, he could not fend off rivals animated by their own desire to profit. No matter his victories against the Dutch or his African neighbors or his brother, there were too many enemies of Eguafo. But it is not polite to speak of the death of a king.

Eguafo descended into a new civil war. On 13 January 1699, Takyi Kuma marched an army of foreign warriors toward Eguafomon. He carried English muskets and powder and paid his troops with RAC goods.[8] King Takyi's general Amo Takyi rallied the *caboceers* and warriors of Eguafoman, and though outnumbered four to one, they met the king's brother in battle. The Eguafo fighters drove Takyi Kuma's warriors from the field. "The Commanians [Eguafo] ow'd this Signal Victory to their General, Amo-Tecki," wrote Bosman, "a Negroe, who in Valour equall'd, if not exceeded their Murther'd King."[9] But the general's forces could not hold back the repeated invasions of Takyi Kuma. In April 1700, Takyi Kuma defeated Eguafo in battle and took the stool of Eguafoman.[10]

Eguafo was but one of many kingdoms plagued by endemic warfare in 1700. To the north, Denkyira's armies invaded their neighbors in an aggressive bid to control trade routes to the coast.[11] In 1701, Denkyira struck the northern forest kingdom of Asante only to suffer a bitter defeat. The Asante retaliated by invading Denkyira, sweeping across their villages, pillaging and taking slaves. Merchant traders marched fresh captives toward the ships waiting at sea.

African merchants sold Court to a British slaver in this period of war, around 1700 or 1701. He was nine or ten years old. He left no record concerning how he was made a slave. On the seventeenth-century Gold Coast, a child could be enslaved in many ways. Barbot, an active slave ship captain in the late seventeenth century, wrote that children were sometimes sold by their parents "because they cannot keep them" or because "they cannot pay their fines." People starving might "sell themselves to rich men" for life. "But of all these," he wrote, "the largest number are those taken in war or seized in their homes and carried off."[12]

Like more than a million West Africans carried by the British across the Atlantic in the first half of the eighteenth century, Court's passage into slavery transformed his status from a subject of an African body politic, a person with ancestral and political rights, to a slave in America, a person who could be bought and sold and harmed with near impunity. In the first passage, from kingdom to coast, African merchants tore him from his home. In the second, on the slave ship, the captain and crew stripped Court of the markers of his past life and renamed him with a number in a ledger. He became an anonymous, naked person in a crowd of strangers. In the third and final passage, the march from ship to plantation, planters made Court a Black slave, a racialized person who would spend the rest of his life laboring in perpetual bondage for the profit of his white master. By the end of these passages, the slavers even took his name, given to him eight days after his birth by his mother's people.

Court's passage into slavery began with his forced journey from his homeland to the sea. His captors took him from his family, his mother and father and his mother's relatives, the matriclan. They stole him from the protection of the kingdom. With each step toward the coast, his captors led him farther away from his ancestors, who watched over him and waited for him in the earth.

Court would have known people who were enslaved in his homeland. As part of "a considerable Family in his own Country," slaves made-up part of his family's wealth.[13] Akan speakers called slaves *akoa,* a male subject, or *adonke,* a foreigner from the north.[14] Akan Twi speakers used a complicated lexicon for specific slave identities (at least by the nineteenth century, when the missionary J. G. Christaller created his English/Twi dictionary). They called a person "met on the way and seized as a slave" an *odwen.* They called a female slave from the north, with scarification marks on her face, an *aburuwa afana;* a short slave, an *akoana;* a strong slave, a *kwaberan.*[15] As specific as they were, they all referred to a person who could be bought or sold, an isolated person who could claim no connection to the Akan matriclans. A slave on the southern Gold Coast was defined not simply by their lack of freedom but by an inability to belong.[16] A slave was a person without ancestors in the village, a perpetual stranger with no place in the kingdom. "When [slaves] die they are thrown in a ditch," wrote Barbot. "I myself have seen instances."[17]

Eguafo was not a kingdom known for its sale of slaves in the late seventeenth century, but English correspondence regularly mentioned slave labor in the kingdom.[18] Only in times of war might ship captains find Eguafo merchants selling large numbers of slaves. "Here is sometimes a brisk trade for slaves when the Commanians [Eguafos] are at war with the upland Negroes, and have the better of it," wrote Barbot, "for then they bring down abundance of prisoners, whom they sell immediately, at a cheap rate."[19]

Enemy warriors would typically march a new captive back to the warriors' town or capital to be distributed as spoils of war and assigned a public fate. They would put many captives, especially women and children, to work in the towns and villages, cultivating the manioc root and millet that fed armies and villages.[20] Court was not chosen to labor as a slave among his captors. With several others, his enemies marched him south, down the forest trails to the coast, and there sold him to the English. If he was taken along the central Gold Coast, roughly between Eguafo and the Fante lands to the east, his captors most likely took him to the headquarters of the RAC, Cape Coast Castle.

The castle was a prison. It sits on a rocky outcropping, stones jutting out into the sea, the walls of the fortress mounted with great guns. Beneath the fortress, the English cut a vast dungeon for holding slaves. Barbot, who wrote of Cape Coast Castle, described the dungeon as a series of "vaulted cellars, divided into several apartments which could easily hold a thousand slaves."[21] A visitor today is struck by the pitch-black darkness of the dungeon and the sound of waves crashing against the walls.[22] A child in such a place must have been filled with fear.

Olaudah Equiano remembered the questions that so troubled him as an eleven-year-old boy waiting on a British slave vessel to sail for America in the mid-eighteenth century. "What was to be done with us?" he asked chained men who spoke his language. "We were to be carried to these white people's country to work for them," they answered. He thought to himself, "If it were no worse than working, my situation was not so desperate," but he still "feared I should be put to death, the white people looked and acted, as I thought, in so savage a manner." He asked the chained men, "If these people had no country, but lived in this hollow place [the ship]?" They told him white people came from a distant country.[23] He wondered at the spirits that drove the ship. He would not be comforted and longed to escape, though he could not find a way.

Court could not escape either. He encountered a vast array of people seeking to profit from the historical forces that had created an Atlantic slave trade on the coast of Africa. He was born into a society under pressure from intense violence and rapid political change. Between 1675 and 1750, the Gold Coast was a crowded region subsumed in wars among petty kingdoms that sought to consolidate their power at the expense of rivals. Behind these wars was a social upheaval brought about by the slave trade, a process of political formation that made Africans from these war-torn regions more astute as slave rebels. In a remarkable way, the peoples carried across the Atlantic Ocean in slave ships continued the process of consolidation and conflict they had known in their Old World. The slaves that would become rebels in the Americas were people who had been given the experience of both violence and political reinvention in western Africa.

The slave trade was the cause of this transformation among the peoples of the western coasts of Africa. At the end of the seventeenth century, the numbers of slaves exported from western Africa began to rise rapidly. For the years between 1650 and 1700, more slaves were sold on the Atlantic Coast than in the previous two hundred years combined.[24] Between 1600 and 1650, current estimates show roughly 680,000 slaves were carried into the transatlantic trade. From 1650 to 1700, this number doubled to more than 1.2 million. By 1750, Europeans had transported an additional 2.5 million slaves out of Africa.[25]

The expansion of the trade was a response to rising prices for slaves along the Atlantic Coast of West Africa. The demand created by the plantations in the Americas coincided with the discovery of Brazilian gold in Minas Gerais, meaning that Portuguese ships competed with merchant vessels of Britain and other European powers hoping to provide human chattel to the labor-hungry provinces in the western hemisphere.[26] For British slave traders, the rising competition on the coast was obvious. Captain William Snelgrave noted the change in his own lifetime trading on the road of Whydah, along the slave coast in modern-day Benin. "Whereas in the Year 1712, there went only 33 Ships from England to the Coast," he explained, "in 1726 . . . there had been there the Year before above 200 Sail, to the great increase of Navigation, and the advantage of our Plantations in America."[27]

Facing increased demand and competition, European factors proved willing to pay higher prices for slaves, doubling and then quadrupling the prices in goods paid to African merchants at the opening of the eighteenth century. This was true from Senegambia on the western Atlantic Coast to the river kingdoms of the Kongo and has been well documented by historians.[28] Whereas a slave cost the RAC £1.72 sterling at the beginning of its trade in 1673, by 1703 slave prices averaged £10.24 sterling. Representatives of the RAC blamed these high rates on both competition and the acquisitiveness of African merchants.[29] It was only the matter of a few coins, but for the peoples of West Africa, it was the difference between life and death.

The rising price of slaves created new economic incentives for African kings and merchants to sell their captives to Europeans. Slavery was indigenous and widespread in sub-Saharan Africa by the late seventeenth century. In the forest interior, slaves both played roles as agricultural producers and held value as chattel that could be sold. The absence of landed property in sub-Saharan Africa made slaves one of the only forms of revenue-producing property.[30] "Slaves are, you might say, a form of money among these Africans," wrote Barbot in the 1680s.[31] Higher prices for slaves made it more profitable to trade a slave than to put them to work in agricultural production.[32] The rising price of slaves also made transport from the interior to the coast far more profitable for African merchants. As historian Joseph Miller argued in *Way of Death*, rising slave prices in the Atlantic economy helped to finance the expansion of the slaving zone in central Africa.[33] From the Gambia

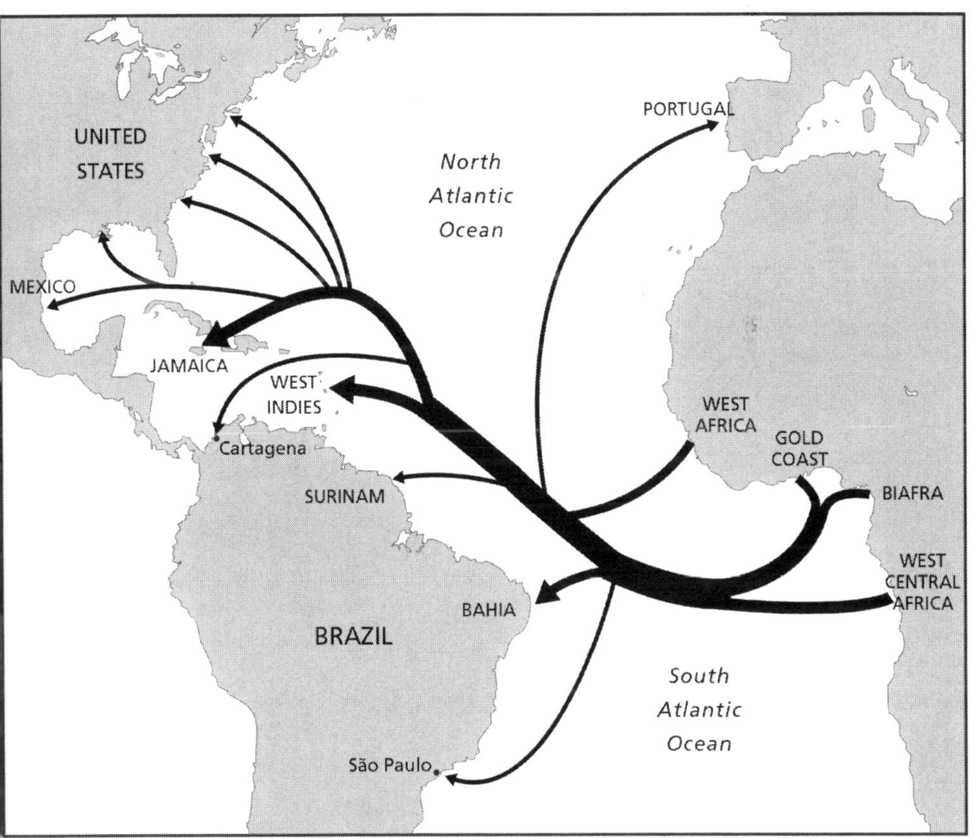

Map 3. Volume and direction of transatlantic slave trade to North America and the West Indies, 1688–1748

River to the Congo, the rising price of slaves allowed the trade to move into new frontiers, bringing Atlantic commodities to peoples far from the sea. By the early eighteenth century, slaves traded along the West-Central African coast originated from regions more than a thousand miles away.[34]

The competition to gain access to Atlantic slave markets—to control the routes of this trade and to demand tribute from smaller states with access to the coast—helped to fuel the expansion of warfare in western Africa. Small kingdoms, and specifically the headmen of those kingdoms, could profit and expand by controlling the routes of trade.[35] The ability to put a large, organized army in the field became crucial for the success of any state, and centralization allowed kings and merchants to demand tributes and duties from both African slave merchants and European traders.

The civil war in Eguafo and the invasion of the kingdom followed a pattern repeated throughout the Gold Coast. The slave trade led to the erosion of older African states; competition and rivalry over trade routes and tribute; and the growth of new, centralized political institutions. The rise of the British African trade, its increasing demand and growth of shipping, were not benign influences on the coast of West Africa. Rather, the slave trade was a powerful force that fueled large armies of organized states as they conquered rival nations and sent millions of new slaves into the western world.

Court's second passage, the "Middle Passage" on the slave ship, removed him forever from his native land. The European merchants on the ship transformed him into a nameless person, a number in a ledger without an origin or people. The passage across the Atlantic Ocean put him in constant physical danger. On the slave ship, a child saw more than a lifetime's worth of suffering and death in eight weeks.

Court cannot be identified on any specific slave ship. Slave ship captains did not record the names of their captives, only the numbers. Of the forty British slave ships that carried slaves to Antigua between 1700 and 1702, only one recorded a mission to the Gold Coast. The

Fauconberg, an RAC ship, departed London in 1699 and anchored at Cape Coast Castle in March 1700.[36] The ship took on 606 captives that spring, 103 of them children, an unusual number of boys and girls under the age of ten.[37] Most of the other known British slaving voyages in these years did not specify their destination on the African coast.[38] The *Fauconberg*, however, is unique because the ship's journal has survived.

Captain John Luke, commander of the *Fauconberg*, had ordered his crew to begin constructing the wooden partition on the deck while still at sea. The partition separated men from women and children on the voyage. On Wednesday, 4 January 1700, the *Fauconberg* dropped anchor at Little Komenda where the RAC ship "sent goods a Shore" for the small English fort. Luke ordered the crew to construct the "furnace," the cooking stove, that would serve to prepare food for the hundreds of slaves he intended to transport across the Atlantic Ocean. He sailed east for Cape Coast. On 19 March, after purchasing small groups of enslaved men and women for weeks, the RAC paddled 130 captives from Cape Coast Castle out to the *Fauconberg*. On 20 March, the *Fauconberg* enslaved 79 more men and women in one day. On 26 March, Luke ordered the ship to weigh anchor, tacking against the wind and heading toward Antigua. At the top of his journal, on the first page, the chronicler wrote they sailed "by ye Almighty Gods Permistion."[39]

Court would form a lifelong bond with a child who traveled with him in the slave ship on their Middle Passage. Coobah, a Fante girl whose day name meant she had been born on a Wednesday, suffered with him on their journey across the Atlantic.[40] Together, they were two small people aboard one of the 371 slave vessels that crossed the Atlantic Ocean in 1700.[41] They became part of a forced migration, a one-way, relentless exodus of near 12.5 million people over more than four hundred years across the sixteenth to nineteenth centuries of which only 10.7 million survived.[42]

The British became the consummate slave traders of the western hemisphere. Their ascent as leaders of the trade was rooted in the expansion of their colonial empire overseas: the demand for labor in the English plantations, the increasing volume of shipping among colonies, and the unique combination of state sponsorship and private enterprise that expanded what they had always called the "African trade." The rise of the British slave trade was an attempt by the British to satiate their need for labor in their colonies and to profit from the lucrative (so it was assumed) trade in human beings. By 1745, the growth in this commerce of people was tied to British imperial expansion.

For the ministers and merchants of the British Isles, it was clear the "African trade" had become part of the foundation of their empire in the Americas. "Will not every British Planter in America, and every West-India Merchant in England," wrote Charles Hayes to the House of Commons, "grant, that the Negroe Trade on the Coast of Africa, is the chief and fundamental Support of the British Colonies and Plantations?"[43] Most Britons agreed. They had celebrated the slave trade for a generation. In 1713, during the reign of Queen Anne, crowds of supporters marked the opening of the British slave trade to Spanish America with a torchlight procession through the nighttime streets of London.[44] By the early 1740s, British economist Malachy Postlethwayt could insist it was "allowed on all Hands, that the Trade to Africa is the Branch which renders our American Colonies and Plantations so advantagious."[45] In the year Postlethwayt published his pamphlet *The National and Private Advantages of the African Trade Considered* (1746), the population of the enslaved had reached proportions never before witnessed in the plantations of the Americas.

Historians might be surprised by the significance I place on the slave trade in the first half of the eighteenth century. Scholars who study this commerce in people generally focus either on the formative era of the seventeenth century or the latter years of the eighteenth century, when British slave trading reached its highest volume.[46] Historians of South Carolina and Virginia have consistently reported the sharp rise of slave imports in those colonies in the first half of the eighteenth century, but far fewer have stressed the increases in Jamaica, the mid-Atlantic, and New England.[47] Their reasons for neglecting the first half of the eighteenth century are obvious. The volume of slave shipments from 1700 to 1750 was less than that of 1750 to 1800. Over the course of the

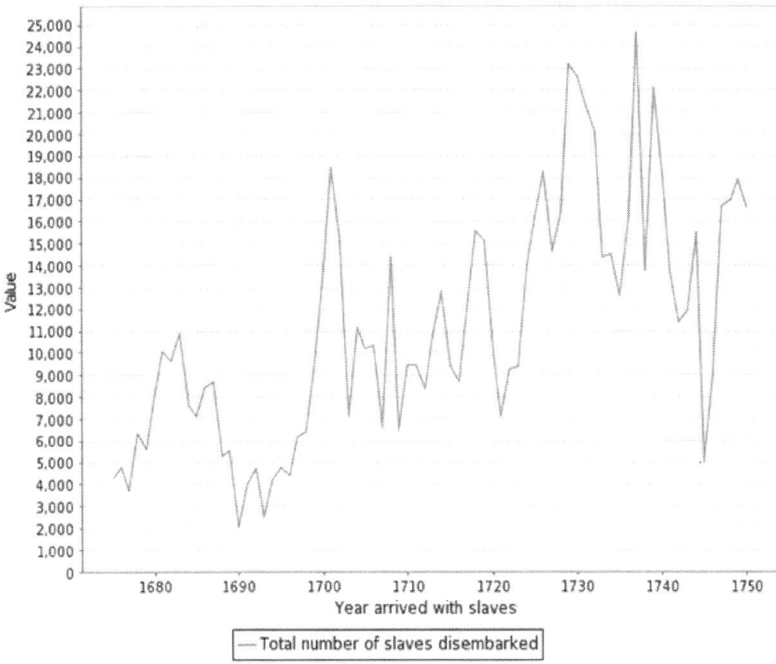

Graph 1. Numbers of Africans carried into British mainland America and the Caribbean on British vessels, 1675–1750 (in thousands). The Trans-Atlantic Slave Trade Database, 2009. *Slave Voyages*. http://www.slavevoyages.org (accessed March 26, 2012)

history of the British slave trade, the first half of the eighteenth century appears only as a step on a long and infamous stairway.

But from the perspective of people in colonial America living in the first half of the eighteenth century—white and Black, free and slave—the demographic shift in slave population meant a great deal. Never in the history of British colonial America had merchants transported so many slaves into the colonies. The numbers of new slaves altered the populations in every province, not only the American South. While in some of the northern mainland colonies the number of white emigrants equaled or surpassed that of Black slaves, the volume of the trade ensured that a population of coerced and abused laborers was a physical presence straining the oppressive fabric of British America. The slave trade in the first half of the eighteenth century was a powerful and transformative force.

At the end of the seventeenth century, private merchants sought to profit from a demand for slaves that could not be satiated by one company. Before 1689, the kings of England had followed a model of slave trading that embraced a state run monopoly, the RAC, for trading to Africa. Despite blessings from the Stuarts and a great deal of investment from merchant interests, the RAC quickly proved inadequate in fulfilling the terrible demand for labor in late seventeenth-century plantations.[48] Up until the Glorious Revolution, the RAC carried an annual average of 6,100 slaves a year to the New World, more than doubling the number of slaves in the Americas, yet planters complained bitterly over its inability to satisfy demand.[49] The "groans" of the planters against the monopoly began almost immediately and grew louder over time. "We must have them; we cannot be without them," wrote the Bajan planter Edward Littleton of the slave supply. "How the Company and Agents Lord it over us, having us thus in their power. We are forced to scramble for them in so shameful a manner, that one of the great burdens of our lives is the buying of negroes."[50] This competition for slaves was especially acute in Virginia in the 1680s and 1690s, as the RAC neglected the Chesapeake for the larger markets of the Caribbean. With the Glorious Revolution in 1689, the RAC discovered that without the support of the Stuart kings, many parliamentarians were less than friendly to the renewal of its charter.

After the revolution, private traders took advantage of the suspension of the monopoly and launched for the coast of West Africa. Between 1689 and 1697, English "interlopers" outnumbered RAC ships by nearly four to one in the African slave trade.[51] In 1697, the RAC negotiated a compromise that ended its monopoly but required every English vessel visiting the coast of Africa to pay a 10 percent duty for maintenance of slave forts.[52] Slave traders could legally send ships to Africa, but they were easy prey for rival European powers.[53]

The acquiescence of the RAC to enterprising merchants and planters ushered in a new era for British slave trading at the opening of the eighteenth century. Over the next fifty years, the British African trade surpassed all others. Table 1 provides estimates of the slaves disembarked by British vessels into the various regions along the Atlantic littoral.

Table 1. Slaves disembarked in the British transatlantic slave trade, estimates by region, 1700–1750

	Europe	Main N. Amer.	Brit. Carib	Fr. Carib	Dutch Amer.	Danish W.I.	Span. Americas	Brazil	Africa	Totals
1700	0	974	17,033	0	0	0	1,318	0	0	19,325
1701–1710	0	13,035	106,455	4,877	0	113	1,390	0	0	125,870
1711–1720	0	11,213	115,294	115	0	0	10,194	979	0	137,795
1721–1730	532	28,251	144,730	0	0	0	12,260	138	259	186,170
1731–1740	2,631	55,120	135,807	321	500	0	6,548	444	166	201,537
1741–1750	0	15,841	119,465	3,000	45	290	4,816	0	90	142,917
Totals	3,163	124,434	638,784	8,313	545	403	35,896	1,561	515	813,614

Source: Estimates, 2009, *Slave Voyages*. The Trans-Atlantic Slave Trade Database

The most dramatic increase in slave trading took place on the American mainland, where slave disembarkation increased more than fourfold between 1710 and 1740. In the British Caribbean, the increase in volume was less extreme, but estimates of the numbers of slaves disembarked still rose from 106,455 from 1701 to 1710, to 144,730 from 1721 to 1730, or an increase of 36 percent in slave-trading volume. After the granting of the slave-trading *assiento*, a contract allowing foreign nations to trade to Spanish America, at the end of the War of the Spanish Succession in 1713, the British also increased their slave trade to the Spanish Americas.

Behind the growth of both monopoly and private slave trading was a broader expansion of shipping and commerce in the British Empire. Between 1675 and 1730, transatlantic crossings tripled from near 500 a year to 1,500.[54] Numbers of slave-trading vessels appear to have grown proportionately during this expansion of commerce, though they were always a small part of a widespread imperial project. Between 1675 and 1680, the British averaged about twenty-six transatlantic slave ships a year, increasing to roughly ninety ships a year between 1736 and 1740.

Merchants trading in slaves benefited from this growing volume as economies of scale lowered the cost of transporting goods and made the slave trade more profitable. It is hard to overstate this critical factor in the growth of the British slave trade. For the merchants and financiers of the slave trade, the profitability of the Middle Passage depended heavily on the costs of shipping. According to historian David Eltis, between 1675 and 1725, efficiency among all ships delivering slaves to the Americas improved by 25 percent. Ships of sail were able to lower costs by shrinking the numbers of crew per tonnage and keeping larger numbers of slaves alive in the Middle Passage. This change in price over time has been cited by Eltis as the "single most important influence over the size and profitability of slave empires."[55]

Between 1701 and 1750, the British imported more than 675,000 people and nearly quadrupled their total slave imports into the Americas. This rapid expansion was a response to the demand for labor in the plantations, one that was ubiquitous throughout the Americas and

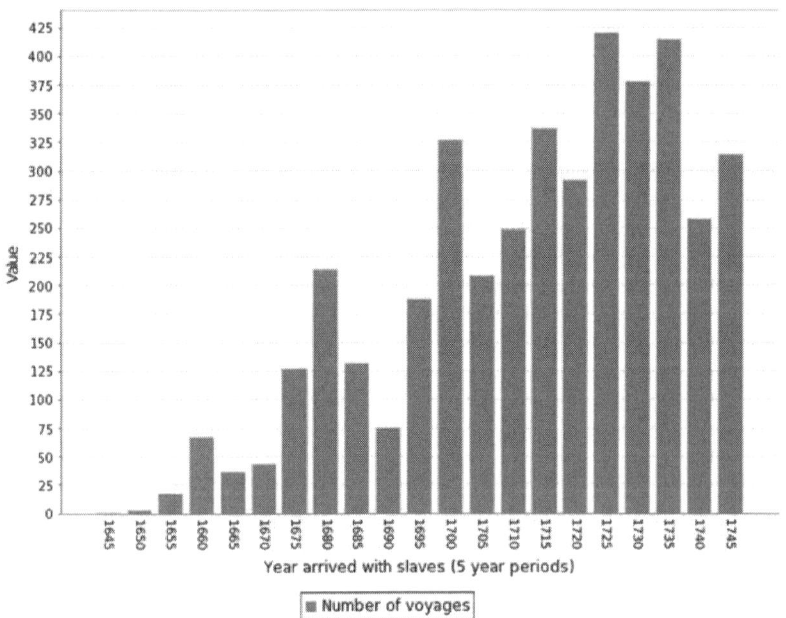

Graph 2. Numbers of British slaving vessels in the transatlantic slave trade, 1650–1750. The Trans-Atlantic Slave Trade Database. *Slave Voyages*. http://www.slavevoyages.org

Table 2. Numbers of transatlantic British ships engaged in the slave trade to mainland North America and the Caribbean, 1700–1750

Year	Mainland North America	Caribbean	Totals
1700	2	67	69
1701–1710	66	469	535
1711–1720	68	518	586
1721–1730	120	591	711
1731–1740	202	588	790
1741–1750	65	507	572
Totals	523	2,740	3,263

Source: The Trans-Atlantic Slave Trade Database. 2009. *Slave Voyages*. http://www.slavevoyages.org (accessed March 30, 2012)

fostered from the northern harbors of mainland America to the islands of the Caribbean. The expansion of the slave trade grew in proportion to British imperial shipping among colonies and through the unique combination of state sponsorship and private enterprise that expanded the African trade. By the middle of the eighteenth century, Britons believed slaves were critical to the colonial enterprise; Black labor was the "pillar" of American commerce.

The ship *Fauconberg* sighted Antigua at 4 a.m. on Friday, 17 May 1700. A sailor spotted the "hie Land" to the north and west. By noon, the ship coasted along the southern shore of the island, passing Falmouth Harbour. Captain John Luke ordered gunners to salute the harbor's fort and the small vessels anchored in the southern bay. The boom of the guns signaled the RAC's return to the British Leewards.[56]

Court likely flinched at the boom of the ship's cannon. Standing on the foredeck before the mast, crowded among the men and boys, the ten-year-old looked for the first time on the Americas. Gazing north, the island appeared as a series of green hills climbing to a ridgeline against the sky. Looking westward, above Rendezvous Bay, he might have seen his first windmills, the great blades turned by the force of the east-north-east breezes noted by Luke in the *Fauconberg*'s journal.[57] In that long Middle Passage, he must have often feared his destination. What did the seventeenth-century child think of this strange new world?

Figure 4. William Brasier, *To the Right Honourable Richard Earl of Temple &c. &c. This View of English Harbour in the Island of Antiqua Taken from the Hill at the Upper End* (London, 1757). Courtesy John Carter Brown Library, Brown University, Providence, Rhode Island

Coobah, partitioned with the women and girls at the rear of the ship, could have looked back to see Montserrat. It appears as a distant mountain twenty-four miles south and west from the coast of Antigua. As the *Fauconberg* rounded Johnson's Point and sailed north, she would have recognized that she moved through a land of islands, surrounded by a vast sea.

If Court and Coobah were on the *Fauconberg*, they had survived a horrendous Atlantic crossing. Even by the murderous standards of slave ships, the *Fauconberg* suffered an egregious loss of captives. Atlantic slave ships averaged a rate of death of 16 percent in the first quarter of the eighteenth century. The ship weighed anchor on the Gold Coast with 606 people chained below deck, 103 of them children. After 55 days in "heavy seas," the ship arrived with only 376 people.[58] Captain Luke "buryed" 230 men, women, and children at sea, or 38 percent of the people in his care. Sailing along the coast, the ship appeared less a prison than a floating hospital, filled with hundreds of sick people and wreaking of human excrement.[59]

Luke followed a well-established routine for the arrival of RAC slave ships. In England, merchants provided the captain with clear instructions concerning his contacts. On 17 May, at 3 o'clock in the afternoon, the *Fauconberg* anchored at six fathoms in the harbor of St. John. The RAC's agent awaited the ship. "I went ashore att St. John's towne and Spoke to Mr. Sampson," wrote Luke. "Soone after went to ye Governors house" to register the ship's arrival and perhaps pay duties. The next morning, Luke returned to town to "gitt some Lymes for ye Negroes" and to "hire a Sloope to Carry one halfe of ye Slaves to Mountseratt to Mr. Parsons." On Saturday afternoon, the Mr. Sampson joined Luke on board the *Fauconberg* and "Mustered the slaves."[60]

The second passage into Court's and Coobah's slavery ended on deck with the muster. They boarded the vessel as subjects of Eguafo or Akyem or Denkyira or Fante, as members of families and ancestral clans. At the end of their passage, they stood before the slave merchant as anonymous enslaved Black people, naked, stripped of their homeland, a number in Captain Luke's ledger. Sampson recorded nothing about whom they had been in Africa. They were chattel slaves, to be fed and cleaned and oiled, so they might be exchanged at a high price for sugar.[61]

Luke and his crew never explained how so many captives in his care had died. At the muster before Sampson, Luke wrote, "We having on board alive Sick and Well 376," and (rather defensively) "then Losted them ffairly We haveing buryed 230 Slaves." Day after day in the ship's journal, Luke noted the direction of the wind, ship speed, passing vessels, and even the daily catch of "Booneto" and "Albecors," but he had not marked the deaths of the hundreds of people in his charge. How did they die on the *Fauconberg*?[62]

Luke and Sampson began the fast work of separating the captives into lots. Luke selected 175 people to be sold in Montserrat, "87 Men/boys" and "88 Women Girls," there "being noe more able to goe." The two hundred remaining captives were too sick or too weak for a day's sail to the neighboring island. He ordered the Montserrat-bound captives loaded into the hired sloop under the command of a Mr. Johnson and two members of his crew, who sailed to fulfill the company's contract.

On Monday, 20 May, Luke transported the last two hundred men, women, and children to St. John's for sale. The sailors rowed the longboats in turns, the slaves climbing down rope ladders on the side of

Figure 5. William Brasier, *To the Right Honourable George Earl of Hallifax . . . This View of St. Johns Harbour in the Island of Antigua* (London, 1757). This engraving depicts an idealized view of St. John's harbor, facing northeast. St. John's, Antigua, is depicted center right in the distance. Courtesy John Carter Brown Library, Brown University, Providence, Rhode Island

the ship, the sailors shouting instructions with open arms as the sickly and weak tried to hold on.[63] "This day landed Mr. Sampsons Lott of Negroes," Captain Luke noted in the journal.[64]

Court and Coobah clung to the rope ladder of the ship, then took their place in what must have been a crowded seat among the adults on the vessel. They would never again see the hold of the slave ship nor would it ever fully let them go. Much later, they would come to call each other "shipmates" and to acknowledge a bond, forged in the trauma of the Middle Passage, that they would share for the rest of their lives.[65] Neither merchant nor planter would sever that bond.

The final passage into slavery began with the sale of captives to planters. Most slave ships in the early eighteenth-century Caribbean sold their human cargo to buyers on board their vessel.[66] Sampson, the agent, sold the *Fauconberg*'s captives on land, in the town of St. John's, over a period of sixteen days. Luke sent three hogsheads of beans and nine hogsheads of corn to feed the survivors of his passage, along with baskets of "lymes." He had grown increasingly optimistic about his profits. "At Param Gold Coast Negroes Sold att 45 l. per head most of ye men and good Women," he wrote in anticipation.[67] Slaves typically sold for thirty pounds a person in Antigua in the 1690s.[68] If Gold Coast slaves were selling at forty-five pounds, Captain Luke could expect a fine return in sugar for his investors in England.

He left no record of the final sale price for each person. From St. John's, Sampson sent the first longboat laden with a hogshead of sugar, a 1,600-pound giant cask, on Thursday, 6 June. The longboats hauled seven more hogsheads to the ship that day. At a going rate of £1.75 sterling per pound of sugar, Sampson had sold about twenty captives for every cask of sugar: twenty lifetimes so that Englishmen might have their bread and coffee sweetened; twenty lifetimes so that African kings and merchants, ship captains and planters, merchants and shipbuilders might profit from the sale.[69] On 14 July, the crew mishandled a line and one of the hogsheads sank into the sea.[70] On 28 July, the *Fauconberg* sailed for England, its dungeon filled with sugar.

In the market, Sampson and the auctioneers introduced each person as an individual slave, valued for their appearance and potential labor. The white slavers stripped the Africans naked.[71] They shaved, washed, and oiled the bodies of every man, woman, and child.[72] They fed them Captain Luke's peas and corn and limes, trying to restore captives who had been so sickly they had not even been able to make the day sail to Montserrat.[73] "They choose them as they do horses in a market," wrote the Englishman Richard Ligon. "The strongest, youthfullest, and most beautiful, yield the greatest prices."[74] The captives who could not recover, who remained sick or infirm, were sold as "refuse" slaves by the "inch of candle," an auction in which buyers could bid until a candle burned down one inch.[75]

Court was ten years old, according to Thomas Kerby, when he was sold to a planter on the island. If his white master's accounting of his age was correct, he lived for five years as a slave before Kerby purchased him. There were at least 170 plantations on Antigua by 1705.[76] The Langford family purchased Coobah. She survived on their plantation, just east of St. John's, to live to adulthood.[77] Court's first five years on Antigua are not recorded.

Sugar planting accounted for a terrible mortality among the enslaved. The expansion of the plantation system was well developed by the first quarter of the eighteenth century but still expanding. In 1734, Governor William Mathew of Antigua wrote to the Board of Trade complaining that only 24,408 acres of the more than 50,000 acres of manured land was under sugar cultivation.[78] He blamed this on the want of slaves, but the truth was that sugar cultivation killed Black laborers. Sugar cultivation had become more intensive and harsher. From January to May, the dry seasons in the Caribbean, slaves cut the cane almost continuously and hauled it to the sugar mills, where the wind or cattle turned the gin that crushed out the juice. The liquor was then boiled in cauldrons in special boiling houses. At times, mills could run up to nine months, the slaves getting less than six hours of sleep a night and working six days a week. From June to December, the rainy season, slaves holed, planted, dunged, and weeded the fields.[79] As plantations became more efficient, the labor only intensified for slaves. At the same time, malnutrition was rampant. As a rule, in the first half of the eighteenth century, planters provided only a small portion of food and expected slaves to provide the rest through personally cultivated fields. The intensification of sugar production cut down on time for food production and forced slaves to survive on barely enough calories to keep them working. Malnutrition led to exhaustion and vulnerability to disease.[80]

Mortality in the cane fields was exacerbated by the introduction of unseasoned African slaves who were extremely vulnerable to the American disease environment. In 1740, Charles Leslie of Jamaica noted that "almost half of the newly imported negroes die in the seasoning," referring to the period of three years thought to be required for a slave to become acclimated to the tropical environment, and historical studies have generally supported his observation.[81] In 1732, Reverend Robert Robertson of Nevis sought to explain the high mortality of slaves in the islands: "The Loss in Slaves (not including those immediately from Guinea, of which about two fifths die in the Seasoning) may well, one Year with another, be reckoned at One in Fifteen; in dry Years when Provisions of the Country Growth are scarce, one in Seven in my plantations; and when the Small Pox . . . happens to be imported, it is incredible what Havock it makes among the Blacks."[82] Robertson did not stress overwork, but he found the combination of disease and lack of provisioning to be murderous to the Black population of his plantations.

The mortality rates for slaves arriving in the 1720s and 1730s may have been the highest witnessed in the British colonies over the entire eighteenth and nineteenth centuries. Historian Richard Sheridan argues that the intensification of agriculture led to growing fatalities among slaves throughout the British West Indies in the first half of the century.[83] In Barbados, the Leeward Islands, and Jamaica, the natural decline in overall population was close to 4 percent annually in these years. "It is computed in the West Indies," wrote philosopher David Hume in 1752, "that a stock of slaves grow worse five per cent every year, unless new slaves be bought."[84] His numbers were a bit too high, but contemporary white Britons were well aware of the tragic mortality in the islands.

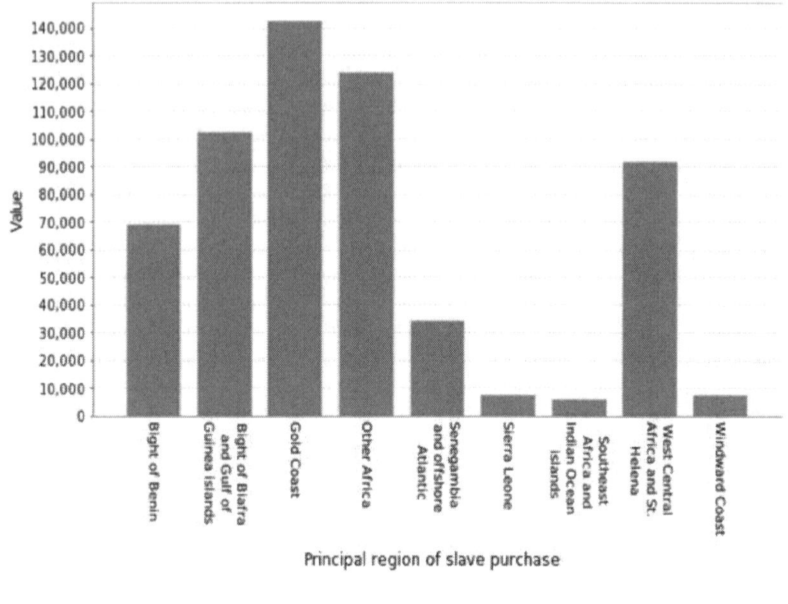

Graph 3. Number of slaves taken from African regions aboard British vessels, 1700–1750. The Trans-Atlantic Slave Trade Database. 2009. *SlaveVoyages*. http://www.slavevoyages.org (accessed March 30, 2012)

Language provided the first and perhaps most important barrier to integration for new arrivals. In the early eighteenth century, Africa held the most linguistically complex population of any continent.[85] Language separated slaves even aboard the slave ship. When in 1725 Captain William Snelgrave discovered the ship's cooper murdered by Coromantee slaves in the dark of night, he did not fear the rest of the African captives, "for above one hundred of the Negroes then on board, being bought to Windward, did not understand a word of the Gold-Coast Language."[86] White observers of the slave population frequently commented on the language difficulties of the new slave population. In 1729, Edmund Gibson, the bishop of London, noted that his missionaries to the colonies complained that the African slaves could not speak English and in 1740, Commissary Alexander Garden of South

Table 3. Average annual decline in slave population (by percentage)

Years	Jamaica	Barbados	Leeward Islands
1676–1700	3	4.1	4
1701–1725	3.6	4.9	4.4
1726–1750	3.5	3.6	4.8

Source: Sheridan, *Sugar and Slavery*, 247, table 11.1.

Carolina still observed the "many various ages, Nations, languages" of the "Body of Slaves."[87]

Slaves arriving in the provinces in the early 1700s could be completely isolated by their inability to communicate. Language remained a great barrier for African slaves across British America. The Chesapeake Bay region of Virginia was particularly prone to isolating new African slaves because of the smaller plantation size and large body of English-speaking creole slaves.[88] In Maryland in the early 1730s, a Wolof man called Job remembered that he grew "desperate" and "disturbed" because of his "Ignorance of the English Language, which prevented him complaining, or telling his Case to any Person about him."[89] English planter Edward Long of Jamaica wrote that slaves "who do not speak the dialect of slaves on the islands sometimes kill themselves in despair."[90] Surviving the despair of slavery required the ability to communicate.

Court survived this gauntlet of mortality and despair. He survived his passage into slavery. At every step, slave traders took him farther from his home and robbed him of his ancestry and people. He survived the brutality of the slave ship and the anonymity of the slave market. He awoke in an Antigua, in some forgotten place, a slave in British America. And it was in that condition that Thomas Kerby purchased Court in 1706.

CHAPTER FOUR

The Waiting Man

13 October 1736
St. John's, Antigua

ROBERT ARBUTHNOT STEPPED TO THE front door of Thomas Kerby's home without invitation and without warning. It was his third visit in three days. Much had changed since Monday, when he presided over a trial of slaves in Kerby's home. Arbuthnot had created a sensation when he announced his investigation of a plot. He ordered constables to search slave quarters for weapons and powder but they found none. He recorded the constable's reports of secret meetings of Black people, carefully noting their accounts of growing "insolence" among enslaved men. Witnesses spoke of one suspect above all others: Court, the "King" of the slaves. Arbuthnot's investigation had led him full circle, back to the place it started.[1]

He stepped into Kerby's merchant house with newfound authority. He had come to interrogate the Speaker of the Assembly and accuse Court of plotting a rebellion.

Kerby greeted Arbuthnot in the front room, his place of business. In Arbuthnot's report two days later, he remembered the conversation in simple terms. He "acquainted [Kerby] with what the Constables told him they had found in Court's Room, and what the world seemed to think of his Slave."

Court was a "a dark, designing, ambitious, insolent fellow," Arbuthnot informed Kerby, with power over the nation of slaves called the "Coromantees." The constables had found "more than 100 pistoles" in

Court's purse, a fortune for a free man, more so a slave. Court would have been valued at forty-five pounds sterling in 1736.[2] With that much money in his purse, he might have purchased his freedom twice over. How and why was a slave holding so much coin?

Arbuthnot leveled his accusations squarely at the Speaker. Kerby had vouched for Court the previous morning and told Arbuthnot that his enslaved waiting man had "always behaved with great Fidelity and honesty." Arbuthnot said he had been credibly informed otherwise. At best, Arbuthnot implied, Kerby was blind to Court's designs. At worst, Kerby had lied to the justice of the peace to protect his bondsman.[3]

Kerby weighed how best to respond to the accusations against his slave. He might have raged at Arbuthnot. Who was this Scottish newcomer to suggest Kerby could not manage his slaves? Kerby might have confronted Arbuthnot with his status and rank, reminded the Scotsman that he was of English heritage and of great estate, born a slave master, elevated by planters to their highest elected office. He was a merchant, a planter, a patriarch.

He might have challenged the evidence. By British custom and law, Court and all his possession were Kerby's property.[4] The constables had entered Kerby's house without his consent, searched his slave without his permission, and smashed Court's "exceeding fine wrought drum."[5] He might have shouted at Arbuthnot to leave his home and not return. Kerby might have said all this and more.

Instead, Kerby invited Arbuthnot to meet with Court. With careful tact, Kerby "Desired the said Robert Arbuthnot to go with him into Courts Chamber." The Speaker called for Court and asked him to show his possessions to the Justice of the Peace.

In Court's private quarters, Arbuthnot met the "King" of the slaves for the first time. There is no record of their first impressions of each other. Court sought to convince Arbuthnot of his innocence. He "Denyed the Constables had seen any Such Purse as they talked of, Of a hundred Pistoles." He presented two purses to Arbuthnot, one with "Six crowns in Silver" and "another with Fifteen or Sixteen Pistoles and Some Silver," an amount worth about sixteen British pounds or a third of Court's value as chattel property.[6] It "was all he had in the World," Court told Arbuthnot. He had no weapons, he added. The two white men returned to the front room while Court waited.[7]

Arbuthnot was not convinced. Whom should he believe: the constables, who claimed Court had a suspiciously large amount of money in his purse, or the slave, the "designing" fellow? Court had enjoyed more than enough time over the last two days to hide anything suspicious. He knew Kerby had searched Court's room before the constable's arrival with the warrant. In his report to governor and council, Arbuthnot did not mention his suspicions of Thomas Kerby, but in that instance, in Kerby's home, he had good reason to suspect the master and slave were working together against his investigation. No, Arbuthnot would not accept Court's innocence.

At that tense moment between the two men, Robert Delap entered Kerby's house. "Delap came in and found us talking about Court," Arbuthnot remembered, as if the young man's appearance was a coincidence.[8] Delap was no passerby. He was Antigua's deputy provost marshal, the official whose duties included serving warrants and committing men to jail. He was only seventeen or eighteen years old (according to christening records) and new to a job granted to him through the governor's patronage.[9] His convenient appearance in Kerby's front room meant only one thing: Arbuthnot had called on Delap to take Court away.

Delap volunteered more damning gossip against Court. "He was very Credibly informed that Court was at Mrs. Parke's Plantation the Sunday Seven night before and there was Crown'd King of the Coromantees in presence of the greatest Number of Negroes that were Ever known to be Assembl'd together, Near Two thousand," Delap said, "That a Great many White People were present and saw the Coronation, That Court set Under a Canopy of State, Surrounded by his great Officers; That he Walked in Procession as King; and had all the Homage and Respect of a King paid to him. And that Tomboy a Slave of Mr. Thomas Hansons sat the Next in honour to him."[10] Delap's account of Court's "coronation" was timely, bolstering Arbuthnot's investigation.

Confronted by both men, Kerby launched into a full-throated defense of Court. He thought "his Slave was incapable of any bad Design, for that he was an Elderly Distemper'd [i.e., sickly] Fellow and had Always behaved like a Faithfull Slave and lived very well," Kerby said, "beside which he was under no Temptation, for that he had Offer'd him his Freedom." Kerby's offer to manumit Court would have been news to Arbuthnot. If it was true, it upset the entire investigation. Why would a slave soon to be freed want to risk his life to rebel?

"And therefore he imagined it to be Only an Innocent Play of Courts Country, and that no harm Could be meant by it," Kerby said, "more Especially as it was Represented before so many White People." Court had performed a "play" from Africa and played his part, Kerby argued. He was not a real king. It was all just a misunderstanding.

"I Could not help taking things in quite in a Different Light," Arbuthnot replied. "That I was Convinc'd that it was a Serious thing, and that Court meant Nothing less than to be King of Antigua. And that [I] thought the State to be in the Utmost Danger."

The two men became angrier, Arbuthnot remembered. They spoke "as they were affected," that is, as they felt. Kerby searched for an argument, any argument, that would save his enslaved waiting man.

Kerby never explained to Arbuthnot why he defended Court. For their part, Arbuthnot and the commissioners would write that Kerby's "Indulgences" of Court "were great, and uncommon," without explanation.[11] But there was a reason for Kerby's trust in Court, a reason why Kerby spoke of thirty years of "fidelity" from his slave. After all, when they were both young, Court had been by his side when Kerby led a rebellion against the governor of the Leeward Islands.

Court's political vision emerged from his experiences in slavery. If his childhood on the Gold Coast provided a memory of belonging to an African community, his life as a British slave shaped his political movement. He lived through the despair of the Middle Passage. He knew the brutality of the plantation. Perhaps most importantly for his political education, he witnessed his master's ascendence, watched Thomas

Kerby join an organized rebellion and survive to rise through the ranks of the planter class. Court witnessed firsthand a winning strategy for political power in the Americas.

More than two thousand years before Kerby enslaved Court, the Athenian philosopher Plato explained the origins of the authority of the slaveholder over his slave. In book 8 of Plato's *Republic*, Socrates asks Glaucon, "Do you know why rich men are free from fear and not afraid of their slaves?" Glaucon replies, "Yes. It is that the whole city comes to the aid and support of each individual private citizen." Socrates responds, "Well said. Now consider: Suppose a God picked out of the city a man who owned 50 slaves or even more, and put him, together with his wife and children and all his property, including slaves, in the desert where no free men would come to his aid. What do you think the quality and magnitude of his fear would be for his own safety and that of his children and wife?" "He would be in every kind of fear," Glaucon says.[12] Plato, who lived in a city of slave owners, understood that a master's authority to own slaves originated from the city, the community of property-owning subjects and their institutions. Slaveholders could not rule over their bondspeople without the state.[13] If removed beyond the proverbial city walls, if dropped by a God into a desert, masters lost their ability to coerce obedience. Where "no free men would come to his aid," the slaveholder's power was lost, and he would fear the slave's wrath.

Kerby was able to enslave Court because the laws and customs of British Colonial America condoned it. If profit was the motivation for white Britons' enslaving Black people in America, it was the collective will of the community that made it possible. British Americans believed it was acceptable for Kerby to hold Court in bondage. They granted status and power to slaveholders. Kerby shared their beliefs.

By the early eighteenth century, British Americans had fully embraced enslaving Black people and American Indians. In Antigua, Britons claimed they could not profit from sugar without exploiting Black slaves. "We think it our Duty to advertise [to] our fellow Subjects of

Great Britain, to consider that slavery is not our choice, but Necessity; it being impossible to carry on our Sugar manufactures by White Labourers," explained Antiguan officials in 1736.[14] But slavery meant more to Britons than simple profit.

British planters maintained a worldview in which they understood themselves as patriarchs, male heads of household with authority over their wives, children, servants, and slaves. Male planters expected obedience and loyalty and, in turn, accepted responsibility for the welfare of everyone in their household.[15] The planter's "mastery" and status could be measured by his ability to rule well over his "people." The most powerful planters had the largest households and the most slaves and commanded the most respect.

Kerby embraced this worldview. He was born owning slaves. He profited from their labor. In the mid-1720s, Kerby became the agent for the Royal African Company (RAC) in Antigua, making him the broker for slaves across the island.[16] He sold slaves for profit. He died owning slaves.

As the only surviving heir of one Dr. Thomas Kerby, he inherited as a boy in the early 1690s a 175-acre plantation in the Falmouth Division in the Parish of St. Paul in the southern half of the island.[17] In 1698, he was still listed as an "infant," a term broadly used for a minor who had not achieved his twenty-one-year-old majority. Kerby removed to St. John's at a young age, perhaps at his parents' death, and never returned to live on his plantation.

He was an ambitious young man and very bright. He trained as a merchant, probably under his guardian, Esay Burges. In 1702, Kerby purchased the patent to become the deputy secretary of Antigua at a time when the acting secretary lived in Nevis.[18] It was a position of remarkable responsibility for a man who could not have been much older than a teenager. He oversaw issuing titles to land, wills, licenses, the orders of the governor, and writs of election. By 1704, he also worked as council clerk, the official who attended the governor and colonial council.[19] He could only have achieved such a position through the permission of Colonel Christopher Codrington, captain general and governor of the Leeward Islands. Kerby must have seemed capable to the elderly officer.

In British colonial America, royal officials obtained their political power through the patronage of the Crown. Queen Anne appointed the governor, and the governor in turn recommended prominent men to serve on the Council of Antigua. The council members recommended to the governor their favorites for provost marshal, secretary, vice-admiralty judges, clerks, and justices of the peace. The offices could be lucrative, extracting fees from the public, but they all came with a price. Each appointed official owed his position and obedience to his patron on the council. Each council member owed his obedience to the governor. The governor owed his position to ministers in London, who owed their positions to the queen. Patronage, the support of high-placed officers, remained the gateway to royal office.

The colonial assembly represented the other center of power in British America. Freeholders—men who met the property requirement—elected representatives to pass the laws of the colony. The assembly controlled taxation and revenue and even the salaries of governors. Kerby, born far from the corridors of power in England, had every expectation that he would one day serve on the assembly. Nevertheless, he aspired to royal office.

His great patron on the council was probably Colonel Edward Byam, commander of the Antigua militia. Kerby would remain close to Byam his entire life, serving as executor of the elderly statesman's will.[20] In 1705, Kerby married Jane Gamble, a relative of Colonel George Gamble, another member of the council.[21] With so many patrons from the council, Kerby needed only the governor's recommendation to secure his own seat in the most powerful chamber of the province.

Kerby purchased Court around 1706, just after his marriage and at a time when his political star was on the rise.[22] Kerby wanted a "waiting man," a personal servant. There were many reasons for a young white slaveholder to want an enslaved person for such a role. The waiting man might be tasked with carrying messages, collecting payments, or delivering goods. A waiting man might fetch and hold a horse. He might even carry his master's gun, or at least the powder and shot. But above all else, the servant waited. He stood behind the master, dressed in fine livery (a bright coat and hat), for all to see.

Court was part of Kerby's ambitions. An enslaved waiting man stood as living proof of Kerby's wealth and authority. When Kerby took his place at the council table, beside Colonel Codrington and Colonel Byam, he could order Court to wait outside with the other personal slaves. Kerby purchased Court to prove his mastery over other men.

There is no record of the first meeting between Kerby and Court, no portraits to reveal their appearance. Kerby would have been in his mid-twenties, perhaps younger, dressed in the British planter style: a broad-brimmed hat, his hair cut short (for wearing wigs at Council) and wrapped in a handkerchief to absorb sweat. He would have worn a brightly colored coat (unless he was out in the sugarcane) and a white holland shirt tucked into breeches, with stockings and buckled shoes.[23] His clothes marked his status as a wealthy man.

Court was about fifteen years old in 1706. He had survived the "seasoning" time, those first few years of slavery in which an African might be expected to die from disease or despair. He would have worn two pieces of clothing, a loose-fitting shirt made of linen or wool and a pair of "drawers," the ubiquitous clothing of male slaves in British America. He wore no shoes. Even in town, slaves went barefoot.[24]

Kerby made an unusual choice in choosing an African as a personal servant. Planters typically chose American-born enslaved children to serve as skilled or domestic slaves. Creoles spoke English and had more familiarity with the customs of white Britons.[25] When Kerby brought Court to St. John's, he would have encountered few Africans among the elite slaves, the skilled artisans and servants of the town.[26]

Kerby introduced Court to a different kind of slavery—the domestic servant rather than the plantation. In the sugarcane and in the yard, Court knew deprivation and the constant threat of overwork and hunger, but he could at least sit within a community of slaves and close his eyes to sleep free from the watchful gaze of the white overseer. As a waiting man, Court would live beholden to the whims of his master.

Kerby could punish Court at will, harm him at will. Kerby could sell Court to another planter or even sell him off island to an unknown fate. As an enslaved waiting man, Court would live the rest of his life anticipating a summons from Kerby.

They would have been strangers to each other at first. They came from two cultures, separated by four thousand miles of ocean. Court would have spoken with a Fante or Twi accent when they met, his English sprinkled with expressions that were strange to Kerby. "I will go and come," he might have said when he left his master's side, even though he was not coming back. (It was rude to leave without promising to return. In the 1690s, the Dutch slave trader Willem Bosman complained of this custom on the Eguafo Coast.) When told to sit, Court might have squatted on his haunches on the floor, rather than take a chair. He might have poured the first sip of water on the earth with a prayer.[27]

Despite their bewildering differences, they had many things in common, the master and the slave, the white Briton and the Black "Coromantee." They were both young, near the same age (Kerby was older by seven or eight years).[28] They were both orphaned, Court by slave traders who took him from his people and Kerby by the death of his parents. They were both said to have been from "considerable family," though neither came from the ruling elite.[29] Most surprising, they both shared a political ambition that would bring them into conflict with the rulers of the island.

On Tuesday, 5 December 1710, the elected members of the Antigua Assembly marched on St. John's Courthouse. Court would have been waiting outside with the other enslaved manservants as twenty-five assemblymen and a "mob" advanced on the seat of government.[30] The crowd pressed into the courthouse. Speaker Nathaniel Crump banged on the door of the council chamber.

Kerby sat inside, taking notes in his role as council clerk. He sat at table with nine of the most powerful men in the province: Antigua's Lieutenant Governor John Yeamans and seven members of the colonial council. At their head sat Colonel Daniel Parke, the captain general and governor of the Leeward Islands.

Governor Parke knew who was at the door. He had reportedly spent the morning tearing up written messages from the assembly.[31] The marshal hurried to the entrance and returned, announcing that the Speaker wished to read a speech to His Excellency. Parke said he did not want to hear it. He told the marshal not to let the Speaker inside the chamber.[32]

Crump pushed his way through the door. He claimed he "had business of great moment to communicate to the General and Councill," remembered Thomas Morris, a member of the council.[33] Crump began to read his speech but Parke refused to listen. The assembly later claimed Parke "clapped his Hand several time to his Sword, charg'd the Assembly with a Riot, and threaten'd to clap their Speaker in Irons."[34] Someone shouted from the doorway that Parke "was no longer Generall, and that they would no longer obey him as such."[35]

The council members tried to intervene. They "begg'd [Parke] not to esteem the Assemblies waiting upon him with their humble Address a Riot, and pray'd him to suffer it to be read."[36] Parke shouted at the Speaker to leave.

At the rear of the crowd, Court would have been one of the first to see the 38th Regiment Grenadiers marching toward the courthouse. They lined up behind the assemblymen, an officer and eight soldiers in conical hats and orange coats, their muskets ready.[37] They came on, pushing through the crowd, up to the doorway, waving off the assemblymen with the tips of bayonets. An assemblymen asked the officer "if they intended to fire upon the Assembly?"[38]

"They only wanted Orders to do so," the officer answered. The grenadiers pointed their loaded muskets.[39]

Parke ordered the assembly to "withdraw." They would be allowed to reconvene in two days, he told them, on Thursday, 7 December. The crowd began to break up, angry, some chanting "No Generall" and others that "they would take him and send him home in irons."[40] Someone shouted "that they would, by that Day, muster up as many Forces as should drive him and his Granadeers, to the Devil."[41] When Parke returned to his seat at the table, several members of the council recommended that he sail to another province.

The power struggle between Antigua's assembly and governor erupted during the War of the Spanish Succession. For nine years, the Leeward Islands had become an important theater of conflict between the British and French Empires. In 1702, Parke's predecessor, Colonel Codrington, invaded French St. Kitts and captured 1,200 French settlers, whom he expelled.[42] Three years later, the French bombarded Nevis and returned to St. Kitts, burning plantations and capturing thousands of slaves. Antiguans feared they would be next. In 1705, Queen Anne and the Lords Commissioners of Trade sought to appoint a new governor who could defend their precious sugar islands. They appointed Daniel Parke.

He was a poor choice. Parke was a ruthlessly ambitious man, prone to anger and quarrels. Born the son of a wealthy Virginia planter, he spent his entire life in pursuit of the governorship of his homeland. Following in the footsteps of his deceased father, Parke secured the patronage of Virginia's Governor Edmund Andros, won a seat in the House of Burgesses, and by the age of twenty-nine had secured his father's old place on Virginia's council. But he was notorious for violence against his enemies. He struck the governor of Maryland across the head with a horse whip. After an argument with Anglican priest James Blair, Parke assaulted the priest's wife in church, pulling her out of her pew and holding her arm, hard, before the entire congregation. He dared the priest to intervene.[43] In 1697, Parke sailed for England with the intention to run for Parliament and win the patronage of the Crown. He left behind his wife, three daughters, and an illegitimate son he named Julius Caesar. He never saw them again.

Parke failed miserably in England. He lost his election. He tried to bribe his way into office, only to be caught and charged with the crime. He might have faced punishment if not for the outbreak of war in 1701.[44] Parke escaped to the continent to serve as an aide-de-camp to the Duke of Marlborough. He quarreled with other officers, even on the march of a campaign, and faced a court martial.[45]

The war changed his fortune. At the Battle of the Schellenberg in 1704, Parke marched with the Forlorn Hope (frontline volunteers) into the French guns of the army of Louis XIV. The French shot him in the legs.[46] Five weeks later, at the famous Battle of Blenheim, as French forces collapsed before the British and their allies, the Duke of Marlborough handed Parke a short note and told him to ride to Queen Anne with news of victory. Park rode through the night, exchanging horses, and sailed to England a step ahead of the news. He arrived at Windsor Castle in the dark. Queen Anne greeted him in her robe and Parke took a knee, handing her the news of victory over the Sun King. She asked Parke what he would like as a reward. He answered he wanted only her likeness, a portrait miniature to carry with him.[47]

But Parke wanted much more. He lobbied for a year to be appointed the next governor of Virginia. When he was passed over for another of Marlborough's officers, Queen Anne granted Parke a consolation prize: governor of the Leeward Islands.

To a young man like Kerby, with his own ambitions, Parke must have seemed the epitome of British political success. He was a planter's son who had achieved a governorship. Parke wore the portrait of Queen Anne around his neck, proof of her favor. He spoke openly of the patronage of the Duke of Marlborough.[48] Parke could tell stories of the Battle of Blenheim, remark on his conversation with the queen, and command the militia with the authority of a veteran. He was the epitome of a young colonist's ambition.

Parke soon began to act the tyrant. He arrived with clear instructions to put the colony in a state of defense, and he came to view the powerful gentry as a threat to his authority. On the council, Codrington, his predecessor, resisted his reforms. Parke challenged Codrington's title to his vast lands. The assembly sought to investigate Parke, so he dissolved their meeting, for years, and resisted ordering them back into session.[49] He set out to create his own sphere of power. Parke passed over the recommendations of the council to pick his own loyalists for office, elevating the enlisted soldier Michael Ayon to the position of provost marshal.[50] Most notably, Parke took control of the 38th Regiment, the poorly paid and demoralized troops stationed on the islands. Parke ordered the soldiers to arrest subjects and confiscate smuggled goods. Parke then demanded bribes to return them. When the assemblyman Edward Chester openly opposed the governor's confiscation of his smuggled trade goods, Parke slept with his wife and moved her to his plantation.[51]

In 1708, just two years after Parke's arrival, the assembly submitted a petition to Queen Anne begging her to remove the governor from office. Bristol merchants submitted a separate petition as well. The twenty-five articles accused Parke of using the queen's troops against the population, arbitrarily jailing nine people, and soliciting bribes, along with many other abuses of power. Parke countered with a long defense that he sent by his own packet to England.[52] Both sides waited for a response from the queen.

Kerby, as acting secretary of the island, soon learned to despise Parke. Kerby stayed closely allied with Christopher Codrington and Edward Byam, Parke's opponents on the council. Writing to the Lords of Trade and Plantations in 1709, Parke accused Kerby of refusing to send the council minutes to England. "My predecessour Coll. Codrington did not care to send home his Minutes of Councill, and the Secretary being his friend and my enemy won't lett me have them to send home," Parke wrote. He accused Kerby of spying for the assembly. "The Councill and myselfe both have reason to believe all along he has told them everything that has passed in Councill," he insisted.[53] Kerby appears to have specifically inspired article 6 of the impeachment, in which the assembly accused Parke of tampering with the writs of election. Kerby, as secretary, wrote the writs and knew that Parke had tried to change the rules concerning the voting districts of assemblymen. "What Mr. Kerby swears for them in their Deposition, No. 91, only shows what kind of man he is," Parke wrote to the Lords of Trade.[54] It may have been a principled stand—resistance against the governor's interference in the rights of the assembly—but Kerby had lost the favor of Colonel Parke.

In May 1710, the governor and planters learned that Queen Anne had ordered Parke to return home to defend himself against the articles of impeachment. The government appeared specifically concerned with

Parke's use of a royal regiment against the queen's subjects. Across the island, the planters celebrated their victory. The Crown ordered both Parke and the assembly to record sworn depositions from witnesses in preparation for a trial.[55] The governor would bring the depositions with him to London. But when the time came for Parke to sail in July, he refused to go.

The planters were amazed. Parke had refused an order of Queen Anne. He stubbornly stayed ensconced in his seat as governor of the Leeward Islands. In the fall, rumors of French ships menacing the coast provoked Speaker Nathaniel Crump to ask the governor to call the assembly back into session.[56] On Tuesday, 5 December, as both the council and assembly met in their respective chambers, Parke insisted that only he could appoint the clerk of the assembly. The Speaker and the assembly exploded at the governor, unwilling to tolerate his authoritarian administration any longer. They marched on the courthouse.

Court was with Kerby when he organized the rebellion. On that Tuesday evening, after the grenadiers had dispersed the assembly, Court saw the leaders of the assembly gather at Kerby's house in St. John's. By candlelight, Kerby worked in his capacity as secretary to transfer the property of each man to his appointed heirs. They all feared that if their rebellion failed, Parke or the Crown would forfeit their lands.[57] Kerby transferred his 175 acres to his neighbor, a Mrs. Willoughby, the clearest sign that he planned to join the rebellion.[58]

On Wednesday, 6 December, Court followed Kerby as he approached Colonel George Gamble, his wife's relative, and asked him to convince Parke to leave the island to prevent bloodshed. As they spoke, ten men carried a summons across Antigua. In the name of Colonel Edward Byam, they called every freeholder to gather the next morning for a muster of militia in preparation for arresting the governor.[59] Back at home, Kerby prepared a proclamation, one that called on free Britons to rise against a traitor.

Parke began his own preparations to defend himself that day. He ordered the 38th Regiment to his plantation, but two of the regiment's captains refused to send their men to the governor's aid. The British naval commander sailed for Barbados.[60] Perhaps fifty men, most of them Parke's loyal grenadiers, took up a position in front of the governor's house.[61] Parke set up four field guns guarding the approach and summoned his appointees, the despised provost marshal Michael Ayon, George French, and others, to prove their loyalty in his defense.

At dawn, on the morning of 7 October, three hundred freeholders assembled at Otter's Pasture, just on the edge of town. Court might have even carried a weapon beside Thomas Kerby. Parke's allies later claimed that many of the assemblymen armed their slaves to fight by their sides.[62] Court would not forget the marshaling of the militia against the governor. Twenty years later, on the exact same spot, Court mustered his own militia of enslaved men.

To the bang of a drum, three hundred militia marched in formation to the marketplace in St. John's. While they stood at attention, Kerby ordered his chief clerk, John Booth, to read the assembly's proclamation against the governor, a proclamation Kerby wrote. According to Parke's supporters, the assembly accused Parke of being a "traytor" and "required all manner of Persons to repair to them, and be aiding assisting to them in taking General Parke dead or alive, or else their Estates should be forfeited." It was a daring assertion of authority by Colonel Byam and the assembly.[63]

Colonel Gamble and Speaker Crump rode to Governor Parke's plantation for a final negotiation. If he would disperse his soldiers and agree to sail to a neighboring island, they would offer themselves as hostages for his protection. Parke countered by saying he would allow the assembly "to make what Laws they should think proper for the Welfare thereof; and that he would pass them, provided they did not touch the Queens's Prerogative." Parke would send away most of his soldiers, he said, but only if the militia would disperse or send him four hostages from their leadership. He would not surrender the post appointed to him by the queen. Crump and Gamble returned to town. The beat of marching drums from the marketplace warned Parke that the militia had not accepted his terms.[64]

The rebels attacked in two columns, one commanded by a Captain Piggott and the other by a Captain Paynter, both elected members of the assembly. Piggott led the frontal assault down from Church-Hill, overlooking Parke's house. Paynter moved to the north and west and attacked the rear of the house.[65] On the approach of Piggott's column, the 38th Regiment gunners fired the field artillery and fled.[66]

The loyalists later claimed that Kerby had started the battle. He stepped out in front of Piggot's men, "advanced some small Distance before the rest, and fired the first Shot against the General." Both sides opened fire. Firing and loading from cover, advancing slowly, the militia shot the grenadiers to pieces in front of the house. Piggott charged down the hill, forty men behind him, and broke through the door. He confronted Parke in the parlor, both men pointing their pistols at the other. Piggott ordered the governor to surrender. Parke commanded Piggot be gone from the house. Both men fired at once, Parke's shot killing Piggott.[67] Loyalists and rebels battled through the house, and Parke fell, wounded in the thigh. The militia came on, their numbers overrunning the soldiers, putting to death many who tried to surrender. The militia shot Michael Ayon through the mouth. George French, who had already been shot twice in opening gunfire, was shot again as he lay on the floor. He later claimed that Thomas Kerby held a pistol to his head and would have shot him if an unnamed gentleman had not intervened.[68]

The rebels fell on the wounded Parke, beating him and breaking his back with a musket. They ripped the portrait of the queen from his neck and tore his clothes. They dragged him by one arm and one leg out of the house, down the steps, and left him "at last exposed to the Scorching sun in the open street." Parke begged for water. When Elizabeth Sweegle knelt to "offer him some water in a Callabash," Samuel Watkins kicked it out of her hands. They shouted at Parke, kicked him, and called him "dog." At last, some men picked him up and carried the wounded governor to his surgeon. He died on the table.[69]

Court was with Kerby at the end of the battle. According to one anonymous account of the aftermath of the fighting, Kerby found Michael

Ayon wounded and called to his "personal slave" to fetch a chair to carry Parke's loyal provost marshal back to Kerby's home in St. John's.[70] The rebels had riddled the governor's house with musket balls, killed fourteen or fifteen soldiers, wounded twenty-five more, and shot or stabbed most of Parke's supporters.[71]

Kerby and the elected members of the assembly had murdered the governor of the Leeward Islands, the Crown's executive officer. They had shot the queen's troops to death. Kerby had made many contingency plans for defeat. It is not clear that he had any plans for victory.

In 1711, Queen Anne ordered General Walter Douglas to take command of the Leeward Islands. She instructed him to arrest up to six ringleaders of the rebellion and pardon the rest. Douglas extorted bonds from the leading rebel planters, especially the assembly members, requiring huge fees before he issued the pardons. He kept the bonds for himself. Douglas issued the queen's general pardon to the rest of the island. Excluded from that pardon was Thomas Kerby, whom Douglas ordered to be arrested as a leader of the revolt and sent back to London on charges of treason.[72]

Kerby fled to Barbados. He lived on the Codrington estate, protected by the Codrington family, until Governor Robert Lowther ordered Kerby arrested and transferred to England in 1712.[73] Kerby would spend the next three year pleading his innocence before English courts.

He was not convicted of treason. Like many of the other ringleaders, he escaped punishment by claiming he had received Queen Anne's general pardon from Douglas.[74] Douglas had failed to send the list of pardons to England, and without contrary proof from the governor of the Leeward Islands, the judges ruled in Kerby's favor on a technicality. Kerby returned to Antigua in 1716, never again to act as island secretary or sit in the council chamber.[75]

The enslaved men and women of Antigua remembered the violent struggle between the assembly and the governor. In 1791, on Dominica, the British governor recorded meeting an elderly slave named Granny Sarah. She had spent her childhood on Antigua, and she told the governor she remembered "perfectly well the rejoicing on the Sacra's [white men] being let out of gaol, who had killed Governor Park."[76] More than eighty years later, the elderly woman could still remember the joy of the leading planters who had escaped punishment for killing Parke.

Court had been closer to the insurrection than a young Sarah. He saw the planters and their assembly overthrow the governor and kill the queen's grenadiers. If Arbuthnot had ever learned of Court's proximity to such a violent revolt, he might have assumed the "King" of the slaves had learned a simple lesson: the Crown and its soldiers could be overthrown. It is possible that Court might have walked away from the bloody scene at the governor's mansion with a profound sense of the vulnerability of white Britons. This might have been the lesson he learned from the killing of Colonel Parke.

But there was another lesson to be learned, a lesson exemplified by Kerby, right before the young man's eyes. Power lay in popular leadership rather than a distant monarch. The planters had won. Court learned that power in British America could be gained by building political alliances and assembling local leaders to resist oppression. Kerby's political ambitions would bear witness to this strategy over the next twenty-five years, as Court watched his master rise through the ranks of the planters on the island. Court would stand behind him as he rose, always the waiting man.

Kerby searched the faces of Arbuthnot and Delap, the men who had come to accuse Court of a new rebellion and take him away. Kerby did not share stories with Arbuthnot. He did not speak of Court's role in the violent rebellion against Daniel Parke, a fact that would not appear in any records from 1736. In the front room of his home, Kerby only insisted that Court was a "faithful slave" with no intentions to hide his "play" from the view of white authorities.

Arbuthnot would not relent. Court meant to be "King of the slaves," he said. "The state was in the utmost danger."[77]

Kerby suddenly relented. He told Arbuthnot that "he might take up Court and commit him to gaol if he thought proper."

Kerby's sudden consent to Court's arrest surprised Arbuthnot. The justice of the peace hesitated. Arbuthnot "did not think it safe or Prudent for a Private Magistrate to go a Step further, not knowing what Bad consequences might attend his Sending the Principal Conspirator (As he looked upon Court to be) to Gaol," he told Kerby. It was a "Matter of State Proper for the General and Council of State that were to meet the Fryday following, before whom he should lay all his Informations." Arbuthnot would take his accusations against Court to the governor.

Arbuthnot and Delap departed Kerby's house without Court. But after they were gone, in the quiet of the front room of his house, Kerby was left to reflect on the growing danger of Arbuthnot's investigation. The governor and council had great power on the island. The investigation had become a threat, not only to Court but to Kerby's household and his precarious place as Speaker of the assembly.

CHAPTER FIVE

The Ambassador

July 1730
Williamsburg, Virginia

IN THE LATE SUMMER OF 1730, a rumor of emancipation swept through the slave populations of colonial Virginia. Planters reported crowds of slaves meeting "in the open and expressing a desire to obtain their Freedom." Determined to discover the cause of the disturbance, Governor William Gooch ordered many slaves "taken up" and interrogated by colonial officials. The slaves had a "Notion generally entertained amongst them," explained Gooch to the Lords of Trade in England, that "his Majesty had sent Orders for setting of them free as soon as they were Christians."[1]

The slaves believed that King George II had issued a proclamation emancipating all bondspeople baptized in the Christian faith. The planters were suppressing the king's edict, claimed the arrested slaves, preventing Black men and women from the king's offer of freedom. Black people embraced the story, gathering in meetings to organize and protest and demand their liberty.

The "Chesapeake Rebellion," as it is remembered by historians, set a precedent for the ways in which enslaved Black people would respond to news of freedom from England. Slaves passed the rumor across plantations and especially between the towns of Williamsburg and Norfolk, the two centers of maritime communication in the Chesapeake Bay. News traveled much slower into other provinces on the Atlantic Coast, appearing only four years later in East Jersey. Black people responded to

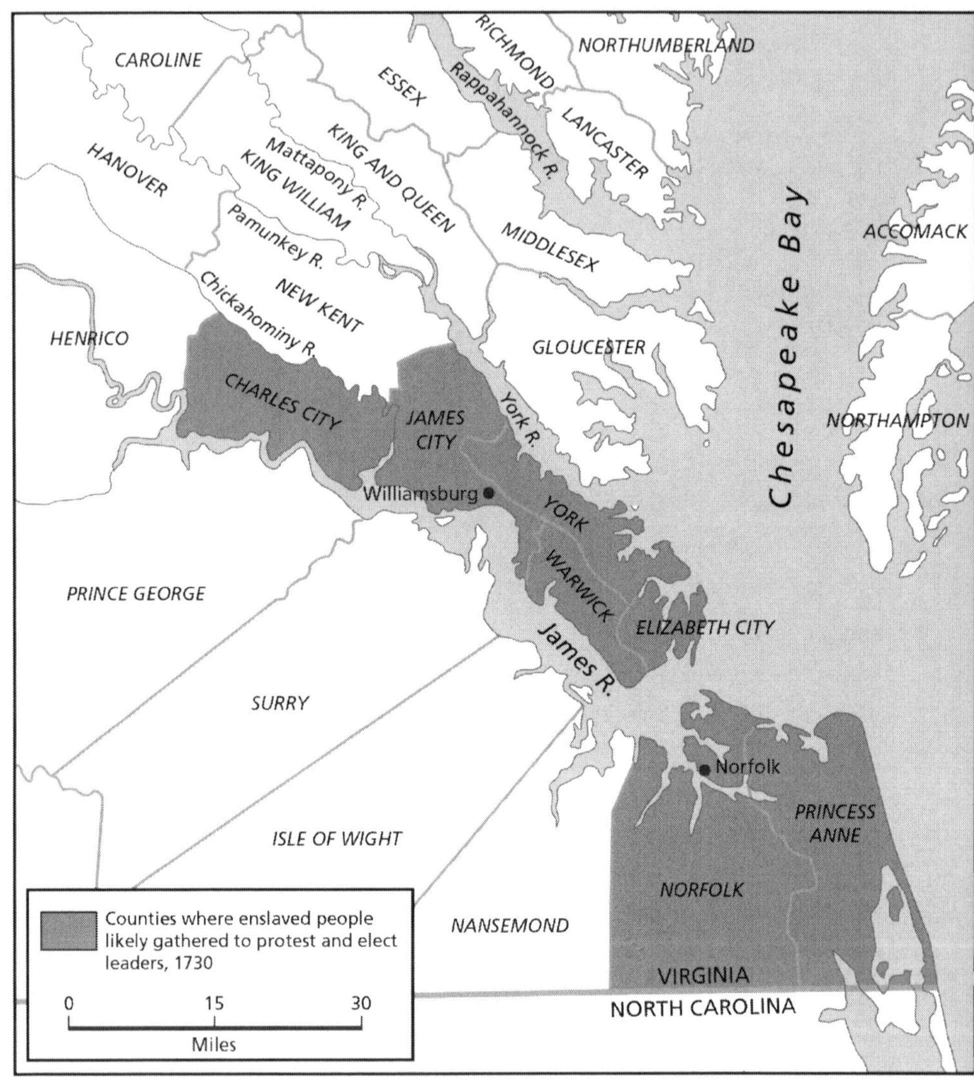

Map 4. Virginia counties where slaves gathered to protest, 1730

the report in great numbers, organizing meetings of hundreds of slaves who elected leaders to take their cause to the king. Their protests became a social movement, one in which a diverse population of slaves invented a new political community all their own. Their movement attracted the attention of white authorities, who attacked the gatherings of slaves and executed their leaders. Examining the Chesapeake Rebellion of 1730 illuminates the possibilities and limits for Black people seeking to respond to a rumor of emancipation in British America.

As the enslaved men and women of Virginia gathered in large meetings along the waterways of the Chesapeake Bay in the summer of 1730, the sailors of the London tobacco ship *Amity* paid little heed to the tumult. They went about their work on the York River, lowering giant barrels of tobacco—called hogsheads—into the hold of their ship. At the end of July, a Captain Wills ordered the crew to weigh anchor and set sail for England.

It came as a great surprise to the *Amity*'s crew when one of their white crew met a Black man in the hold. The stowaway had hidden among the hogsheads and escaped detection until the *Amity* was underway for London. The sailor brought him up on deck, into the wind and light, a slave, surrounded by twenty-one white English sailors. Wills confronted the stowaway. Why had the stranger dared to hide aboard his London-bound ship? The Black man had a surprising answer. He "was going Ambassador from the Negroes to his Majesty King George," he announced. He had been sent by the slaves of Virginia to inform the king of their plight.[2]

Captain Wills thought the idea absurd. Slaves could not have an "Ambassador." They labored all their lives at the will of their masters. They could not elect leaders like English freeholders. They had no state and no ambassador. And no slave could ever hope to speak to the king. But while Wills and the sailors had spent the summer months loading tobacco along the York River, Black men and women had created a new politics of their own. Surrounded on the deck of the *Amity*, the "Ambassador from the Negroes" represented a new movement that had taken hold among the enslaved people of the Chesapeake Bay.

The first historical evidence of the rumor appeared in the correspondence of Anglican commissary James Blair, though he did not understand what was happening. On 20 July 1730, Blair reported crowds of Black people asking him for baptism at his church. He was pleasantly surprised. For more than a year, the commissary had been trying to instruct and baptize Virginia's slaves after receiving a directive from Edmund Gibson, the bishop of London. Blair had found few takers.[3] Suddenly, at midsummer, it seemed the slaves had discovered a passion for his lessons. "There is a very great number of Negroes lately instructed in the Church catechism," Blair wrote the bishop. Unaware anything might be afoot, he celebrated that "great Numbers of them attend the Church."[4]

Enslaved men and women held their first open meetings over the next ten days. They met in the hundreds near the capital of Williamsburg according to London newspapers, and along the James River in the most densely populated region of the province.[5] By 30 July, a white Virginian writing to London described slave meetings across "five counties."

Virginia governor William Gooch appears to have been unaware of the meetings as late as 23 July. On that day, at his desk in the governor's mansion in Williamsburg, Gooch was hard at work responding to queries from the Lords of Trade and Plantations. Asked the number of inhabitants over whom he ruled, Gooch wrote, "The number of souls in Virginia will amount to 114,000 at least," with Black slaves accounting for about a third of the total population. Asked by the Lords "what places and forts of defense" existed in Virginia, Gooch responded, "There are no forts in this colony, nor any places of defense." He could look only to the militia, he explained to his masters in England, whose numbers of foot and horse he hoped "would be in a little time under a very regular discipline."[6]

Gooch learned of the meetings sometime between the end of July and early August. The gatherings of so many slaves created a sensation among the white planters of the James River, who crowded around the governor in alarm. Determined to discover the cause of the meetings, Gooch ordered slaves "taken up" and interrogated by justices of the peace. "There was a Notion generally entertained amongst them," he wrote, that "his Majesty had sent Orders for setting of them free as soon as they were Christians."[7] King George had promised Black people freedom, the prisoners explained. The planters suppressed the news, holding slaves in bondage still.

Gooch knew the rumor was not true. King George II had not freed the baptized slaves of the American plantations. Gooch could find no basis for such a story in his correspondence, nor could he determine the story's origin. "I have not been able to learn who was the first Author of it," he complained in a letter to the bishop of London. And yet the governor could not stop Black people from sharing the story across Virginia. The meetings of slaves grew in number and so too did the fears of the white colonists.

By September, Gooch had "discovered many Meetings and Consultations of the Negroes in several Parts of the Country in order to obtain their freedom." He mustered out the mounted militia "with Orders to Secure all the Negroes found off their Masters Plantations." For the unfortunate people caught up by white troops, Gooch ordered a "severe Chastisement by Whipping." He hoped the severity of physical punishment would "deter them [the slaves] from any such unlawful Meetings, and to Convince them that their best way is to rest contented with their Condition."[8]

But many slaves "refused to rest contended." As autumn brought an end to the stripping of tobacco and labor lessened across the plantations, they continued to share the story of freedom and to meet in secret. "There was a general rumour among them that they were to be set free," the Anglican commissary Blair would remember. "And when they saw nothing of it they grew angry and saucy, and met in the night time in great numbers, and talked of rising; and in some places of choosing their leaders."[9]

On a Sunday afternoon in the winter of 1730–1731, several hundred slaves gathered in a great meeting along the border of Norfolk and Princess Anne Counties. Planters raised the alarm. The "Negroes had the boldness to Assemble on a Sunday while the People were at Church, and to Chuse from amongst themselves Officers to Comand them in their intended Insurrection, which was to have been put in Execution very soon after," Gooch wrote later.[10]

The mounted militia attacked the meeting. The horsemen captured many of the slave leaders. "This Plot being happily discovered, the Ringleaders were brought to a Tryal, and four of them, on clear Evidence convicted, were Executed," Gooch wrote.[11] There were many other Black men and women who escaped mounted militia, fleeing south and west into the Dismal Swamp. There they lived free for months. The

Virginians enlisted the help of Pasquotank Indians who hunted down the escaped slaves and ended their desperate attempt at freedom.[12]

Britons remembered the violence against the Norfolk meeting as the "Chesapeake Rebellion" of 1730. Historians sometimes describe the tumult as the largest slave revolt in British American history.[13] But it was no such thing. There is no record of slaves attacking their masters. No rebels burned buildings or set the precious tobacco crop on fire. British officials did not mention weapons in the hands of slaves—no muskets or knives, not even hoes or farm implements. It is not clear the protesters sought to overthrow the colonial government at all. That slaves met in violation of the law and against their master's will was rebellious, to be sure. Virginia's laws forbade slaves from meeting in large numbers. And there is reason to think that some slaves advocated for "rising" against the planters, whom they believed had disobeyed the proclamation of the king. But calling the protests a "rebellion" or "insurrection" conceals the political moment that took hold in the slave communities of America in the fall of 1730. For white Britons, the slaves' crime in Virginia was not overt insurrection; it was political expression.

The rumor of the king's edict set in motion a new politics among the slaves of the Chesapeake. Black men and women acted together in hope of freedom. They grew "saucy," according to Blair, indignant that planters would hold them against the will of the king. Slaves met in open meetings across Virginia in the hundreds to complain and protest. Factions grew in their ranks, some speaking of "rising," others wanting to petition the king so he might know the plight of his most oppressed subjects. They spoke of "choosing their leaders," wrote Blair.[14]

Theirs was a social movement, one of the earliest initiated by Black people in British America.[15] They spread their movement across the plantations and rivers of the Chesapeake Bay and along the eastern coast of the Atlantic. The rumor of emancipation became the slave's cause, generations before the revolutionary fervor of Europeans.

Social movements empower ordinary people to change their fates. They are sustained campaigns waged by people who share a common cause. A social movement is larger than a single revolt, more public than a plot. It begins when individuals recognize a shared grievance. It grows as they campaign together, challenging authorities or elite opponents to address a perceived wrong. Social movements produce leaders, men and women who inspire others by articulating the moral purpose of the campaign. From their struggles, participants can forge a greater sense of collective identity—they can recognize each other as similar because of their common plight. For the Black slaves of the Chesapeake, a social movement helped create a new political culture.

Historians have long assumed social movements began in Europe as early expressions of democratic fervor. The social scientist Charles Tilly, who has influenced generations if scholars with his studies of social movements, traced their beginnings to the British Isles in the 1760s. It was during the "Wilkite controversies," when poor workers mobilized across England to support John Wilkes in his campaign for civil liberties, that Tilly believed English people began to invent the social movement. Mobs and rebellions had been common expressions of political anger for ordinary English people for centuries, as had appealing to local elites to represent their interests. But the supporters of Wilkes engaged in a campaign to convince the public and political leaders to embrace universal male suffrage and expose corruption. "They fashioned a new sort of campaign: the sustained challenge to authorities on behalf of a relatively well-defined program in the name of an aggrieved population by means of coordinated public performances," Tilly and fellow historian Lesley J. Wood explained. With "meetings, demonstrations, petitions, electoral participation, strikes, and related means of coordinated action," the English workers challenged authorities "without necessarily attacking them physically."[16]

The Wilkites insisted their cause transcended any single riot or protest. In May 1768, when perhaps forty thousand protesters clashed with English soldiers in St. George's Field, an anonymous supporter of the movement penned a letter to the newspaper *North Briton* denying the violence had been an insurrection.[17] "Is every little tumult of the people, every little riotous assembly, to be branded with the odious and dreadful epithet of rebellion?" the writer asked. "If it is, I will venture to affirm, that there have been, I do not say one, but 20 different rebellions in England within these 4 months."[18] If the slaves of eastern North America had possessed a newspaper of their own in 1730, they might have dismissed the planters' accusations of rebellion in similar terms.

Black slaves in the British colonies began to invent their own social movements in the second quarter of the eighteenth century. Their politics did not emerge from English legal traditions of Magna Carta or the philosophes of the Enlightenment. Nor was their movement born from the political conflicts of West Africa. Rather, Black people created the movement from the necessity of uniting a diverse and oppressed population of slaves in common cause against their slavery. The spark that lit the fire was a rumor of freedom.

Why had Black people embraced the rumor that King George II had freed the baptized slaves of the plantations? The rumor of the king's freedom inspired slaves to organize for good reason. Slaves wanted their freedom. The story gave them hope. But enslaved men and women believed the rumor because of a controversy that had persisted in the English colonies for at least a century.

The rumor of monarchial emancipation originated from the longstanding debate surrounding the baptism of slaves in the British Empire. Planters had argued against slave baptism out of the opinion that it would make slaves less manageable and that it was irreligious to enslave another Christian. The Church of England insisted it was the first duty of Christians to convert heathens to their Protestant faith. Despite the insistence by church authorities that slavery was endorsed by the Bible, planters stayed reticent, refusing to allow slaves to participate in Protestant services.[19] As early as 1711, missionaries for the Church of England noted that Black ferrymen on the James River complained of being forbidden from baptism, their "Master not admitting it" despite the "great desire" of slaves.[20]

Virginia's slaves attempted to take the issue into their own hands in 1723. In one of the earliest documents written by a slave in British America, a mixed-race man wrote a letter to the newly appointed bishop of London asking him to "Releese us out of this Cruell Bondegg." In the letter, the author explained that enslaved Blacks lived in "Sevarity and Sorrowfull Sarvice." They were "hard used on Every Account," kept in ignorance of the teaching of the Bible, denied holy matrimony, and "to be plain they doo Look no more upon us then if we ware dogs." The anonymous author apologized for his "riting," which was "vary bad," but he hoped the bishop would forgive him as he was just a "poor Slave that writt it and has no other time but Sunday."[21] If the letter demonstrated anything, it was that in 1723 Virginia, freedom had become deeply interwoven in the minds of slaves with the rites of Christianity and baptism.

In 1729, Anglican missionaries sought to quiet the protests of planters and settle the debate over slave baptism by securing an opinion from London. The philosopher George Berkeley lobbied Attorney General Philip Yorke and Solicitor General Charles Talbot to clarify whether the rite of baptism would free slaves within the British Empire.[22] From their chambers, Yorke and Talbot issued a legal opinion in January 1730 "that a Slave, by coming from the West-Indies to Great Britain or Ireland, either with or without his Master, doth not become free, and that his Master's Property, or Right in him, is not thereby determined or varied." Their opinion also stated "that Baptism doth not bestow Freedom on him, nor make any alteration in his temporal Condition in these Kingdoms. We are also of Opinion, that his Master may legally compel him to return again to the Plantations."[23] The Yorke-Talbot opinion, as it came to be known, would be dismissed by Lord Mansfield in his Somerset decision forty-three years later.

The evidence for the influence of this opinion on the emancipation rumor is entirely circumstantial. The opinion appeared in January 1730. Slaves were sharing the emancipation rumor by that summer. They were contradictory ideas, of course, with Yorke and Talbot declaring baptism would not free a slave while the rumor insisted King George II had emancipated the Christians. But the timing of the opinion and rumor suggest that the controversy in England had somehow fostered a false report in British America.

Contemporary white Britons remained equally confused about where the story had started. In Philadelphia, Benjamin Franklin reported that it had all started with a sailor. "This uneasiness among the slaves, tis thought, was occasioned by a sailor, who said in the hearing of some of them, That the King of England had ordered they should all be set free," Franklin reported in his *Pennsylvania Gazette*.[24] If this were true, it is possible a sailor had learned of the controversy and misunderstood the outcome, setting sail before learning of the Yorke-Talbot decision.[25]

Printers in London believed the return of Virginia's former lieutenant governor Alexander Spotswood had started the rumor. It began sometime the previous year with "a Report at Col. Spottwood's Arrival, that he had Direction from his Majesty to free all baptiz'd Negroes," the printer Samuel Nevil explained.[26] Spotswood had returned to his Virginia plantation in the spring of 1729 after a seven-year absence living in England. He had advocated against unrestrained violence against slaves in his time as governor.[27] Perhaps his arrival had somehow been conflated with news in England of the Yorke-Talbot opinion the following year. And yet the real origins of the rumor lay not in the legal chambers of London but the open-air cooking fires of Virginia, where slaves gathered at the end of long days to share news.

When the rumor took hold in midsummer, slaves quickly shared the story between Black communities on the Chesapeake Bay. Black communication in the British Atlantic closely followed the routes of trade. Exchanging news in the second quarter of the eighteenth century depended on the mobility of people, whether between plantations or across oceans. Even a printed newspaper or private letter had to be carried by someone.

In Virginia, Black slaves provided the maritime labor force for the commerce of the Chesapeake. Tobacco cultivation had dispersed plantations along the deep rivers of the region, and water served as the highway between settlements. In his correspondence to the Lords of Trade and Plantations on 23 July 1730, Gooch himself noted "shallops," or small vessels, were "constantly employed in the Bay and in transporting the Country's commodities from one River to another," but "their Crews can't properly be termed Seamen; being for the most part Planters with

Negros and other Servants."[28] Black watermen dominated transportation among scattered plantations in which canoes carried "Goods, Horses, and other Cattle from one Plantation to another over large and spacious Rivers."[29] Planters maintained their own small docks to deposit their hogsheads of tobacco aboard sloops waiting in the James, York, and Rappahannock Rivers.

But there were also limits to slave mobility in Virginia. Tobacco merchants owned few deep-water vessels. As Gooch explained to the Lords of Trade, the province's entire fleet "consists of one Ship, Six Brigantines, and Sixteen Sloops, which are all that usually go to Sea." These vessels were directed toward the tobacco trade between London and Virginia and rarely traded to other provinces.[30] There is no known evidence that Virginian slaves worked aboard these deep-water vessels in the 1730s. Like South Carolina merchants, most Virginian slave owners were unwilling to risk the possibility of their slaves' jumping ship in a London port.

Black people had to get their foreign news from visitors to their shores. Enslaved sailors had already become a significant presence on British colonial ships by the first half of the eighteenth century. Between 1720 and 1743, Black mariners made up an estimated 25–40 percent of all seamen aboard maritime vessels based in the island colonies of the British West Indies and Bermuda.[31] The presence of Black sailors aboard so many island vessels placed them at the center of the commercial activity of the British Empire in the first half of the eighteenth century. Ships crewed by slaves were part of an expansive intercolonial trade that crisscrossed the Atlantic. In 1726, William Byrd noted that the largest harbor in Virginia, Norfolk, maintained a trade that "is Chiefly to the West-Indies."[32]

Bermuda's enslaved sailors were especially well placed to disseminate news because of the centrality of the island's maritime trade. According to a report by Governor John Pitt of Bermuda, slaves made up more than 40 percent of sailors on Bermudian ocean-going vessels in 1733.[33] In the eighteenth century, Bermudians were the consummate intercolonial traders of the Atlantic world. George Berkeley noted in 1725 that Bermudians were the "only people of all in the British plantations who hold a general correspondence with the rest of America."[34] It was a Bermuda ship—almost certainly crewed by Black slaves—that first carried news of the slave conspiracy on the island of Antigua to Virginia in the winter of 1736.[35]

The movement of the rumor of emancipation provides evidence for the routes of Black communication as they existed in the 1730s. Like blood in the water, following reports of slave meetings illuminates the extent to which slaves had shared the story of the king's edict. White officials first described meetings near Williamsburg, the capital of the colony, situated between the York and James Rivers.[36] A Virginian noted the meetings spread to five counties within days, though he did not list which ones.[37] The centrality of Williamsburg on the Virginia Peninsula made at least eight nearby counties likely locations for the meetings discovered by white authorities. By September, Gooch had learned of "Meetings and Consultations of the Negroes in several Parts of the Country," suggesting the gatherings had spread beyond the peninsula.

Seven months after the first reports of slave gatherings, Gooch described a meeting of hundreds of slaves near Norfolk, between Princess Ann and Norfolk County on the Elizabeth River.[38] Positioned south of the great harbor of Hampton Roads and close to Virginia's largest port town of Norfolk, the meeting took place at the locus of trade and communication on the Chesapeake Bay. There was no better place to organize a movement and spread the word to Black communities in the province and beyond.

In 1734, the rumor of freedom continued beyond Virginia's shores. Black men and women in Somerville, New Jersey, shared a story that would have been quite familiar to the enslaved communities of Virginia. "The English-men were generally a pack of Villains, and kept the negroes as slaves," an enslaved Black man supposedly shouted at a white colonist named Renolds. The white men were holding the slaves in bondage, "contrary to a positive Order from King George, sent to the Governor of New York, to set free, which the said Governor did intend to do, but was prevented."[39] The slave promised the white man that he "was as good as a man as himself" and "in a little time he should be convinced of it." Fearing a widespread plot, Jersey authorities arrested the slave and forced him to name others.[40]

In the interrogations that followed, the accused slaves professed belief that planters had suppressed a royal order of emancipation. The slaves of the mid-Atlantic embraced the rumors that had gripped the Chesapeake only four years earlier. It is roughly two hundred miles by sail along the Atlantic Coast from the mouth of Chesapeake Bay to Somerville on the Raritan River. Outside the riverine trade of Virginia, the rumor had slowed and evolved, but the promise of freedom persisted.

The slave's system of communication, the networks of laborers and ferrymen that traversed the rivers and bays of the Chesapeake and mid-Atlantic, would persist through the next generation. In 1775, Massachusetts's delegate to the Second Continental Congress John Adams recorded in his diary the observations of Georgia officials, who insisted "the Negroes have a wonderful art of communicating intelligence among themselves; it will run several-hundred miles in a week or fortnight."[41]

It was no small feat for an oppressed people to share a rumor of freedom across so many dispersed communities. There were great barriers to organizing the slaves of the Chesapeake in 1730. They were not one people but many. Guineamen captains purchased slaves in distant lands, some more than eight thousand miles away (Madagascar), and carried their prisoners across the Atlantic Ocean to the rivers of the Chesapeake. Probably forty thousand Black people lived in Virginia in 1730, about half born outside the province.[42]

Most of Virginia's new slaves arrived directly from Africa. Merchants from London and Bristol favored the Bight of Biafra for slave trading to Virginia in the 1710s and 1720s, so much so that more than half the Africans arriving in the Chesapeake were sold from that coast.[43] The British slave ships from Biafra became part of a larger forced migration. In the decade before the rumor of the king's edict, between 1720 and 1730, at least 167 British Guineamen carried African-born slaves into Virginia.[44]

Planters dispersed the new slaves across the peninsulas and rivers and swamps of the Chesapeake, a geography that scattered Black populations and impeded large gatherings. The English had carved off small plantations for more than a century, foregoing villages and towns for private landholdings that might elevate their status. Planters purchased African slaves in small lots, with even the richest white colonists rarely buying more than three or four slaves from any ship. In the 1720s, the majority of slaves lived on plantations with fewer than ten Black people.[45]

In 1724, a minister in Christ Church Parish noted the difficulties Africans experienced in communicating. There were "a great many Black bond men and women infidels that understand not our Language nor me their's," he wrote to England.[46] White observers of the slave population frequently commented on the language difficulties of the new slave population. In 1729, the bishop of London noted that his missionaries to the colonies complained that the African slaves could not speak English.[47]

This forced migration created powerful divisions in slave communities. Separated by ancestry and language, Africans sought out members of their own slave "nation" and often competed against other slaves suffering in the deplorable conditions of tobacco slavery. Enslaved people fought for positions on plantations and for resources like space and food. These differences could be pronounced. In Virginia in 1728, Robert King Carter felt that he had to warn his Creole drivers not to brutally harm his African fieldhands.[48]

In 1730, in response to a false report of emancipation in England, the slaves of the Chesapeake began organizing their diverse and oppressed peoples into a political community. The rumor empowered slaves to try and change their fate. Black leaders waged a sustained campaign across the waters of the Chesapeake in common cause with people whom they had never met. Their meetings were larger than a single revolt, more public than a plot. The slaves elected their own leaders, men and women who inspired others by articulating the moral purpose of the campaign. From their struggle, the Black slaves of the Chesapeake invented a movement in which they all could agree they shared a common plight and common purpose. Theirs was a social movement, rather than a rebellion, the product of sharing a rumor of emancipation among an oppressed people.

White British colonists crushed the Chesapeake emancipation movement. They dispersed the open meetings of enslaved Black people who sought freedom from their king. White authorities hanged the leaders of the grand gathering in Norfolk and Princess Anne Counties. They hunted down the slaves who ran to the Dismal Swamp. Even aboard the tobacco ship *Amity,* Captain Wills refused to offer any mercy.

In late September, the *Evening Post* of London reported the story of Wills's encounter with the stowaway who claimed "he was going Ambassador from the Negroes to his Majesty King George." Wills refused the Black man passage. Instead, Wills told the *Post,* "his Excellency was turn'd ashore and whipt thro' every County to the Place from whence he came." Meant to be humorous, the captain reassured the newspaper's London subscribers that he had done his part to ensure there would be no ambassador of slaves to King George II.[49]

From our vantage point, looking back on an era of unrest in the British Atlantic, we can see the origins of the enslaved man's idea. His response was born from the monarchial emancipation rumor of 1730. It was an attempt to appeal for protection from the British king, as a Briton might hope to do within the British Empire. And yet it was also something more. It was an expression of a shared cause and a shared purpose and an attempt to make an appeal for all the "Negroes."

It is in such watershed moments that we discover the origins of the first Black Atlantic. The "Ambassador" desired to be both Black and British, and of course free. Like thousands of slaves circulating news and rumor throughout the colonies of North America and the West Indies, he understood that he shared a common fate with the enslaved people of African ancestry. In such moments the Black Atlantic was born.

CHAPTER SIX

News of St. John

23 November 1733
St. John, Danish Virgin Islands

IN THE WEEKS LEADING UP to the New Jersey conspiracy of 1734, a Bermudian ship—almost certainly crewed by slaves—arrived from the West Indies with news of an island-wide slave rebellion on the Danish province of St. John.[1] The captain of the vessel reported a massacre, and the news moved quickly through the populations of New York and New Jersey. On 18 March, the *New York Gazette* published a letter from a colonist who had witnessed the interrogations of the accused slaves.

Displaying a heightened awareness of news from the West Indies, the white colonist who carried the news to New York alerted the people there that the latest slave conspiracy was part of a wider spate of rebellion sweeping through the British Atlantic. "How very necessary it is for every Colony to make proper Laws and Ordinances for their own Security," he warned. "The late Massacre perpetrated by the Negroes in the Island of St. John's, the very great head they are come to in the Island of Jamaica, and the general Melancholy Apprehensions of his Majesty's Subjects in the West Indies, gives but too much room to fear there is some great Fatality attends the English Dominions in America, from the too great Number of that unchristian and barbarous People being imported."[2] The British colonist warned his white New York readers to cast their eyes a thousand miles south, to another region of tumult and rebellion.

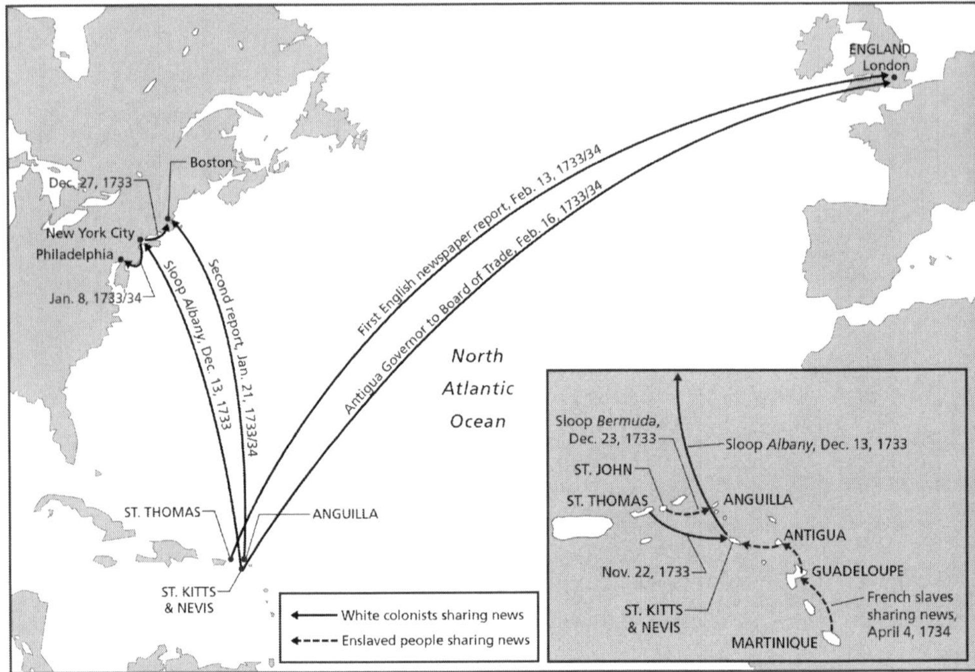

Map 5. News of the St. John's insurrection, 1733–1734

News of the St. John insurrection of 1733 circulated quickly through the slave quarters of the islands, transcending imperial boundaries with the urgency of rumor and the possibility of freedom. The geography of the Leeward Islands produced interconnected slave communities in which slaves could travel in less than half a day between islands. Despite these many connections, the disparate African populations of forcefully transported slaves and the polyglot populations of Creoles born to diverse nations made alliances surprisingly difficult. These differences among slave communities created a crisis between islands as slaves shared news of the first successful island-wide slave revolt in the New World.

In 1730, on the Gold Coast of Africa, the kingdom of Akwamu collapsed before an invading army from the west. The nation of Akyem surprised Akwamu during a period of widespread discontent within the kingdom. Like the many victims of the warring state, the Akwamu people abandoned their capital and attempted to flee east and south, away from the invading army.[3] The Ga people of Accra turned on their former masters, fighting alongside the Akyem soldiers and enslaving the Akwamu as they attempted to seek refuge among the European castles with which they had traded for so long.[4] The Ga sold their Akwamu to the European forts, including the Danish Fort Christiansborg. Historian Ray Kea argues the Danish slave ships *Haabet Galley* and *Countess of Laurwig* were loaded with Akwamu slaves in 1731 and 1733, the two ships carrying together 357 people to the Danish islands of St. Thomas and St. John.[5]

The newly enslaved Akwamu captives arrived on the island of St. John during a period of intense settlement. The island is six miles across and mountainous, with the most fertile regions on the leeward (western) side of the island. The Danes began moving from nearby St. Thomas to St. John in 1717. By 1733, there were 208 white settlers and 1,087 Black slaves on the island of St. John with approximately ten slaves on each plantation. Because the Danes lacked settlers, they invited Dutch, French, and English planters to purchase land and raise sugarcane under the authority of the Danish West Indian and Guinea Company. The planters scattered over the island, maintaining small herds of cattle and aggressively planting sugar. They were encouraged by their king in Denmark, who in 1729 passed an edict requiring all national refineries to use only company sugar from the West Indies.[6]

On 23 November 1733, the Danish magistrate John Reimert Soedtmann awoke to the sound of his breaking door in the early morning.[7] The sources are silent as to whether the men who entered his room bore torches or entered the chamber in darkness, but the magistrate must have recognized his own slaves very quickly. They forced him to stand up and then stripped him naked.[8] The men told Soedtmann to sing and dance, almost certainly in mimicry of the way the Guineamen captains forced slaves to dance for exercise on ship decks during the Middle Passage.[9] The magistrate performed for his slaves, naked, in what must have been a pathetic show, and then one of the men ran a sword through his body. After he had fallen to the ground they severed his head and cut open his torso and "washed themselves in his blood." The men took hold of his thirteen-year-old stepdaughter, named Hissing, and killed her. They laid her dead body on top of her stepfather before they left.[10]

As the Soedtmanns died, a party of slaves carrying bundles of wood approached the entrance of Fortsberg, the garrison on the eastern side of the island. "Werdae?!" called out the sentry in the dark. "Company Negroes with wood," answered the men. The sentry opened the doors and the slaves filed into the fort. From the bundles of wood, the slaves suddenly drew forth bills and cane knives. There were six soldiers in the fort that night. The lone survivor hid under his bed and then escaped while the rest of the soldiers died.[11] The slaves, now freemen, raised the flag over the fort and fired the cannons out over Coral Bay. The Akwamu signaled the beginning of their conquest of St. John.

News of the St. John insurrection of 1733 dropped like a stone into a pond, with waves of rumors moving west and north and east. These avenues of slave communications were a product of the growing commercial activity within the British Empire in the first half of the eighteenth century. There were few innovations in shipping between 1675 and 1740, which meant that the growing number of migrants and the subsequent expansion of trade depended on an increased volume of vessels traveling across oceans.[12] In an age when news could only travel as fast as a ship of sail, the arrival of more ships meant the expansion of communication among colonies. Colonial American historians have long celebrated this growth of commerce as an important development in the making of a British American people. There has been less appreciation of the role of this commercial expansion in fostering a Black British Atlantic in the first half of the eighteenth century.

The journeys of slaves along coastal waterways and among British colonies created a complex and extensive network of communication. In his study of African American seamen *Black Jacks* (1997), historian W. Jeffrey Bolster provides a graphic description of the interconnected routes of these many mariners at the end of the eighteenth century during the Age of Revolution. He asks the reader to imagine a map of the Caribbean archipelago: "From each island radiate short spokes that dead-end, like antennae: the out and back voyages of daily fisherman. Each island, too, is encircled by loops from point to point along its shore: the coastal trips of slave boatmen. Bold lines connect virtually every island to others: the inter-island voyages of black and white crews and runaway slaves. Finally, even more prominent lines arrive at most islands from (and depart to) African, American, and European ports: international voyages on which blacks sailed."[13] Bolster's depiction of Black maritime activity captures the overlapping routes of commerce that brought slaves together. Like most scholars of the British Black Atlantic, Bolster was more concerned with the late eighteenth century, but nearly sixty years before the American and French Revolutions, enslaved men and women lived within their own distinctive Atlantic world.[14]

Black communication in the British Atlantic closely followed the routes of trade. Exchanging news in the second quarter of the eighteenth century depended on the mobility of slaves, whether between plantations or across oceans, and the labors of Black people determined the extent of contact between regions. This was especially true for Black sailors. In regions where white labor was scarce, such as the Caribbean and Bermuda, slaves had far more opportunities to work aboard vessels and travel among provinces. Enslaved mariners moved in and out of smaller Black diasporas shaped by geography and coastal trade.

In 1738, Royal Officer Don Manuel de Montiano ordered a proclamation read in the Spanish town of St. Augustine, Florida. With "Beat of drum," the town crier moved out from the shadow of the walls of the still unfinished Castillo fortress and down the streets of the garrison port. When near enough to the harbor to be heard by sailors and dockside laborers, the crier announced the Spanish would provide "Liberty and Protection to all Slaves that should desert thither from any English Colonies."[15] There were English people within earshot to hear the proclamation, but according to a report later made by South Carolinians, the audience for the crier was not the white ship captains and sailors trading along the harbor. Instead, the Spanish intentionally announced their proclamation to the "many Negroes belonging to English Vessels that carried thither Supplies of Provisions &c. had the Opportunity of hearing it."[16] Don Montiano spoke directly to the group of people most likely to spread news of emancipation and protection to the slave societies of the British colonies. The "Negroes belonging to English Vessels" were the Black sailors of the Atlantic, a people that traveled among colonies and played a critical role in the spread of slave resistance during this period of intensified unrest.

Significant evidence suggests Black mariners made up between 25 and 40 percent of all seamen aboard maritime vessels based in the colonies of the British Caribbean and Bermuda between 1720 and 1743. Black crews aboard ships based in mainland colonies made up a much smaller percentage, but scattered references to black sailors suggest that at least in Rhode Island, there were a great many slaves aboard ships. Because historians have understood so little about the extent of this important population in the first half of the eighteenth century, it is worthwhile to explore the evidence in detail.[17]

Records for slave mariners in this period are quite rare, but at least three critical documents produced by royal governors offer evidence for the extensive numbers of Black sailors aboard ships at sea. In 1720, Governor Walter Hamilton of Antigua produced a list of all ships at port and a description of their crews. On the right edge of his list he drew a firm line, creating columns labeled "white" and "negro" and listing the numbers of each group aboard each ship. His numbers reveal that "negro" sailors made up about 98 of 235 crewmen. No Black people worked on the largest brigantines and snows, but they did make up about 25 percent of the crews of sloops, deep-sea vessels that made the bulk of the carrying trade among colonies. Sloops were the most popular ship on the island. On one fifteen-ton sloop, the *Plunkett,* the entire crew consisted of four Black sailors and no whites.[18] On smaller boats or droghers, typically used to move goods around and between the Leeward Islands, Blacks outnumbered white sailors by about three to one. In short, the lists provided by Hamilton in 1720 indicate that slaves dominated the local carrying trade.[19]

In 1743, Governor Edward Trelawny of Jamaica provided numbers for Black mariners in Kingston almost identical to those of Antigua twenty-three years earlier. His census of North American ships at anchor found crews comprised 41 Black and 135 white sailors. At nearly 23 percent, this number appears remarkably close to the percentage of Black sailors who worked aboard deep-sea sloops in Antigua in 1720.[20] Despite the fact that these two reports spanned more than twenty-three years and were written by different governors at opposite ends of the Caribbean, the comparable number aboard ship suggests that Black mariners represented about a quarter of the sailors aboard Caribbean-owned ships in the second quarter of the eighteenth century.

Black sailors made up a larger percentage of sailing crews in the island colony of Bermuda, located approximately 640 miles east of North Carolina. In 1733, the island's Governor John Pitt counted 200 white sailors and 150 slaves aboard local vessels, putting the percentage of Bermuda slave mariners above 40 percent. Because the ocean-going carrying trade was so extensive in Bermuda, it is likely that the vast majority of these Black mariners crewed ships that traveled throughout the Atlantic Ocean.[21]

Bermudian slaves were the consummate Black sailors of the British Empire during the 1730s. Tobacco agriculture had declined on the island by the late seventeenth century so that white colonists abandoned plantations for ships and made sailing the labor of their slaves. The Bermuda sloop emerged as a favorite carrying vessel because of the native cedar construction of its hull and shallow draft, which allowed for trade far up inland rivers.[22] As Philip D. Morgan explains in his article "Maritime Slavery," Atlantic islands that did not develop a sugar trade put far more of their slaves to work on boats and ships.[23] The fact that slaves worked aboard so many of these ocean-going vessels meant that they had access to a variety of plantations in the mainland and West Indian colonies. Perhaps no other British colonial slave society ranged so far. Bermuda slave mariners could be found aboard sloops on the slave coast of Whydah in Africa, in the harbors of the French West Indies, and anchored along the crowded docks of Boston.[24]

On the continent, the number of Black mariners on ocean-going vessels is less clear from this time period. Colonial governors simply did not respond to the queries of the Lords of Trade in the same manner as Caribbean governors Hamilton and Trelawny. South Carolina's overseas trade in rice provided limited opportunities for Black mariners to work in the colony. After 1736, Charles Town cleared more ships for Britain than any other port in mainland North America. Although the population of Charles Town was only about 6,800 people in 1742, the number of ships that weighed anchor in its deepwater harbor equaled the clearances of the much larger towns of Philadelphia and New York. Ships from the northern ports more often stopped in the harbor during their passage south than on their return. Up until the mid-1730s, according to historian Ian K. Steele, the highest number of entries arrived from West Indian islands, almost 25 percent of all vessels, to trade sugar for rice.[25] Charles Town was the closest sail to the Caribbean islands and a key source of provisions for the slave-heavy populations of the West Indies. Because the port dominated trade in South Carolina, providing a deepwater harbor between the broad Ashely and Cooper Rivers, the town was a critical point of communication for the British mainland southeast.[26] The increasing importance of the port for exchange of news was made evident by the establishment of the first newspaper, the *South-Carolina Gazette*, in 1733 and the inclusion of the colony in the mainland postal route by 1738.[27]

Despite the extensive shipping of Charles Town, the merchants of the province maintained few deepwater vessels of their own in the first half of the eighteenth century. This meant that vessels in their harbors were predominantly staffed by sailors from other ports.[28] Local Black watermen ferried goods from ships anchored in the harbor into the interior of the province, directly encountering white sailors from Britain or the mixed-race crews of the Caribbean. Black pilots commanded a special amount of respect for their ability to guide arriving ships and enjoyed the autonomy of commanding their vessels as they moved between town and plantation.[29] In 1737, during a period of pronounced and growing slave unrest in the colony, a white grand jury bemoaned "Negroes going in Boats and Canoes up the Country trading in a clandestine manner."[30]

South Carolina merchants appeared to fear the mobility that sailing aboard deepwater vessels might provide their slaves.[31] Unlike New England slave owners, who sometimes hired out slaves to ships, rice merchant Robert Pringle worried over the lack of sailors available to carry his shipment of rice to London without suggesting slave watermen instead. The *Richard* had been detained, he explained to a correspondent in London in 1741, "purely for want of sailors." Pringle maintained his own slave watermen in port, however. To assist Captain John Evans of Boston, he sent "Four Stout Negro Men to assist" the New Englander's stranded ship and guide it to Charles Town. Pringle's slaves were "used to be upon the Water," he said, "& understand to Work on Shipboard."[32] The rice merchant asked that the Boston captain provide the men food and drink, "as I have agreed with them."[33] By the 1770s, Charles Town merchants owned far more merchant vessels, but they appear to have maintained their reticence concerning allowing slaves to sail on the wider seas.[34]

Like Charles Town, the tobacco merchants of the Chesapeake maintained few deepwater vessels of their own. In response to a questionnaire from the Lords of Trade and Plantations in 1730, Governor William Gooch explained that the entire fleet "consists of one Ship, Six Brigantines, and Sixteen Sloops, which are all that usually go to Sea."[35]

As Gooch sought to explain to English officials, plantation settlement in both Virginia and Maryland was organized around the river systems springing from the broad Chesapeake Bay. After his journey through North Carolina and Virginia in the 1730s, John Brickell explained that "[Rivers] make very necessary Vessels for carriage of their Commodities by Water, which are called in these parts Periaugers or Canoes." Along these waterways, "Vessels likewise they carry Goods, Horses, and other Cattle from one Plantation to another over large and spacious Rivers."[36] As in South Carolina, planters depended on periaugers (flat-bottomed sailing vessels) and canoes to transfer their goods along creeks and narrower rivers, but the Chesapeake differed in that trade was not so concentrated in a single port as it was in Charles Town to the south. Large plantations maintained their own small docks to deposit their hogsheads of tobacco aboard sloops waiting in the broad James, York, and Rappahannock Rivers. The largest and most important port town of Norfolk, located at the mouth of the Chesapeake Bay and with the large harbor of Hampton Roads, was still quite small. "Norfolk has most ayr of a town of any in Virginia," wrote William Byrd in 1726. "There were then near 20 Brigantines and Sloops riding at the Wharves, and ofterntimes they have more." Byrd explained that Norfolk "Trade is Chiefly to the West-Indies."[37]

Virginia's maritime slaves were largely confined to the Chesapeake, but the extent of riverine travel increased significantly with the passage of the Tobacco Inspection Act in May 1730.[38] In the late fall and early winter, Black waterman sailed to the inspection sites along the rivers and Chesapeake Bay, where they met with other laborers as the tobacco was inspected and sold.[39]

The limits imposed on slave watermen in the Chesapeake found no parallel in the large port towns of the northern colonies. The mid-Atlantic colonies of Pennsylvania and New York and the New England ports of Newport and Boston maintained a considerable number of slave sailors who, like the slaves of Bermuda and the West Indies, had a presence aboard colonial owned deep-sea vessels. Historian Charles R. Foy, who has done considerable research on Black sailors in the northern ports in the eighteenth century, found that slave mariners were the most common occupation of fugitive slaves in the newspaper advertisements of Pennsylvania, Rhode Island, and New York between the years 1720 and 1782.[40] White mariners who owned slaves were likely to take their slaves with them to sea. In Suffolk County, Massachusetts, for example, 18 percent of male slaves were owned by sailors and most would have been involved in some form of ship work.[41] Rhode Islanders maintained many Black men aboard their crews of privateers. Slaves often made up more than a third of a crew on ocean-going vessels from that colony. An article published in the *Boston Gazette* in 1734, for example, described a Rhode Island sloop shipwrecked in Spanish Florida. Aboard the vessel were nine white sailors and five Black. Spanish allied Indians killed four of the white men but made captives of the three Black sailors "to make money of 'em."[42] The famed privateer *Revenge* left Newport, Rhode Island, in 1741 with four Black men aboard its crew of forty-five.[43] It is difficult to determine the exact numbers of Black mariners aboard the vessels based in these colonies, but the trade of the British Empire sent them to the far-off ports of Europe and the Caribbean.

Many of the slave conspiracies of the 1730s bore witness to the almost ubiquitous presence of Black mariners in the avenues of communication that conveyed rumor and news. In most accusations against these sailors, it is not at all clear that they conspired to rebel, only that they bore a proud autonomy which put them into contact with a great many people. The slaves accused were men like Jack, the boatman from Antigua who complained to a white woman on the night of 10 October 1736, "What Do the Baccararas mean by Punishing the Slaves?" When the woman warned he could be taken up, Jack proclaimed he did not care, and when she replied, "Court is king and you are to be one of his officers?" he replied, "Court is King and I am to be one of his generals." Escaping aboard a boat for a day, he was promptly jailed by the magistrate when he returned.[44]

Slave mariners were directly accused of spreading rumors among colonies. Less than a month after the last slaves had died by fire in the New York City slave conspiracy of 1741, the arrival of Manhattan vessels in Bermuda sparked a rumor that the island's Black mariners had somehow been involved in the New York conspiracy. On 1 September 1741, Governor Alured Popple of Bermuda "communicated to the council" a letter purportedly written by Black New Yorkers to conspirators on the small island. The author of the letter, "Negro" Joseph Hilton, warned Black Bermudian Benjamin Hunt that "timese were very dead in New York and that they were hanging six or seven negroes of a day." Hilton warned that "free Joe and Charles Cuff" should not come to the city because they were "named and would be taken up."[45] The letter was not produced for the government. The governor asked the council's advice on how to proceed. Its members responded that the governor should send for a Captain Morgan, whose ship had supposedly brought the letter from the mainland. Standing before the council, the captain "declared he knew not of any such letter coming in his Sloop but that he knew all the Negroes therein named and afterwards withdrew." Perplexed, the governor and council penned a letter to New York, asking Lieutenant Governor George Clarke if the mariners had been implicated in the slave conspiracy. Nine months later, Clarke responded from New York that he knew of no such men and that the interrogations had now ended.[46]

This complicated episode demonstrates a great deal about the difficulties of tracing the relationship of Black mariners to slave conspiracies. The enslaved sailors Joe and Charles Cuff were familiar with Black society in colonial New York City, at least enough to be warned to avoid the port by a friend in the colony, but their involvement in the conspiracy is far from certain. The Black author warned that the two mariners were "threatened" and might be "taken up," but it is much less clear whether that indicated any kind of actual involvement in the supposed slave plot in New York. The mobility of slave mariners emanated throughout the letter, but direct evidence of rebellion is absent. In the fearful heat of the New York conspiracy trials, Joseph Hilton might have simply been warning his friends to stay away from the city.

During the hot month of August 1741, while slaves burned in New York City and rumors of a suspicious letter circulated through Bermuda, an enslaved sailor supposedly set fire to the roof of a Charles Town home with "malicious and evil Intent of burning down the remaining Part" of the port city. Only a few months earlier, the city of Charles Town had been swept by a massive fire and white colonists expressed repeated fears that the fires had been started by slaves.[47] The accused man was a boatswain, or "bos'un," a leader among enslaved sailors, responsible for a crew's handling of sails and rigging. This boatswain supposedly "looked upon every white Man he should meet as his declared Enemy."[48] On the evidence of an old slave woman named Jenny and the man's eventual confession, British authorities burned the boatswain alive. As historian

Peter Wood noted of this incident, the attempted act of arson occurred five days after the *South-Carolina Gazette* printed the news of the New York slave conspiracy, indicating that word of the fires to the north had reached the city. In collusion with his fellow suffering slaves, the convicted boatswain may have been trying to coordinate his attempt to burn down Charles Town with the supposed act of slave arson against Fort George in New York City. At the very least, if he really did declare "every white Man he should meet as his declared Enemy," he should be described as a determined person resentful of his treatment as a slave. As in Bermuda and New York City, Black sailors appear to have been at the center of many accusations of conspiracy that swept through the colonies during the 1730s.[49]

Enslaved sailors entered in and out of regions of Black communication. As part of the crews aboard deep-sea trading vessels, they were a critical component of the growing intercolonial slave community and a population that we can quantifiably measure. And yet in the second quarter of the eighteenth century, responses to rumors were often confined to specific geographic regions. The British Black Atlantic in the 1730s resembled a collection of overlapping diasporas rather than a single, transnational unit. Black sailors moved through these regions and played a considerable role, but they were only a small number of people among the many thousands that traveled in these places.

The British believed the St. John rebellion had inspired the slaves of the Leeward Island. As the insurrection swept through St. John, Captain General William Mathew, governor of the Leeward Islands, reported to London that Black men and women on nearby Nevis had supposedly learned of the Danish rebellion from traveling French slaves.[50] "This day we had News of the Negroes of St. John holding possession thereof still," wrote an anonymous Antiguan to Boston in January 1734. "This has encouraged the Negroes at St. Kitts, and the Week before last they attempted the same in that Island, by setting six Houses on fire, but were prevented of their Design, by a Negro that had a peculiar

Regard for his Master, who disclosed the Plot."[51] The evidence that slaves set fire to houses or plotted to rise in St. Kitts is remarkably limited. The April meeting of the St. Kitts Common Council, after no meetings in January and a series of brief February meetings without mention of conspiracy, noted the receipt of an urgent letter from Governor Mathew in Antigua. The St. Kitts Council passed a series of resolutions for defense, the first in years, but the brief record does not mention a conspiracy.[52]

British authorities believed the archipelago of islands on the eastern edge of the Caribbean was especially vulnerable to slave coordination. Writing in January 1737 during the secret trials and public executions of Antigua slaves, Mathew penned a letter of warning home to England. "The Contagion," he observed of the slave conspiracy, "is spread further among these islands than I apprehend is discovered."[53] He had learned from mariner John Hanson of a supposed rebellion on the island of St. Bartholomew and of a conspiracy on the French side of the island of St. Martin. The captain general had Hanson swear in an affidavit that while in St. Martin, an island divided by the Dutch and French, Hanson and his brother had read a letter from the French government describing the arrest of slave conspirators.[54] According to Hanson, the French governor had learned of an ongoing slave rebellion on the nearby possession of St. Bartholomew to the north in which eleven white colonists had been killed, but the governor could not send soldiers to help because of his own impending slave conspiracy. Hanson claimed that the slaves of Anguilla had intended to rise on 26 December 1736 in solidarity, but the arrest of the slaves in St. Martin had stopped the rebellion.[55] The accuracy of Hanson's account is questionable. I have discovered no such rebellion in recent histories of the French Caribbean and the extent of the hearsay suggests the events as he related should be treated with skepticism.

The white British rumor of slave conspiracy did, however, accurately reflect the interconnected slave communities that existed in the Leeward Islands during the 1730s. In the age of sail, the British described the islands of the Lesser Antilles in relationship to the trade winds, which blew from the northeast. The islands south of Montserrat were designated as Windward, or closer to the origins of the wind, while the island of Montserrat and those to the north and west were called Leeward. By 1736, the Leeward Islands constituted one British colony, composed of Antigua, Barbuda, St. Christopher (St. Kitts), Nevis, Anguilla, and Montserrat, all together stretching more than one hundred miles from the capitol of Antigua north and west.[56] The path of the conspiracy among islands described by Mathew and Hanson matched the direction news would travel by sail. The trades blowing from the northeast allowed vessels sailing northwest to ride perpendicular to the wind.

Contemporary British observers remarked on the close connections among the Leeward Islands. Writing a history of Jamaica in 1740, four years after the Antigua slave conspiracy, Caribbean planter James Knight explained that the Leeward Islands were especially vulnerable to coordinated rebellion due to their close proximity and dense populations of slaves. Black rebels had a high "probability of success" in their insurrections because of the easy travel among and across colonies.[57] Knight was a contemporary observer with a good deal of experience in the islands. Many other observations originated accidentally out of the complaints of English and British planters. For more than forty years before the Antigua slave conspiracy, planters passed laws attempting to prevent slaves from running away to other islands. In 1694, Captain Samuel Horne of St. Kitts complained to the assembly that several of his French-born slaves had escaped, and the rest "hath been Severall plotts contrivances & Combinations" to flee together off the island. The Dutch at St. Eustatius were "intolerable neighbors," complained Governor Walter Douglas in 1712, for the crime of "protecting our Negroes deserters," who had been fleeing Antigua. In 1722, Montserrat passed a law ordering all planters to keep their boats stowed away to prevent slaves from stealing them and traveling among colonies. As far north and west as Vieques, or Crab Island off the coast of Puerto Rico, British slaves gathered to hunt wild cattle and live free from the Leeward Islands.[58]

The archaeological record similarly bears witness to a trade network that existed among the slaves of the Leeward Islands during this period. The archaeology of early Caribbean slavery is not extensive because of the poverty of enslaved people, but excavations have revealed the exchange of slave-crafted pottery among most of the Leeward Islands and extending all the way to Anguilla in the north during the eighteenth century. Archaeologist James Petersen, David Watters, and Desmond Nicholson have explained that clay in several Afro-Caribbean ceramics found in Anguilla and St. Martin appear to have had origins in Montserrat and St. Christopher. Slave-made ceramics dated roughly from the middle of the eighteenth century and discovered in Barbuda were probably made in Antigua. Borrowing from archaeological evidence discovered in Dutch St. Eustatius and Nevis, Petersen and his colleagues have reconstructed an extensive network of locally made Afro-Caribbean exchange during this period.[59] All of this suggests a trade in goods among slaves in the Leeward Islands.

Perhaps the simplest evidence for slave communication among the islands is the Black boatmen listed by Governor Hamilton in 1720. Although the Antiguan described thirty sloops on the island, he also noted twenty-two boats. Seventeen of these boats listed only one white sailor on board and five had no white person in the crew at all.[60] Every boat listed was worked by slaves. Boats were intended for sailing short distances around or between the islands.[61] These vessels gave slaves tremendous autonomy to communicate throughout the Leewards.

The slave rebellion on the island of St. John was the first successful island-wide slave revolt in the western hemisphere, at least for a little over six months. Beginning their rebellion on 23 November 1733, the slave rebels managed to fight off four European expeditions and to control, at various times, the length of the island. For the white Danes and their English and French allies, the insurrection was simply a "negro rebellion." For the slaves who lived on St. John, there were two struggles: the first a war against the planters and the second, a civil war between the Akwamu and the rest of the Black population.

There is considerable evidence that the slave rebels on St. John were led by Akwamu men taken in the great war that destroyed their kingdom. The Danes described the rebels as mostly "Aminas," their designation for slaves from the Gold Coast, but in January 1734, at the height of the rebellion, Danish governor Philip Gardelin sought to correct the record. He said the rebels were "here so called Mina, but actually of the Aquambo nation."[62] Unlike the English, the Danes confined their slave trading to the monopoly of the Danish West India and Guinea Company, which carried slaves from Christiansborg Castle in Accra directly to the Danish West Indian islands of St. Thomas and St. John. In his article "'When I Die I Shall Return to My Own Land,'" historian Ray A. Kea compared the company records from Christiansborg Castle and the Danish West Indies to establish the identity of the "Amina" slaves forcefully carried into St. John. The Danes called the slave leader of the rebellion King Juni, Kea explained, but in some of the sources noted his "bussel" (African) name was Jama. This matched well with a *caboceer* named Nyamma, who served on the court of the king of Akwamu and traded extensively with Fort Christiansborg in the 1720s. During the war of 1730, Nyamma had commanded between one and two thousand men for the Akwamu king as a rearguard before these last forces surrendered in 1732. Kea argued that King Juni was probably taken in these last engagements and carried to St. John in the spring of 1733. Kea found many similar Akwamu names among the long list of St. John rebels.[63]

The St. John rebellion was to the planters a "negro rebellion," but it was also an attempt by one nation of Africans to conquer and rule over others. From the very outset of rebellion, it was clear that the insurrectionists had excluded hundreds of the island slaves from their conspiracy. The first plantation attacked by the conquerors of the fort was defended only by slaves, the widow who owned the property residing on a neighboring island. "These Negroes, who had armed themselves defensively," wrote Pierre J. Pannet, a French planter, "received the rebels with indescribable courage." After cutting down several rebels and losing one of their own, the bondsmen retreated to a planter stronghold on

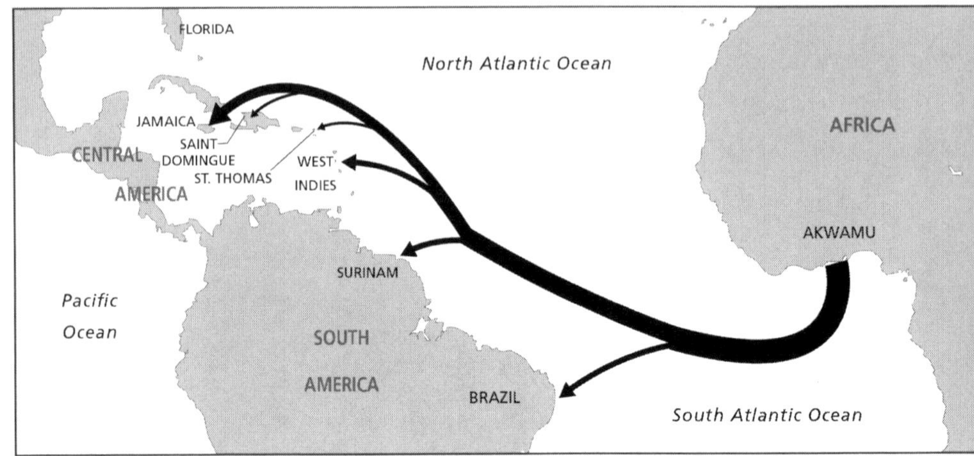

Map 6. The Akwamu diaspora in the Americas, 1730–1733, representing volume and direction of transatlantic slave trade from eastern Gold Coast to South America and the West Indies.

the island. Slave men and women carried news of the rebellion to their plantations and warned white colonists from attempting to run to the garrison, the principal place of defense on the island.[64] The insurrectionists had clearly not warned these resistant slaves of their intention to rebel.

The St. John rebels did not find common cause with the rest of the Black population on the island. Pannet, who lived on St. Thomas in November 1733, wrote that interrogations of captured rebels had revealed their intention to reenslave the people of St. John. "The Negroes from other nations were to be provided to them to do their labors and were to belong to them as slaves," he explained. "This is the reason why they preserved all the sugar factories and other buildings." Pannet claimed that the St. John rebels had tried to coordinate their rebellion with the "Aminas" of St. Thomas and the "Coromantee" on the nearby English island of Tortola.[65] As in Antigua, a shared African "nation" appears to have been more important than the idea of racial unity.

In fact, the idea of race appears to have confused the rebels. In December, after only a couple weeks of freedom, several of the St. John insurrectionists approached a Dutch Captain Vessup as he was attempting to rescue goods from one of the St. John plantations. They offered to trade "ten negroes" for powder and shot. According to Pannet, they also offered to make the white man their leader if he would help them conquer St. Thomas. Vessup accepted the "ten negroes" on "account" and promised to return with powder, then promptly sailed to St. Thomas with the story and his ten new slaves.[66]

As strange as these actions might have seemed to the Dutch Vessup and French Pannet, the offer of trade and alliance was entirely in keeping with the Akwamu experience with Europeans on the coast of Accra. For half a century, the Akwamu had traded rival Black African slaves to white men for gunpowder. For decades, the Akwamu had fought alongside the Dutch or Danes in the small wars that erupted along the Gold Coast. It must have been a rude awakening for King Juni and his people to realize that on the other side of the Atlantic Ocean, being Akwamu meant little to the Danes. In the Americas, the Akwamu were Black men and slaves and the Europeans were white men and free. Race mattered a great deal to the Europeans on the opposite side of the Atlantic.

The last stand of the Akwamu began on 23 April 1734. Two French barks arrived at the island of St. Thomas with more than two hundred Creoles armed and led by white French officers. The enthusiastic Danes responded by supplying seventy-four Black slaves and thirty white Danish volunteers for the expedition. During the month of May, the French scoured the island, working night and day in large parties so that the rebel slaves could not escape. At the end of April, the insurrectionists had sought to surprise and ambush advanced expeditions, and in bloody fighting left behind three men before being beaten off by the Danes. As they sought to flee, it became obvious to the French that the Akwamu were running out of gunpowder. The St. John rebels used bows and arrows in several skirmishes. As waves of armed Black Creoles and European sailors swept across St. John over the ensuing months, the insurrectionists ran out of gunpowder and broke their weapons.[67] According to the British, "Most of the Negroes that were scattered about upon the Island, took all the Canoes and other small Craft they could find, and quitted the Place." British newspapers reported that fleeing slaves had "gone to Cape Fransway," referring to Cape Francaise on the northern coast of Saint-Domingue.[68] The accounts of the end of the rising by Danes and from other British sources relate a different outcome.[69] While the colonists "flea'd" or burned many of the rebels they captured, other free men and women escaped to prominent escarpments on the edge of the island.[70] In the 1690s, an African-born Amina slave had once told a Danish official he had no fear of death, for "when I die, I shall return to my own country."[71] At the end of the rebellion on St. John, several of the last rebels committed suicide in great circles, facing east toward the Gold Coast of Africa.

The leaders of the St. John rebellion oriented themselves toward Africa and sought to reestablish connections familiar to the world they had known. They looked not west to the Americas but east and over the heads of the enslaved people of African ancestry that were not of their nation. Although they might have identified with "Amina" or "Coromantees" who spoke Akan languages, and we might even refer to them as members of an "African Atlantic," they did not hesitate to fight and enslave rival Black people and they do not appear to have sought common cause with other slaves not of their nation. They exhibited what historian Eugene Genovese has called the "restorationist" sentiment of unrest, meaning slaves did not reject the idea of enslavement but instead sought to rebel against or escape from their particular condition.[72] The rebels of St. John were little concerned with a shared Black ancestry. They were determined to rediscover their lost status in Africa.

CHAPTER SEVEN

The Jamaican War

August 1733
Jamaica

FAR TO THE WEST, A second region of Black communication had taken shape around the colony of Jamaica. The island was thirty times the size of Barbados and the Leewards combined and the principal destination for new planters and slave ships in the Caribbean during the first half of the eighteenth century.[1] The large expanse of the island made Black communication distinctive and quite different from the Leeward Islands to the east. Already in the 1730s, Jamaican slaves circulated in two diasporas, the first a decidedly contained, internal, island-wide network of roads, markets, mountain trails, and western rivers that connected plantations. The second diaspora stretched as far as New York and London, where news of events in Jamaica could inspire violence far away.

The First Maroon War in Jamaica was the largest internecine conflict in the British Empire during the 1730s. Over a period of more than ten years, the descendants of escaped slaves fought against the combined forces of the British Empire in a desperate struggle that engulfed the interior of the island. For the planters, the Maroon War was at first simply an insurrection, a continuous struggle against escaped slaves who would not submit to white authority. The British held more than 90 percent of the island's population in slavery, roughly 100,000 people. The significant victories of the Maroons over white colonial militias led the assemblies to alert their governor to the "greatest apprehension of a general rebellion," warnings repeated in the halls of the Lords of Trade and Plantations in England.[2]

But the First Jamaican Maroon War never actually became a general slave rebellion. Black slaves in Jamaica and the Maroons of the mountains did not express a shared sense of purpose and identity during the 1730s, at least not compared to the British. Marronage, the practice of slaves fleeing bondage to establish their own rule in wild places, created new communities struggling for survival against European empires that sought their ruin. The Maroons of Jamaica did not necessarily view the survival of their new peoples as synonymous with the liberty of slaves throughout the island. The continued success of the Maroons was widely reported across the British Atlantic world and was known to slaves as far north as New York and London. The First Jamaican Maroon War became news of a more general revolt across the Atlantic world of the 1730s.

White colonists on the island shared an obvious and immediate interest in suppressing both the Maroons and all plantation slaves. The Maroons could inspire slaves to rebel and rebellion could mean the end of the colonists' lives and livelihoods. White Jamaicans also shared an identity as Britons protected under the auspices of their king. As Britons, they spoke the same English language, prayed at their Anglican church, and accepted the legitimacy of the officials sent to rule. Coupled with the shared determination to control the slave population and the military might of their empire, it was a significant and intimidating advantage.

The Black societies of Jamaica enjoyed no such advantages. The slave population and Maroon villages were not united in common cause. Had even one-tenth of the 100,000 slaves on the island taken up arms, the rebels would have outnumbered the entire white population of 8,000 people. But like Black communities throughout the British Empire in the 1730s, they were a people forced together from hundreds of African kingdoms or born into slavery in a number of American colonies.[3]

These differences among Black people in Jamaica became conflicts that exploded during the First Jamaican Maroon War.

This was true from the very beginning of maroonage on the island. During the conquest of Jamaica by the English in the 1650s, the escaped slave Lubola and his people chose an alliance with the invaders and waged war against rival Spanish Maroon villages.[4] The Maroons shot Lubola in battle, but they had together set a precedent of internecine conflict. There is little sign that these tensions had abated in the early eighteenth century. By the 1720s, the Maroons had developed distinct villages in the interior of the island that exhibited strong ties to Gold Coast origins. To the Windward, or eastern, side of the island, the Maroons lived in several large but separate towns with Nanny Town said to be the most powerful. Hidden in the Blue Mountains, Nanny Town attracted the attention of British colonial authorities throughout the war. The villages' spiritual leader, Nanny, had taken the name of the mythological Akan trickster spider Ananse for her own and sought to protect her people with magic. To the west, or leeward, side of the island, the famed Maroon Cudjoe (Kwadwo, meaning Monday-born) led a second and larger community. The Leeward Maroons occupied the remote Cockpit country, a craggy and labyrinthine region in the northwestern interior. Cudjoe exercised powerful authority over his people and organized his town and surrounding villages around lieutenants with Akan day names like his own.[5]

Although the Maroons sought to use Gold Coast traditions to unite their communities, they did not recreate Africa in America. They were forced to build a very different life in the colony. Maroons suffered under vagaries specific to their conditions on the island. Their fear of reenslavement forced them to live in the most difficult and remote regions. They planted and hunted and yet lived at a level of subsistence and isolation that would have been foreign to the crowded commercial centers of the Gold Coast.[6] Perhaps most importantly, the Maroon villages suffered from a lack of women that would have been quite rare on the coasts of Africa. This fact encouraged the Maroons to raid plantations to liberate female slaves. It was just such a raid that began the First Jamaican Maroon War.

In 1729, the Windward Maroons raided a plantation on the northeastern side of the island. They shot and wounded the plantation's white overseer and then withdrew into the forests, escaping with six enslaved women. This was not a new challenge to British authority. The fertile lowlands of the northeast had for many years been vulnerable to small raids from Maroons. In response to the raid, a company of thirty-eight white men and eight Black slaves—assigned to carry baggage—launched a pursuit of the raiders. The pursuers quickly became the pursued. The Windward Maroons ambushed the company in the Blue Mountains and sent the white militia and baggage slaves fleeing down from the mountain. In their wake, the militia left behind twelve men lost or dead.[7]

When newly appointed governor Robert Hunter learned of the defeat of the company, he ordered the creation of a "Grand Party," an expedition of ninety-five militia men and twenty-five Black baggage handlers with the express assignment to destroy the Maroon villages. The king had ordered Hunter to place the colony in a state of defense against Spanish invasion and he was determined to secure the island. "The Assembly," wrote Hunter to the Lords of Trade and Plantations, "must be induced to provide better for their Security both from within and without."[8] There was silence for weeks, and then the soldiers began appearing again in the town of Kingston. They spoke of ambushes, terrified and confused officers, and men so panicked they had drowned in the flooded rivers. "One fourth part of them are destroyed," wrote Governor Hunter to his masters in England. In the halls of the king, the Board of Trade endorsed sending two British regiments to save the island from the "rebellious and runaway negroes."[9]

Over the next nine years, the Maroons inflicted heavy losses on the white planters as they warred across the interior of Jamaica. Hunter and the assembly sought to create ever larger expeditions, each with orders to destroy the "Negro towns" of the Windward Maroons. Hunter attempted to raise funds to construct a series of barracks, or forts, along the interior of the north and to garrison these barracks with white and Black soldiers. In 1731, an early expedition captured Nanny Town for three days, but the Maroons simply fled their village once the fight had turned against them. The company of militia burned the town and then retreated. Maroons responded to the destruction of their villages and their crops by raiding plantations throughout the north. The violence escalated. Raids ended with white overseers or Black slaves shot to death. The Maroons lit plantation homes on fire and slaughtered livestock.[10] By 1733, the British planters had begun to lose control of the war. The Windward Maroons broke into smaller raiding parties that were difficult to find. Desperate for provisions, they raided plantations at will. Small companies sent out against them often found no one to fight. At other times, the Maroons ambushed their enemies so ferociously that soldiers and baggage slaves fled in a panic, leaving weeks' worth of powder and shot behind.

In this declining condition, the governor and assembly sought to form yet another "Grand Party" to attack the Windward Maroons. Taking advantage of the arrival of the Royal Navy, the assembly equipped one hundred soldiers and fifty sailors to attack the villages of the Blue Mountains. It also created a company of free Blacks and armed more than two hundred slaves to join in the expedition. On a late August afternoon in 1733, the Maroons ambushed the Grand Party as it advanced toward Nanny Town. The fighting was by all accounts fierce, with eight of the white officers dying almost immediately and at least one of the Maroon leaders falling in battle. Over time, the Maroons proved to be far better fighters. The soldiers and sailors began to desert and then fled en masse. A Captain Swanton, shot through the chest, gave orders that the baggage slaves flee with their supplies as he and only eleven men—out of four hundred—prepared to fight to the last. By close of night, a heavy rain fell on the dead and dying and the Maroons withdrew, leaving the wounded Swanton and his men in the dark.[11]

When news arrived of the defeat of the Grand Party, a kind of panic swept through Kingston and Spanish Town. Government officials began packing up records in the capital and old women ran "flying to the protection of the squadron for safety."[12] The enslaved, 90 percent of the population, must have learned of the victory of the "negroes in rebellion." The assembly issued an official statement to Governor Hunter warning of the "greatest apprehension of a general rebellion."[13] Planters filled their letters with despair. "God only knows what will be the Event of this Miscarriage," wrote one to England, but he was sure the colony would soon be lost. "Its Gods Mercy they are not joined by our own Slaves," wrote an assembly member of the Maroons. "If that should happen this country must be cut off."[14]

Despite these significant victories, no unity emerged within the Black population of the island. The Windward and Leeward Maroons fought their battles separately, demonstrating little coordination. Cudjoe, the undisputed leader of the Leeward Maroons in the Cockpit country, sought to incorporate or destroy any rival settlements that emerged near his village. According to one account at the end of the war, Cudjoe had attempted to adopt a separate band of Madagascar slaves into his community around the year 1720. But he had struggled to rule them and apparently killed several of their number.[15] As the Maroon War progressed into the 1730s, Cudjoe harassed and intimidated rival settlements. In 1735, a captured slave reported that a small Maroon village under the leadership of a "Captain Goome" was willing to surrender to planters in exchange for protection from Cudjoe, who "troubled him very much." Captain Goome "could not sitt down in one place but was forced to goe Every day to a new one."[16] The Windward Maroons of Nanny Town also discovered that Cudjoe was not willing to join in common cause against the planters. As Nanny Town became too dangerous for the Windward Maroons, several hundred sought to cross the mountains and join Cudjoe for protection in 1735. According to an "anonymous account" written after the treaty, Cudjoe refused to shelter the people from the eastern half of the island, blaming them for the war with the white planters and insisting that he would not have independent villages living in the Cockpit country.[17]

These tensions among Maroons also suggest the limits of shared membership in the Coromantee nation. Slaves from the Gold Coast dominated the slave populations of Jamaica in the early eighteenth century, and this should have created an important political and cultural unity among both Maroons and plantation slaves. Between 1700 and 1750, slave traders to Jamaica carried more than twice as many slaves from the Gold Coast as from any other region, making up roughly 32 percent of all Africans living in Jamaica. Because of the incredible mortality among the Jamaican slave population, it is possible that tens of thousands of Gold Coast–born slaves lived in Jamaica during the Maroon War. Not surprisingly, there is some evidence of Coromantee runaways joining Maroons over the course of war. During the victorious era of the Maroons in 1734, forty "Coromantines" rebelled in the parish of St. Thomas and fled into the interior. Historians Orlando Patterson and Mavis Campbell use some of these instances to stress African national unity during the First Maroon War, but these moments are important exactly because they were exceptions to the rule.[18] The vast majority of Coromantee slaves, tens of thousands, did not join the Maroon villages and did not rise in rebellion. The lack of unity among the members of the Coromantee nation may in part be explained by the clear tensions between Maroons and plantation slaves. The British descriptions of raids often included accounts of slaves killed in the violence. In 1732, the governor reported to the assembly an attack on the Barclay plantation in St. Elizabeth in which the Maroons killed six slaves and took eight slaves with them, including one small child who they bashed on a rock and left for dead. In a similar attack in St. Elizabeth Parish that same year, Maroons left two slaves dead and took eight others.[19] In 1734, a planter and his two white overseers fled a plantation under attack by Maroons in the northeastern corner of the island. In the process, the planter abandoned his wife. With two plantation slaves, she secured herself in a building and fought off repeated attacks by the Windward group.[20] In this case as in many others, the plantations slaves clearly chose to fight against the Maroons.

In most situations, though, plantations slaves appear to have sought a middle course between planters and Maroons. British officials believed the slave populations were biding their time to see if the Maroons would emerge victorious. As the assembly explained in its address to the governor, the slaves "want but a favourable opportunity to withdraw from their servitude."[21] After the defeat of several of the Grand Parties in 1733 and 1734, the planters in the northeast announced they could no longer tolerate the "Insolent behaviour of our own slaves."[22] On the plantations, slaves refused to do their work, "nor dare their master punish them for the least Disgust will probably cause them to make their Escape."[23] Although most slaves did not run away to the Maroons, slaves did sometimes sell the "rebellious negroes" gunpowder or goods in the slave markets.[24] Perhaps the best example of the ambivalent attitude of the slaves toward the Maroons was expressed in the actions of a slave named Sam, as recounted by the slave Sarra in an examination by white authorities. According to Sarra, Sam had lived on a Colonel Nedham's plantation from which the Windward Maroon Cudjoe had fled. Sarra claimed that Sam hosted Cudjoe on Nedham's plantation overnight, and when Cudjoe asked Sam why he did not join the Maroons, Sam answered, "Master uses us goodee yet, but when he uses us ugly we'll come."[25] As Mavis Campbell noted, the slave Sam had made a conscious choice to live life on the plantation rather than live among the Windward Maroons.[26]

Despite the middle ground chosen by many enslaved people on the plantations, there were those among their number who were determined enemies of the Maroons. By 1732, the planters were relying on companies of fighting slaves they called Black Shots. The leaders of these slave companies were mostly Creoles, Black men born into slavery in Jamaica with the ability to track and fight in the mountainous forests of the island. In 1732, two of the earliest successful expeditions sent against the Maroon villages included a majority of armed slaves. The campaign resulted in three villages taken. The heroics of the Black Shot officer Sambo, who held his ground when the white officers ran away, led the Jamaican assembly to reward the Creole with the command of four Black Shot companies who were sent out again by the governor.[27] "You'll think it strange but it is true," wrote Hunter to the Board of Trade in England, "my Chief Dependence in Case of an Attempt was upon the trusty Slaves for whom I had prepared Arms."[28] The Black Shots proved murderous against the Maroons. In 1733, the slave Cuffee shot to death Nanny in an attack on her village. In the same year, a Creole named Scipio killed the dynamic Windward Maroon leader Kishee.[29]

The motivations of the Black Shot soldiers are not obvious in the historical record. Part of the limited evidence suggests that many Creole Black Shots did not speak African languages and did not share a culture with the decidedly Gold Coast–oriented Maroons they faced in battle. A white officer named Ayscough complained to the assembly in 1733 that the leader of the Black Shots could not speak the Coromantee language of the Maroons.[30] There were also financial rewards for fighting that may have motivated creoles who hoped to profit from the war. The governor and assembly offered money to slaves who served well and promised them the plunder taken from Maroon villages. Slaves who brought in the ears of dead Maroons were offered cash prizes. Most important, however, was the promise of freedom. As a reward for Sambo's service in 1733, for example, the assembly passed an act that freed his wife and children.[31] These acts were rare, but the possibility of freedom must have served as a powerful impetus for enslaved soldiers.

These many tensions between the Black peoples of Jamaica were enshrined into law by the Maroon Treaty of 1739. Governor Edward Trelawny landed on the island with the intention of forming a treaty with the Maroons. Without the permission of the Jamaican assembly, he instructed a militia colonel named Guthrie, already involved in previous attempts to contact Maroon villages, to march on Cudjoe and negotiate a peace. The treaty Guthrie and Cudjoe signed promised that the British would accept the "perfect state of Freedom and Liberty" of the Leeward Maroons in exchange for the Maroons' agreeing to accept the authority of King George II. Most significant to the planters, the Windward Maroons agreed to "take, kill, suppress, or destroy all Rebels wheresoever that be throughout this island; and to submit to the orders of the Commander and Chief on that Occasion."[32] In effect, Cudjoe and his men agreed to fight against all slave rebels and other Maroons.

The treaties allowed the planters to once again take control of the island. Governor Trelawny sent new expeditions to the eastern Blue Mountains with instruction to burn villages and sue for peace, but the militia enjoyed the distinct advantage of fifty Maroon fighting men from Cudjoe's town serving as rangers and guides. Within three months of the Leeward treaty, the villages of the Windward Maroons had also negotiated peace with the British government.[33] Trelawny insisted that the end of the war would open Jamaica to a new wave of planting. Indeed, looking back forty years later, Edward Long wrote that he dated "the flourishing state" of Jamaica "from the ratification of the treaty; ever since which, the island has been increasing in plantations and opulence."[34]

Among the slaves, there was great despair. The assembly had insisted that slaves were biding their time to wait to see who might win between the Maroons and planters. The treaties made it clear that the only real losers would be the slaves. The treaty made the Maroons the allies of the Britons and the official enemy of any slave who sought to escape their condition of slavery. In March 1740, slaves met in large crowds near the capital of Spanish Town and would not disperse. According to Long, the crowds met at night for days and elected captains to lead them. Fearing rebellion, Governor Trelawny ordered the cavalry out against the crowds. The soldiers arrested slave leaders, executed some, and banished others.[35]

The Maroons began working closely with white militias to control the slave population. Cudjoe continued to enforce his will as brutally as the planters. Looking for bounties, Cudjoe's Maroons killed so many runaway slaves that the assembly passed new laws attempting to pay more for slaves taken alive.[36] In May 1742, Cudjoe appeared before Trelawny with four captives, claiming he had discovered a conspiracy among his number to rise in rebellion. When Trelawny sought to appear magnanimous by pardoning the Maroons and giving them back to Cudjoe, Cudjoe publicly killed two of the men and sent the others back to the governor with instructions that they be sold off the island.[37]

The largest accusation of conspiracy emerged from a male slave named Hector in late January 1745. He approached his white mistress warning that "diverse drivers on four or five plantations" were planning a slave rebellion in which she would be killed. The location of the conspiracy was probably in St. John Parish, part of modern-day St. Catherine Parish in southeastern Jamaica, near the old capital of Spanish Town.[38] According to a newspaper account in the *Boston Evening Post*, the white woman sent a message to her husband in town and when she received no reply, contacted her neighbor Simon Clarke, a member of the provincial council. Clarke rode to Spanish Town and rushed in on the governor, who immediately and secretly called out his fighting men. The next day, the company of soldiers ambushed the conspirators in a field described by the informant as the rendezvous for the rebellion. According to Benjamin Franklin's *Pennsylvania Gazette*, the militia captured "12 or 14" slaves "and continu'd to take more of them by Degrees." The wrath of the planters was terrible. Some of the conspirators were "hang'd, some burnt, some hung in Chains, and some sent off the island."[39]

The violence of the Jamaican Maroon War and the despair that appears to have swept through the slave communities reached a terrible pitch in August 1745. In an act that evinced great desperation, a group of twenty African-born "Coromantee" and "Popo" slaves, most of whom were publicly owned by the "King's Navy Yard," broke off from a palisades construction project on the eastern side of the island and began marching west, attacking plantations as they went. According to the author of a letter from St. David's Parish, the rebels set out with a "Design to kill all they met with." They were led by a man called "King's Cudjoe," his name indicative both of a slave owned by the Crown and, because of his day name, probably of membership in the Coromantee nation. The rebels killed a "Negro man" at the palisades and then, according to the writer, a "free Fisherman Negro and four old Negro Women about a Mile from Bull-Bay." The reasons for these killings were not explained by the author. The rebels continued westward, attacking the Innis plantation and killing the white overseer and "two or three slaves." At the next plantation of a Mr. White, the insurrectionists killed three more slaves and burned the plantation to the ground. By that time, planters had spread the alarm throughout the region. The author of the account described a second party of twenty more slaves who had "agreed to join" King Cudjoe's rebels at the palisades but were prevented by a "breach" created by a storm.[40]

It was the Windward Maroons, the people once described by the planters as the "Rebellious Negroes," who destroyed the rebellion of the desperate Coromantee and Papaw slaves. "A few days later," explained the author of the letter, King Cudjoe's party was "met by our friend Negroes (who had been formerly Rebels) under the command of one Colonel Bennet, of Spanish Town, who soon defeated them, killing four men and one woman and taking three women prisoner, the remaining Thirteen making their escape into St Thomas Paris on the back of Negro River." In open battle, the people the Jamaicans now called "the friend Negroes" opened fire on the African peoples rebelling against their condition as slaves.[41] Over the next weeks, the planters relied on the plantations slaves to finish the work of the Windward Maroons. Colonial authorities put a bounty of five pound for each dead rebel and ten pound for each taken alive. "The Other Twelve were soon after brought in or killed by the plantation Negroes," wrote the Jamaican author, "Scarcely a day happening without one or other being brought in dead or alive." The band of twenty slaves accused of seeking to join Cudjoe were also "taken up." The planters banished a few slaves who gave evidence against the others, but most were burned or hanged, their heads displayed along the freshly cut roads constructed by slaves on the new plantations.[42]

The violence of the insurrectionists suggests the differences and frustrations that pervaded the slave communities in Jamaica by 1745. "Tis believed the cruelty with which Cudjoe's party proceeded," wrote a Jamaican author, "was the chief means for its being so soon quell'd, as it exasperated all the plantation negroes against them."[43] If the African-born Coromantee and Papaw slaves killed as indiscriminately as the planters described, then this violence might indeed have incurred the wrath of other slaves. But the insurrection in St. David's Parish presented the chasm that had developed between the Black communities of Jamaica. Coromantee slaves attacked and killed slaves on nearby plantations. The Windward Maroons, once the intrepid enemies of Spanish Town, now fought alongside white officers serving under the British Crown. In the decades to come, there would be new conspiracies and insurrections in Jamaica, but there would be no alliance between the Black communities of the island.

During the 1740s, the slave communities of Jamaica were connected mostly by coastal travel and a limited network of roads. Because the colony was so large—English settlement only began in earnest at the end of the seventeenth century—much of Jamaica had not been cleared for planting and was still forested in the second quarter of the eighteenth century. The research of archaeologist Mark Hauser into the roads demonstrates that as late as 1744, the road system had hardly changed on the island from 1678. A southern road stretched from Kingston in the mid-southeast to Negril on the west coast, and another road from Kingston ran directly north along the edge of the Blue Mountains to St. Anne's Bay in the center of the northern coast. Outside of narrow forest trails, no other roads were available for travel.[44] Addressing the assembly in 1745 and looking back at the First Jamaican Maroon War, Governor Trelawny credited the survival of Jamaica on the inability of slaves to communicate across the island. "The Negroes can have no communication together," he explained, "or if they had it, would be almost impossible . . . to execute their designs." As Edward Long noted years later, the defeat of the Maroons actually allowed planters to intensify development.[45] As early as 1757, the road system throughout the island was much more extensive, creating at least twelve new avenues for travel across Jamaica.[46] Was it a coincidence that the largest Caribbean insurrection before the Haitian Rebellion, "Tackey's Revolt," swept through Jamaica in 1760?

As in many colonies, the great meetings of slaves took place in the markets of Jamaica. Sunday market day, the traditional Protestant

Sabbath day in which slaves were excused from their labors, played an important role in the formation of Black society in the Caribbean. On these days, slaves could congregate free from the supervision of their masters. Hauser's archaeological study of the Black markets of Jamaica in the eighteenth century has established the considerable amount of trade that took place among slaves from different parts of the island. His depiction of the growth of slave markets throughout the island, however, skips from 1707, when there were only four markets around Kingston, to the 1770s, when fully thirteen separate markets stretched along the coasts of the colony. Between 1729 and 1746, there were four markets located around Kingston with perhaps one or two on the west coast and another two in the center north.[47]

Planters recognized these Sunday festivals as a dangerous threat to their plantation slave system. In Jamaica, rebellious Maroons moved through the Black markets, searching for supplies in their ongoing war with the white plantation elite. As Long explained, "It is well known that many of them resorted every Sunday amongst the vast crowds that assemble there from all parts of the country."[48] He feared that besides the trade in fowl and fruits, Maroons secured the critical gunpowder necessary for slave resistance. As early as 1730, the Jamaican assembly passed laws for "better regulating slaves, and rendering free negroes and mulattoes more useful, and preventing hawking and peddling."[49] Yet Jamaican authorities also worried that slaves were securing more from the markets than simply food and gunpowder. In the same year, the assembly passed another law, this one "for preventing communication or trade with rebellious negroes." Jamaican planters feared that market days were opportunities for plotting unrest.[50]

The markets of Kingston and Spanish Town were the sites of the first full rebellious meetings of slaves in 1740. The Maroon treaties of 1739 established the Maroons as legitimate client peoples of the British Empire on the condition that the formerly "rebellious negroes" policed the enslaved Black population. The assembly had insisted that slaves were biding their time to wait to see who might win between the Maroons and planters.[51] In March 1740, slaves met in large crowds in the markets of the capital Spanish Town and refused to disperse when ordered by the constables. According to Long, the crowds met at night for days and elected captains to lead. Fearing rebellion, Governor Trelawny ordered the cavalry out against the meetings. The soldiers arrested slave leaders, and white officials ordered the agitators executed and banished others.[52]

Whatever the limits of communication within the interior of the island in the 1730s, the Jamaican diaspora was surprisingly extensive during the same period. In 1704, British North American shipping at Jamaica consisted of only thirty-one ships a year at harbor in Port Royal. By 1729, the same port was averaging ninety-five mainland ships at anchor. Ships entered from November to May and departed by the end of the sugar harvest in early August.[53] As Governor Trelawny demonstrated to the Lords of Trade and Plantation in 1743, his census of North American ships at anchor found that 23 percent of the sailors aboard ships were enslaved.[54] There were also a great deal of boatmen on the island, and they did demonstrate the capacity to sometimes travel to other islands. During the Maroon War, Major John Richardson complained bitterly "that it became of late so frequent for Negroes to go off for the island of Cuba, that for some weeks last, several had stole off in canoes."[55] The northern Jamaican parishes of St. Ann and St. Mary maintained an illicit trade in cattle with Spanish coastal traders, making escape all the easier. But for the most part, Jamaica's Black diaspora stretched much farther, all the way to London and New York.

In 1741, British colonists accused several Jamaican slaves of conspiring to burn the city of New York. In May of that year, an enslaved Jamaican named Jack, a cooper, sat before the Supreme Court justices of the colony attempting to save his own life. He was a popular man among the slaves of the port of New York and a compatriot to many Black Jamaicans sold aboard ship and carried into the town. Jack had presided over the center of slave communication: the freshwater well on his master's property that supplied the best drinking water in southern Manhattan. Slaves from throughout the island congregated at the well daily, visiting and sharing news.[56]

That afternoon, 8 June 1741, the Supreme Court condemned Jack to be burned alive for conspiring to set the city of New York on fire. His accusers, two slave men named Quack and Cuffee, had included Jack in their dying confessions at the stake, and as dead men had left the Jamaican with few options for refuting their claims. After the court ruled Jack be burned the next day, he returned to his jail cell and announced to the guards that if the judges would spare his life, "he would discover all that he knew of the conspiracy."[57] In his testimony, he claimed to know a great deal.

For the justices, the first problem with Jack's confession was that they could not understand it. His "dialect was so perfectly Negro and unintelligible," wrote Justice Daniel Horsmanden, "'twas thought, that 'twould be impossible to make any Thing of him without the Help of an Interpreter."[58] In an early example of the development of the distinctive Jamaican dialect, the justices had to engage an interpreter to make sense of his testimony. Historian Jill Lepore suggests that Jack may have been born in Africa before his transfer to Jamaica and then to New York. Perhaps his Akan accent made him hard to understand.[59] It is possible, but Jack demonstrated little of the hesitance of a native-African speaker uncomfortable with a foreign tongue. Jack was a talker.

He hosted slaves from throughout the city on a daily basis, and when he confessed to the justices, he spent three days telling them stories and filling journals. He entertained the white Supreme Court justices with his use of popular Jamaican sayings. "His master live in Tall House Broadway," Jack said of his Jamaican friend. "Ben ride de fat horse."[60] Finding the aphorisms entertaining, Horsmanden made the rare footnote in his published journal of the proceedings and quoted Jack's dialect directly.[61]

But there was nothing amusing about the situation for Jack. His testimony was life or death. To save himself from burning the next day, he had to confess to the accusations slaves made and accuse others in a believable way. "He was advised not to flatter himself with the Hopes of Life," wrote Justice Horsmanden, "without he would do the utmost in his Power to deserve it." Jack replied by looking "very serious," noted the justice approvingly.[62] But we know better. The coercive situation made his confession completely unreliable, and though the justices accepted it as evidence, we should not. And yet at the same time, his confession did reveal a hidden transcript, a network of contact and communication among slaves.

In nearly every confession that emerged concerning Jack, he was described as a conveyer of news. "Countryman, I have some good news," Jack remembered Ben saying to him at his master's well. "What news?" Jack remembered asking the slave Cato on the night of one of the fires.[63] As Lepore explains, Jack's role among the slaves of New York was as a collector of news.[64] We might imagine him as an oral newspaper man, not unlike printer John Peter Zenger, who collected rumors from seamen for his *New York Weekly Journal*, just on the opposite side of town. This point was highlighted by the justices at the time. In his introduction of Jack in his *Journal of the Proceedings*, Horsmanden described him as a captain and noted, "There was a Well in his Yard whereto many Negroes resorted every Day; Morning and Afternoon, to fetch Tea Water . . . and Hughson [the supposed leader of the plot], no doubt, thought he had carried a great Point when he had seduced Capt. Jack."[65]

"Captain Jack" bore a special place in the slave community because he presided over the center of commerce and communication at a local well. As many historians of New York City have noted, the water of colonial Manhattan was notoriously foul.[66] Slaves from throughout the city could beg off from their labors to fetch tea water for their masters, and in the process visit with Black people from throughout the city. For the wealthy of New York, their slaves had to walk from the merchant houses of the East Ward across the port town to Gerardus Comfort's house near the Hudson River. Comfort labored as a cooper, or barrel maker, constructing and repairing casks for ships anchored in the river. He enslaved two men, Jack and Cook, and a woman named Jenny. Sometime after 1733, he dug a deep well beneath his property that was well-known for its pure water. Many of the conspirators accused by the justices—Cuffee and Adam, Caesar and another slave named Jack—were all described as regulars at the well.[67] London, an enslaved mariner, confessed that his master had sent him ashore to fetch water at the well, as had at least ten other confessed or accused conspirators. Their presence did not make the accusations of conspiracy true, but it did demonstrate the mobility of slaves and the importance of the meeting place. Aware of the importance of Comfort's well as a center for Black communication in New York, a grand jury on 12 June, just two days after Jack's confession, asked the assembly to ban slaves from traveling across the city for water.[68]

In New York, Jack played a pivotal role in the meeting places of slaves. His proximity to the well allowed him to develop close relationships with other Jamaicans and many of the enslaved people of the city. His central place at the center of news also ensnared him in the conspiracy accusations in New York in 1741. In the interrogations, Jack's confession played a pivotal role in the conspiracy. He was the first person to confirm every accusation of the young white servant girl Mary Burton, and he implicated many of his fellow slaves.[69] He had been accused alongside five other people, one of them tellingly named Jamaica.[70] Robin, Cook, Caesar, and Cuffee refused to confess and were all chained to stakes and publicly burned by the British.[71] Jack and Jamaica confessed and were banished into the wider Black Atlantic.

By the 1740s, the British Black Atlantic was alive with stories of unrest. Enslaved Jamaicans found they could not escape episodes of rebellion in the wider empire. In Jamaica in 1744, the enslaved Hector warned his mistress that drivers on neighboring plantations were planning to rise in rebellion. According to a newspaper account of the incident, the slave informant revealed the meeting location of the conspirators, and the Jamaican militia discovered the slaves gathered together in an open field. For his reward, the Jamaican assembly granted Hector his freedom and payment of thirty pounds a year for life.[72] Despite his newfound status, Hector felt himself in "daily danger" from angry Black Jamaicans and so gained transport to England. But he could not escape the wrath of Black men and women who learned of his betrayal, even in the British Isles. In a petition he submitted to the Jamaican assembly less than a year after his departure, Hector complained that Black people in England persecuted him and prevented him from his business. He begged leave of the assembly to return to Jamaica despite his fear of the wrath of the island's slaves.[73] Hector's experience suggests that as early as 1745, Black men and women in England knew a great deal about events in Jamaica and shared a sense of purpose and cause with the enslaved on the island.

As rumors of slave unrest gathered in the British Atlantic, colonial officials became increasingly aware of the dangers of transporting convicted slaves to locations within their empire. This represented both an awareness of a growing Black Atlantic and a shared project among magistrates to control slave populations. As late as the 1720s, officials still believed that slaves exiled from the Caribbean to the mainland provinces—or vice versa—would be far enough removed to no longer pose a threat to their colony. When the Antiguan assembly exiled slaves to "the Spanish Coast or to Maryland and Virginia" in 1729, they specified that conspirators be sent to "a place from whence they cannot carry on a Correspondence with the Negros of this Island."[74] The Chesapeake Bay seemed very far away to Antiguans. By the late 1730s and early 1740s, the laws passed to transport convicted slaves looked like that of the assembly in Philadelphia, which ordered the slave Sampson be sent to a "Colony Not of the Dominion of Great Britain."[75]

Governor Edward Trelawny of Jamaica exemplified the growing British determination to control the transatlantic slave population. He warned the Duke of Newcastle of a "dangerous Spirit of Liberty" within the slave populations of the British Caribbean and negotiated a treaty with the Jamaican Maroons that required their oath to fight against slaves in rebellion. In 1744, when New York justice Daniel Horsmanden published his account of the conspiracy trials in the city, Trelawny ordered a copy and had it delivered to Jamaica. When Hector revealed the conspiracy in St. John's Parish in 1744, Trelawny sent forth his militia and then read through Horsmanden's *Journal of the Proceedings*. It was in that document that he recognized the slave called Hanover, a man accused in New York who had escaped prosecution. Trelawny "caused him to be apprehended" and ordered Hanover be transported back to New

York for trial.[76] As the smoke of burning men rose over the island of Jamaica, the brigantine *Mary Anne* weighed anchor, carrying Hanover northward to face the wrath of the men of the mainland colonies.

In February 1745, Hanover stood on the deck of the brigantine *Mary Anne* anchored in the East River of New York. His was a brutal homecoming, a return to the city he had escaped four years earlier during the conspiracy trials of 1741. Hanover had been arrested outside of Kingston, Jamaica. He was twice condemned, first as a chattel slave to be bought and sold all his life and again as a prisoner accused of conspiring against the British king.[77] Hanover had survived two conspiracy trials in two separate provinces and probably lived through the violence and uncertainty of the First Jamaican Maroon War. Aboard the *Mary Anne,* waiting for the skiff that would carry him to shore, he carried with him the lived experience of the unrest that had swept through the British Atlantic.

CHAPTER EIGHT

Organizing the Islands

12 October 1736
St. John, Antigua

"Then strove the candidates to gain their seats / Most heartily, with drinking bouts, and treats."

—Robert Mumford, *The Candidates* (1775)

COURT LAUNCHED A CAMPAIGN TO organize the slaves of Antigua in 1735 and 1736. He had a twofold strategy: He embraced British political culture to win over enslaved craftsmen of the towns. As he had learned from Thomas Kerby, Court performed the English rituals of "treating," inviting men and women to partake of his table in exchange for a promise of support. He relied on the endorsements of local leaders, a practice required of any candidate in the colonies, and made great use of toasts. To the crowds who gathered at his "merriments," he expected praise and a pledge of service.

Court adopted a second strategy to secure support among the people from the Gold Coast. He looked back to his homeland for lessons. He chose an ennobling ceremony and learned its steps from an old man. Court invited the Gold Coast slaves—many of whom were field slaves on plantations—to support his ascendance as their leader. In an astute political moment, he included the leaders of the enslaved craftsmen in his dance. With the stroke of his sword and a public oath, he united the slaves of Antigua into one people.

It is possible to reconstruct Court's campaign across the island. Enslaved men and women remembered Court in the examinations and interrogations of Robert Arbuthnot and the judges.

Together, these interrogations tell a story of a drunken, wild romp that lasted nearly a year. Court crisscrossed the western half of the island as he bribed and cajoled and endeared himself to enslaved Black men. He brought people together with feasts and drink or led his entourage to the feasts of others. Sometimes he appeared at gatherings uninvited, where he was certain to take control and lead a toast and expect a toast in return. By the middle of the summer of 1736, several months before his dance, there were slaves raising their stone mugs to "King Tackey."

As he campaigned, Court navigated the complex political alliances of Black people in early eighteenth-century British America. The examinations reveal a new political culture: There were the enslaved craftsmen of St. John—Court's peers. Most were island-born English speakers. Out of town, the plantations had hierarchies of their own. Slaves gained authority through their proximity to their white masters and control of others. Drivers, the leaders of the "field slaves," were well-represented at Court's feasts. There were alliances of kin, extended families with children spread across many plantations. And there were neighborhoods, communities that emerged clearly from the witness testimony: "the Windwards," "Dickinson's Bay," and "Pope's Head."

African identities still influenced the political culture as well. In 1736, the majority of slaves in the empire were African-born. This was true in Antigua as it was throughout the Caribbean and southern mainland. Africans had memories of loved ones they had known and lost. They remembered the places where their ancestors rested in the earth. For newer arrivals who spoke little English, the shared languages and customs created an important ethnic community that aided survival in the plantations. Their children and grandchildren had a very different relationship to Africa. The continent was an imagined homeland brought to them through the stories of elders or acted out in customs.

Court campaigned on these memories. He presented himself as both an African noble and British patron. The history of his campaign lies hidden in Arbuthnot's examinations and trials.

By the end of the second day of his investigation, Arbuthnot had "Conceived Strong Suspicions of the Negro's Designs of Rising." He believed the testimony of Mrs. Brown; he was sure she had overheard Johnny speaking of a list of slave officers. Arbuthnot believed the constables; the slaves were meeting together in the dark of night, armed with guns, rehearsing for revolt. Arbuthnot believed the worst of what was said about Court too. Court was the leader, and he had a plan.[1]

But each accused slave denied the existence of a plot to rebel. Johnny denied mentioning a "list of officers," as did the other men. Jack, the mariner, confessed to saying "Court was King and I'll be his general," but he had not meant he was actually an officer in a slave army. He had spoken in "jest," he said, or more accurately anger. Jack had never heard of any slave officers or any plot, he insisted. Arbuthnot ordered Jack to jail but still no confession was forthcoming.

Arbuthnot later recounted that moment to the council. "Arbuthnot putting all the Circumstances together was in great Perplexity of mind to know what to Do or how to proceed to Come to the Bottom of the Negros Designs," the clerk wrote.

He was certain the slaves were plotting a rebellion. He just needed a slave to confess.

Arbuthnot "was Casting about what honest slave he Could Consult on this Occasion." He settled on "Emanuel a Negro of Mr: Gregory's whom he lookt Upon as a faithfull and sensible Slave." Arbuthnot sent for Emanuel "purely to Ask his Opinion about the behaviour and Designs of the Slaves" in the hope that he "might be Able to furnish him with some lights."

Emanuel waited on Arbuthnot at the justice's home. It was common in British colonial America for a slave or poor servant to enter at the back entrance. He was a native Portuguese speaker, sold into English slavery long ago. Arbuthnot knew he was owned by the sickly Mr. Gregory, the cooper.

Arbuthnot asked Emanuel pointed and leading questions. He asked Emanuel if he thought the slaves were growing more insolent: "Yes," Emanuel said. "He never had seen such freedoms as they took, that Droves of them would often pass by their House in the Night Time. That many of them would Ride a Horse back, That they Often Diced in the Church Pasture and had often heard them Say I have lost Seven Shillings and such like Sums at Playe."

This was not the answer Arbuthnot was looking for. He was searching for proof of a plot. Emanuel, a slave, complained slaves had too much freedom. They moved about too easily and rode horses and bet too much money.

Arbuthnot tried again.

Had Emanuel "not within this Fortnight or three Weeks heard a Conk Shell blow at unseasonable hours of the Night and Seen or heard of Assembly's of Slaves about the town in Dead of the Night, & what he thought the meaning of all this to be?"

Emanuel said that "he believed the Conck Shells were to Assemble the Negro's together, and that they met & consulted together in the Pastures and Places about the Town at and after Midnight."

This was not the right answer either. Arbuthnot was asking if the slaves were organizing a rebellion. Emanuel said the slaves blew horns to "consult together."

Arbuthnot persisted. But what was their design?

Emanuel did not know: "He never went Amongst them but kept himself at home and Declined the Company of other Slaves."

Arbuthnot cut to the point. Had Emanuel "heard any thing of their Intentions to Rise?" he asked.

"Not," Emanuel answered.

"Whether he Did not Suspect some such Design?" Arbuthnot asked again.

"Within himself, he knew not what to Think," Emanuel said. "[The slaves] were grown very Imprudent, the White People gave them too much Freedom."

Did he know "anything about Darby's Jack?" Arbuthnot asked.

"Not," Emanuel said. Arbuthnot explained that Jack had publicly proclaimed he was a general. Emanuel did not know him.

Arbuthnot gave it one last try.

"Do you know anything of this Court?" he asked the cooper's slave.

Emanuel remembered Court very well.

He remembered the first time Court called on him. It was on a Saturday night "little of this Side Last Christmas," Emanuel said, the winter of 1735–1736.

Emanuel was "sounding his trumpet" in his master's cooper shop in St. John. "I was there alone," Emanuel said. "It was a Dark Rainy Night." Court rode up on his mare, dismounted and shook off the rain. "Court had on a Great Coat but upon his Entering into the Shop, he unbuttoned his great Coat and threw it Open & their appeared a fine hanger by his Side with a Red handle. Court Drew it Out and flourished it," Emanuel reported.

"Look here you Dog is not this a fine thing?" Court asked.

"He also had a handsome Green Silk cap on his head with a Large Bunch of black Feathers sticking up from it behind," Emanuel remembered.

Court wanted Emanuel to play a trumpet at his gathering at the Langford plantation. He "asked me if I would go to the Widow Langfords, where he said he was to have a Feast and a Merriment." Court said he had more work for Emanuel in the future too, "at the Other Feasts to Sound to their healths."

"I told him my Master was perpetually calling to me in the Night Time being a Sickly Man, & therefore Excuse my Self from going to any of their Feasts without my Masters Leave," Emanuel replied. He would not play at Court's parties.

Court did not like this answer. "Upon my Refusing to wait on Court he seemed very uneasy," Emanuel noted. He was born off island (probably in Brazil) and was older and not closely aligned with any group of slaves.

Court announced he would speak to Emanuel's wife, Sabella, and went looking for her. "I Accompanyed him to my Masters Yard where my Wife was," Emanuel said.

Court asked Sabella "how she did?" and went straight to the point. He wanted Emanuel to go to Widow Langford's to "Sound the Trumpet at their Merriment."

"My Wife told him the Trumpet belongs to the King, and is for the White People, And is not Proper for Negros, so go along about Your Business," he remembered.

"Emanuel shall not go along with you," Sabella said.

"Well Woman," Court said, "they say you are not good, And I find you are not good."

"Ay. Ay. go Along," Sabella replied.

"You may take your Husband and Tie him upon your Back," Court said—as an African woman carries a child.

"And then Court in a great Passion went to his Mare and Rode to Mrs. Langford's Plantation," Emanuel remembered.

Court was not finished with Emanuel.

Arbuthnot scratched out notes.

Court's and Tomboy's campaign lasted at least nine months. The judges reported that it had started in November 1735 at a supper hosted by Treblin, a Creole slave owned by Samuel Morgan in St. John's. In January 1736, Court hosted a feast at the Widow Langford's plantation, which lay north of town on Pope's Head Road (Fort Road today). He had friends at the Langfords' plantation and returned there again and again over the next few months. In May, Court rode seven kilometers south and west to the tip of the Five Islands and the Lydserf plantation for another merriment. In July, he hosted a feast at his master's house in St. John, and in August he rode north again to Fargut's supper on the Lyndsey plantation. In September, Tomboy hosted another feast in town.

Between these merriments, Court traveled far inland, east and south down the old highway (Sir Sydney Walling Highway today), ten kilometers to the Pares Plantation in the Old North Division on the eastern side of the island. Court acted as a merchant there, selling "Butter, Bread, and other things" through an elderly matriarch named Queen.

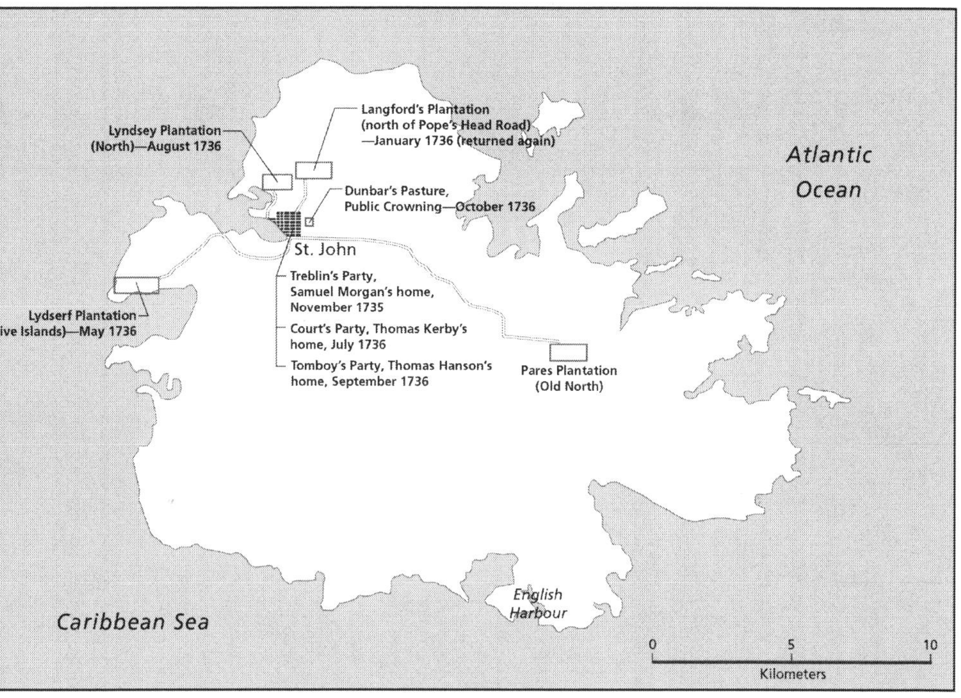

Map 7. Court's campaign across Antigua, 1735–1736

It was there too that he visited with Gold Coast peoples, especially old Quawcoo.[2]

Tomboy rode with Court to most merriments. They worked together, Court leading the crowd and drawing attention to himself while Tomboy sought pledges of support and service. The judges later wrote that the two men had been rivals, and that their relationship had suffered "a long Coldness" in the past.[3] Whatever their relationship had been, they were great partners the year of the campaign.

The two men adhered closely to the practices of British political candidates. Across the colonies, any free British man could run for office in any parish where he was a freeholder. In Antigua, a freeholder was a man, at least twenty-one years old, with ten acres of land or real estate that incurred ten pounds sterling a year in taxes.[4] Those who met the property requirement could vote and hold office. Planters with more land and slaves were especially expected to serve in the assembly. As

Samuel Martin wrote in 1765, a planter "born into a large estate, or has acquired it by industry, he must expect to be a member of the legislature."[5]

The candidate began his campaign by gaining the support of the leading men in his parish. There was little hope of success without public support from the ruling gentry. Powerful planters shared close family connections. They controlled boiling houses and merchant shops and vessels for transporting commerce. They were surrounded by lesser freeholders, men who depended on the support of the great planters to sell their crops and purchase necessaries. A candidate needed the ruling gentry to speak publicly in support of their election and to bring the many men in the gentry's service to support the candidate. As the historian Rhys Isaac wrote of mid-eighteenth-century Virginia, it was "an entire social system based on personal relationships—kinship, neighborhood, favors exchanged, patronage given, and deference returned."[6]

Campaigning in the colonies required candidates to host freeholders at public events and suppers. Gentleman sought to show their generosity by "treating," in the eighteenth-century English vernacular, or providing "merriments and feasts" to their poorer neighbors. As Isaac noted of Virginia, "treating was not simply a way of buying support." It was a political ritual. The candidate publicly accepted an obligation to his voters, represented through food and drink. The leading gentry attended the treats and brought their followers to throw their support behind the candidate. The gentry raised their glasses to the candidates and the lesser freeholders followed suit. "For humbler men," wrote Isaac, "voting was less an opportunity to confer a favor than a chance to show gratitude or to secure the goodwill of a powerful neighbor."[7]

Elections began with formal pledges of support and ended in the cups, with supporters and candidates professing their service to each other. There were no secret ballots in British America.

Court and Tomboy campaigned like British freeholders. There would be no formal election, of course. Both men were slaves. By British custom and law, they had no legal right to a peculium or to property of their own. But they had acquired money through their labor, and they were determined to gain support. They "treated" the leading slaves of the island. Tomboy, long the acknowledged leader of the enslaved craftsmen of the town, brought his supporters to feast and raise their cups to Court.

The two men faced a sea of obstacles on their journey to unite the slaves. At merriment after merriment, both Court and Tomboy took note of the many enslaved men and women who refused to attend. They raised their glasses and shouted, "Damnation to those who failed."[8] They pushed and exhorted their followers for support, with British political customs on full display in early September at Treblin's.

In his testimony before the judges, Quashee remembered that he had not wanted to go to the "merriment" at Treblin's house. But Tomboy had organized the feast and "Deluded me to go" to "tend upon him at a Supper." Tomboy and Quashee were both owned by Thomas Hanson, though Tomboy was the master carpenter and higher in rank. When Quashee said he did not want to go to Treblin's, Tomboy threatened him.[9]

In the evening, the two men set off from Hanson's shop at the corner of Wilkinsons Street and Wapping (the southeast corner of Newgate and North Street today) and made their way across St. John.

Court was at the supper, calling for "helths" and raising his cup. They drank "Madera Wine, Punch, Claret, Ale, & Cyder," Quashee said. There must have been music. Hercules was there, as was the enslaved craftsmen called Venture.

"Court got upon the table Jumping about," Quashee remembered, "saying he would have St. Georges health Drank!" (St. George is the patron saint of England.)

Quashee was made to "tend" or wait on Tomboy throughout the supper. He remembered there were a "Dozn: Cranberry or Gooseberry Tarts, 6 at the head & Six at the foot of the Table—A Cheese—Some Oranges—Grapes—Pine Cashews, I can't tell whether any Sweetmeats or not." There were "Watter Glasses to wash their hands," a formal English custom that must have meant more to an island short on water. It was quite the feast.

"I told Tomboy he had a very fine Supper," Quashee remembered.

"Well it might, when it Cost him So," Tomboy replied in his cups.

Someone called out for liquor. "Things were brought to Drink, the Liquor was poured Out," Quashee said.

"Damnation to those Who Failed," Tomboy shouted, referring to those who had not come.

Everyone agreed to forgive the other Quashee in the room, "Hoskin's Quashee," when he resisted the punch poured into his tumbler. "He said that his Constitution would not bear Punch, but he would—Drink it in water," Quashee recalled. "Then they Drank a health to Dickensons Bay," the community north and east of town.

Court had invited more than the townspeople to his feast. There were Coromantees in the room. Quashee noted the strangers. "Court Drank in Cormantee to the Coramantee's," Quashee said, referring to the Fante language spoken on the Gold Coast. He recognized the tongue, as his mother was Coromantee, and she had given him his day name Kwesi (born on Sunday).

Court finished his toast with the Coromantees and turned to note the empty places in the rooms, the seats of those people he had invited who had not come. Court "said In English it was Damnation to the failers!" just as Tomboy had earlier, "and they Drank Out part of the Bottle of Rum."

"The Coramantees took the rest of the Rum & Bottle & Carried it away," Quashee remembered. "The Coramantees seemed ordinary, Field Negro's."

Many witnesses remembered the subtle tensions between Black communities at these many feasts. Quashee was not alone in noticing the Coromantees and their lowly status as "ordinary, Field Negro's."

These tensions had been on full display the previous month at the Lyndsey plantation. In August, Court and Tomboy imposed their entire entourage on Fargut, who lived as a slave seven kilometers south and west at the tip of the Five Islands. Fargut had asked "the Managers leave for a few Friends only on Sunday" and expected "only a few viz. five or six and was Surprised to see so many." Court and Tomboy "came there without Invitation at Almost Sunset and styed nt above half an Hour,"

Fargut later told the judges, though Jemmy, a slave from St. John owned by Samuel Martin, would claim they stayed much longer. Fargut was forced to press two long tables together and cover them with a cloth.[10]

His meal might have been a formal British dinner with clearly defined English manners and customs on display. Jemmy told the judges that he arrived at Fargut's merriment with his wife, Maria. "I went into the Old House with Maria and others, & we Drank Cool Drink, the Cloth was laid in his New House & at Length I was called in," he remembered. Jemmy felt underdressed and unwashed. "I was very dirty," he told the judges. Fargut put on an unbelievable feast: "A boiled course was served at first and then a Roast Course, there were Two Dishes almost of Every Sort—There were Fowles, To Sorts of Pies. Turkeys boild and Roast porke Boild and Roast Kid & the sorts of Puddings Boiled, Baked, & Custard Puddings."[11]

Even with such a fine meal, Jemmy was distinctly aware of the Coromantees who had arrived for the feast. "Maria Sat at the Table and She looked very Black on Seeing so many Coromantees there," Jemmy said, "and She I made Signs of contempt to Each Other." His testimony did not make clear who had invited the Gold Coast people, but it seems unlikely they were the original "five or six" invited by Fargut. The Coromantees had come as guests of Court.

Following the prescribed customs of the English, the women excused themselves and left the men to drink and smoke. "After Dinner Maria & all the Other Women went away then Fargut brought in Punch, Sangaree & Wine & we Drank," Jemmy recalled.

Tomboy brought immediate attention to his fine coat. "Tomboy said some of them were not Men Because they had not Double breasted Jackets," Jemmy remembered, and the men "were Bantering One Another on that subject." Fargut "then went Out and Brought in two Bottles of Liquor, & put them on the Table. No white person was there at that time. There were Glasses, Stone Muggs etc. on the Table, & a good Deal of cool Drink."

"Gentlman," Tomboy said, raising his glass, "I am going to Toast a Health & Damnation to them that won't Plege it or won't give their Assistance."[12]

Treblin remembered that "Courts health was Drank by Name of King Tackey's," and then he "went out of the House to Dance." There was music in the yard.[13]

Court and Tomboy had turned Fargut's dinner into another stopping point on the campaign. They asserted themselves, though uninvited, brought their own followers, and finished the night with toasts to "King Tackey."

It was an evening replete with British customs and political rites, like that of countless other suppers held by white candidates across the island. The only difference was that the attendees were not free.

Sometime in early March, Court began a second political campaign: uniting the Coromantees behind his leadership. He focused first on the traditional political symbols of his Gold Coast home: the shields, the spears, the canopy. He sought out craftsmen who might help him construct these items.

Court returned to Emanuel's cooper shop around March 1736.[14] He had come for help constructing the canopy. "He told me he brought Sticks to me and wire to make an Umbrella for him and Desired the favour of me to make it," Emmanuel told Arbuthnot. "The Sticks were about Three foot Long and and Inch broad and the Wire was to fasten them." Court had also "brought some blew Cloth and White Ozenbriggs to make it of."[15]

"What Do you want with this?" Emanuel asked.

"Ye Shaw, I want to play my Country Play," Court replied. Emanual said Court "Pressed me very much to make it, and put it together, and stay'd till I did it, and I made & fasten'd the Frame together & Cut Out the Cloth and gave the Cloth to Court to have it Sowed, and then Court went away."

When Court had departed with the cut cloth for the canopy, Emanuel said he "took the Frame and threw it behind my house not Caring to be concerned about making any Such thing."

Court returned to Emanuel about two days later. He had brought "the Cloth Sticht together and Desired me to See it fitted to the Frame and told me to paint a Pidgeon at Top, and gave me Paint and vial of Linseed Oyle to Do it with."

Emanuel said he would finish the canopy but then did not: "I told him I would & he often Called for it but I put it off, from One time to another, and Never did it and was Determined never to Do it, but I did not tell Court so, I always made Excuses to him of want of time." All through the dry season, Emanuel kept the unfished canopy. "I kept the things by me a long time without ever putting my hands to it."

"At Length," Emanuel remembered, "Court fell Out with me upon that Account and for several months together, whenever I passed by him he Either took no Notice at all of me or else spoke Abusively to me, 'As you Damn'd Drunken Son of a Bitch you Dog,' and Such names."

In the examination, Arbuthnot asked Emanuel "what Reason he had not to finish this Umbrella, as he called it?"

My "mind Misgave . . . that it was for no good Purpose," Emanuel said. But it is worth noting that Emanuel feared to say no to Court. Emanuel kept the materials for a long time.

Court sought the people from the Gold Coast. He knew he would not find their numbers in St. John. He maintained close friendships on the Widow Langford's plantation, north out of town on Pope's Head Road, and he turned to that plantation most often.

It must have been Coobah (Ekua in Fante) who drew him to the property.[16] She was his "shipmate," one witness testified, a woman who had been on the same ship as Court as they suffered in the passage across the Atlantic Ocean.[17] "Africans throughout the Americas accorded the highest possible regard to those whom they designated as 'shipmates,'" notes historian Stephanie Smallwood. For a people who had lost their families and people, shipmates were treated like kin.[18]

Court also began to rename Black people at this time. On the Langford plantations, he took a young enslaved person named Robin under his influence. "Robin was Daily with Court, Neglected his Business, Came home several ties half Drunk," noted Billy, a witness against Robin. Court bought Robin a "very good Suit of Cloths" and gave him a new name: "Quamina Jumper," after a young man Court had known in his homeland. Court would be called Tackey. Robin would be Quamina Jumper.[19]

Sometime between the end of the harvest in July and the beginning of the planting time in September, Court began to work closely with Quawcoo, the "Old Oby Man and Physician & Cormantine."[20] He was a practitioner of JuJu, called Obayi in the Americas, the magic used to heal or harm in West Africa. Quawcoo was owned by William Hunt, whose plantation lay far to the south in the Shekerly's Mountains.[21] Court must have sought him out.

It was Quawcoo who taught Court the shield dance. Even if Court remembered it from his childhood, he could not have known the movements or steps. He relied on Quawcoo to show him how to use the shield and sword and spear. "I saw him Once at Kerby's Warfe with Court about a Month before Courts Dance," said the notorious informer Billy, "shewing Court how they played with the Ikim, in his Country." Quawcoo placed a sheep skin on his and sparred with Quawcoo. They "blowed with an Oban," Billy said, a horn made of elephant's tooth.[22] They trained many times, practicing the motions with sword and shield, sparring like Gold Coast warriors.

Emanuel remembered the last time Court visited him at his master's cooper shop. It was about a week before his great dance. Emanuel was "very Sick and Confined to my bed."[23]

"Court then came to me, in a very kind Manner stood by my bed side and Asked me how I Did," Emanuel remembered. Court said he had come to check on him. He "believed my sickness proceeded from Drinking hard."

"I told him it Did not for that I had a feaver & a Pain in my stomach and Side," Emanuel said.

Court asked for the canopy that Emanuel had never finished. "I said I would Do it by and by," Emanuel remembered, but Court said "he would Come to Morrow noon for it to finish it himself or get some Body Else to do it."

Court then spoke to Emanuel "very Seriously," and bent low to the ground beside the cooper's slave. "Well Emanuel," Court said, "if you had taken my Advice and kept close to me you would be a Better Man than you are Now. If you was to see me do good, you would Do good, If I Do bad you Do bad."

"Gods Blood and Sons; if you go to hell must I go there to?" Emanuel asked.

Court saw limes under Emanuel's bed and "Asked me for Some. I told him he might if he would, and he put some into his Handkerchief and after bidding Good by, went away."

Court never returned to Emanuel's shop: "The Next Day Court instead of Coming himself sent a Boy for the Frame; I Directed Our boy Quashee to go behind my house for it and give it to the Boy, which he Did. And just as the boy was out, I bid the Quashee to Call him back, and told him that there was some Cloth besides, but the Boy would not Carry it." Emanuel had Quashee deliver the cloth to Court the next day.

On 3 October 1736, Court dressed like the Big Men he remembered from his childhood. He set aside his livery, his bright coat. He assembled his royal habit in his back room in Kerby's home. He had been waiting for this moment for many years.

He had assembled his political coalition, an alliance of Creole slaves from St. John, organized through a British colonial campaign of feasts and public pledges of support. He had learned something from waiting behind Kerby for the last thirty years. And he had called the Coromantees to him, recruiting them in meetings at Treblin's and Langford's parties, traveling to the outer plantations to win their support to make him king.

They all waited for him in the pasture, his people. "Takyi! Takyi! Takyi! Kukroo Takyi [Great Takyi]!" the people cried.

CHAPTER NINE

Trials

20 October 1736
St. John, Antigua

LIEUTENANT GOVERNOR WILLIAM MATHEW BELIEVED the slaves of the Caribbean were rising in rebellion. From his plantation home on the island of Antigua, he could look west toward Otto's pasture where, only two days before, planters had burned two enslaved men alive, darkening the skies with smoke from execution fires. The burnings had been a warning to slaves in all directions, a punishment for conspiring against the British and their king. Writing to the Lords of Trade and Plantations in England on 17 January 1736, the man responsible for defense of the Leeward Islands insisted he sat in the middle of a conspiracy stretching beyond the shores of the island of Antigua. "The Contagion," Mathew wrote, "has spread farther among these Islands than I apprehend is discovered." The lieutenant governor had just finished with the deposition of John Hanson, a British mariner only recently returned from the French islands to the north. "By an Enclosd Affidavit [the contagion] actually has taken Effect in St. Bartholomews, & is discovered in Anguilla & St. Martins." If Mathew traced his finger along a map of the eastern Caribbean, he could see that slave rebellions appeared to be traveling with the currents, moving ominously toward the colonies of British North America.[1]

Mathew was but one of many Britons who coordinated their efforts to control slave populations even as they created environments of heightened racial fear in the British Atlantic. The fierce determination of colonial officials to interrogate more slaves and commit elaborate, public executions can be explained, in part, by this growing transatlantic climate of fear in the 1730s. The methods of interrogation and coercion and the choices made by justices of the peace determined the extent to which a conspiracy might grow from an accusation into the egregious trials that stand out as some of the worst travesties of justice in early American history.

Over the course of the week following Robert Arbuthnot's report to the assembly, constables arrested slaves and extracted confessions. At some point, a Coromantee named Cuffee testified that he had overheard Court and the Creole named Tomboy speaking of a conspiracy at the back gate of Thomas Kerby's home.[2] According to Cuffee, they were plotting to blow up the governor and the leading planters of the island in a gunpowder plot. On 19 October, the assembly created a special court consisting of four justices of the peace. That very night, the four justices conducted a trial and convicted Court and Tomboy of an unspecified crime relating to conspiracy.[3] Court was ordered to be executed the following morning.

As common as the conspiracy trials were in these years, they varied drastically in their outcome. Only five out of thirty-one conspiracies resulted in the British executing more than two slaves. With the exception of a small Antigua conspiracy in 1729, all of the deadliest conspiracy trials took place after 1735, in the second half of the decade. The intensity of the trials in the latter part of the 1730s, as colonists gathered and then disseminated news through port towns, suggests growing anxieties weighed on the white public. Despite these fears, the large majority of conspiracy trials did not produce the waves of egregious killings that took place in Jamaica, South Carolina, Antigua, and New York.

The most violent conspiracy trials can be split into two types of incidents. In South Carolina in 1740 and in Jamaica in 1745, colonial officials learned of impending conspiracies from planters who had been warned of the supposed danger by a slave. In these incidents, authorities adopted the unusual strategy of ambushing the planned gathering of accused conspirators instead of simply conducting arrests. The militias discovered mass meetings of slaves, just as they suspected, and set about condemning and executing people immediately. The laws of the two colonies required justices of the peace to try the assembled slaves in ad hoc slave courts, typically called freeholder's courts. The minutes of these special trials were not taken or the records have not survived. Georgia pamphleteer Benjamin Martyn related that two hundred slaves were discovered in an open field in South Carolina in 1740. The justices ordered fifty slaves hanged, "ten a day," to "intimidate the other Negroes."[4] In the case of Jamaica, newspaper reports citing an "Extract from a Letter from Jamaica" described authorities' discovering "a great many Negros, took 12 or 14 of them, and continu'd to more of them by Degrees as some have been hang'd, some burnt, some hung in chains [gibbeted], and some sent off the island [banished]."[5] In both South Carolina and Jamaica, the wrath of the militias was terrible and the duration of the trials brief and brutal.

The trials in Antigua and New York were a different matter. In both 1736 and 1741, the authorities found no one in open rebellion. Instead, governors and assemblies formed special committees of officials tasked with interrogating slaves and discovering the extent of the "accursed Negro plot." In Antigua, on 19 October 1736, the legislature appointed four justices of the peace, including the attorney general and members of the council and assembly, "Sworn to act according to their knowledge, their Consciences, and the Laws," to conduct both interrogations and formal trials "of such Slaves as they shall think there is Matter enough against." On 23 October, the assembly passed a new act allowing the committee to investigate all slaves and to use "pains or tortures." The assembly justified the new law by noting the growing threat from slaves: "Rebellions and Treasons being of late more frequent among Slaves than heretofore this being the Second plot formed in this Island within these Seven years." Over the next four months, the committees ordered the execution of eighty-eight people and banished another forty-eight to foreign provinces.[6] In New York, four years later, the colony appointed a grand jury to investigate the conspiracy, interrogating slaves in secure meetings closed to the public. The Supreme Court conducted the public trials.[7] They had similar results to those of Antigua four years earlier. Over fewer than four months, colonists executed thirty-four people and banished another eighty-four men and women.[8]

These were the most murderous trials. In all twenty-six of the other conspiracies, the executions did not exceed two people and in most cases only one. This was true throughout a remarkable range of British provinces, including the Leeward Islands and Bermuda, Maryland, New Jersey, and even at a different time in New York. What was the difference between a conspiracy that ended with one convicted conspirator and the mass killings that emerged in these other places?

The simple answer is that the decisions of governors and their councils determined the extent of a conspiracy in any given colony. They chose the course of conspiracy trials indirectly by deciding whether to create special investigative committees, and they decided the outcome directly by determining when the interrogations of these committees would stop. The burden lay on governors and judges to decide when the trials had run their course. During each slave conspiracy, there were several critical moments when confessing witnesses produced new versions of the conspiracy and accused new people. The governor and his officials had to decide what to believe. Their choices decided the outcomes of the trials.

By 1730, most British colonies had enshrined slave conspiracy into law. Unlike the French and Spanish Empires, which maintained general slave codes based on old Roman law, each English province passed its own code for governing slaves. The most important was the Barbados "Act for the Better Ordering and Governing Negroes" (1661), a comprehensive statute designed to control and regulate slave populations on the island. In the act, planters singled out "Negroes and other slaves" for possessing "Wild and Salvage Natures" that justified separate treatment under the island's law.[9] The 1661 law and the 1688 revised version, entitled "An Act for the Governing of Negroes," essentially made a slave conspiracy "any gathering of slaves in which a crime was discussed."[10] Barbados set a precedent for other colonies. Jamaica (1664) and the Leeward Islands (1697) adopted similar codes for slave conspiracy before the end of the seventeenth century.[11] The mainland colonies of Maryland (1717), New Jersey (1712), and New York (1712) did the same in the early eighteenth century.[12] Virginians charged slave conspirators with treason until 1723, when a unique law defined conspiracy as six or more slaves who "consult, advise, or conspire, to rebel or make insurrection, or . . . plot or conspire the murder of any person or persons."[13] In many other cases, slaves accused of conspiracy might be charged with committing petit treason (a master betraying a servant) or arson, both laws that represented betrayal and usually included the capital punishment of burning.

There was a strong precedent for colonies to form special and extraordinary committees after the discovery of a slave conspiracy. The 1688 Barbados act required its governor to create a special council if "any Negroes or other Slaves" should "make Mutiny or Insurrection" or "hold any Council or Conspiracy." The governor was to select any four officers from the militia, which might include men from his Common Council or the assembly, "to meet in Council, and to proceed by the Marshal Law against the Actors, Contrivers, Raisers, Fomenters and Concealers of such Mutiny or Rebellion, and them punish by Death or other Pains."[14] With the full powers of martial law, the special council was tasked with finding the "Contrivers" and punishing them with "Death or other Pains." Four years after Barbados officials signed the law, the incredible powers of this special council became quite clear. The Barbados Conspiracy of 1692 lasted for more than a month and led to the interrogation of two or three hundred slaves.[15] The Barbados Assembly formed its own investigative committee, the "Commission of Inquiry," to complement the martial law council, which in turn helped identify and interrogate numerous accused slaves.[16] The end result was ninety-five people executed, "a great many burn'd," and at least forty-two men castrated.[17] The special martial law councils and investigative committees proved very effective in delivering accused conspirators and exhorting confessions.

The English method of prosecuting slave conspiracy trials depended on witnesses and confessions. If the authorities believed the witness, then there was little the accused could do to prevent a conviction. Conspiracy, however, was not like other slave crimes. By its very nature, it involved a pact with others. In Barbados in 1692, an informant overheard slaves Ben and Sambo discussing a "wicked design." The special council ordered them gibbeted until they starved or confessed. After just four days, both men offered to confess and name their fellow conspirators. Sambo died from the gibbeting before he could speak. Ben named "most of the chief officers."[18] This was a typical outcome. English authorities required convicted slaves to implicate their fellow conspirators in order to be considered for mercy. There were many exceptions. Slaves often denied the charges to their death, and colonists resurrected egregious methods of execution from early modern Europe, like breaking on the wheel, to make an example of an unrepentant slave. But when faced with burning alive chained to a stake or the possibility of banishment to another colony, many of the accused were willing to confess to the crime and name others. Judge Josiah Smith pointed to this problem in his letter to Cadwallader Colden in 1741. "Any body," he explained, "would chuse rather to be hanged than to be burnt."[19]

Most colonies did not adopt the Barbados method of special councils for interrogating slave conspirators. By the 1730s, provinces with large populations of slaves had adopted Barbados's separate innovation, the freeholder's court, as the means by which slave conspirators were tried. Evolving from the 1661 slave codes, slaves were denied juries and instead were tried by two justices of the peace and any "Three Able, Good and Legal free-holders of the Place nearest where the said Crimes were committed."[20] In the second quarter of the eighteenth century, freeholder's courts were used by all the colonies in the British West Indies and in South Carolina and Virginia.[21] Pennsylvania adopted freeholder's courts in 1700, and New York and New Jersey followed suit after 1712.[22] Bermuda adopted the freeholder's court in 1730 to deal with the poisoning conspiracies that swept through the island. The New England colonies and Maryland did not create special courts for slaves, but instead, in the case of Maryland, tried slaves in the county court.[23]

The freeholder's courts were by their very nature quick to pass sentence. The Barbados law of 1688 instructed the courts to be assembled "with all convenient speed" nearest "where the crimes were committed," and to order punishments on the spot.[24] Virginia followed with the creation of their slave court of oyer and terminer (literally, to hear and determine) in 1692, as part of the "Act for the More Speedy Prosecution of Slaves Committing Capital Crimes." Slaves had to be tried quickly, the law explained, in order to make other slaves "affrighted to commit the like crimes."[25] Because the freeholder's courts were ad hoc in nature and quick to pass judgment, they did not produce the interrogations and elaborate confessions of the special committees created by a governor. Magistrates heard evidence and passed summary judgments. In some cases, justices of the peace could even be discerning, excusing slaves for lack of immediate evidence. Historian Philip J. Schwarz shows that courts of oyer and terminer in the Virginia county of Spotsylvania, for example, had a higher conviction rate of free whites (66.7%) than of Black slaves (60%). This depended on the crime, however. In cases of conspiracy, in which very few whites were ever charged in the history of colonial Virginia, the slave conviction rate was more than 89 percent.[26] As the Virginia Act of 1692 explained, the court's justices of the peace endeavored to make slaves "affrighted to commit the like crimes."

For the most part, the officials on the freeholder's courts were responsible for condemning slave conspirators. Justices of the peace tried poison conspirators in Bermuda in 1730; the slaves in the Virginia rebellion of 1730; and the accused conspirators in South Carolina in 1730, 1734, 1737, and 1740. Freeholders probably tried the conspirators in New Jersey in 1734 (the records are lost) and most other incidents of accused plotting in colonial America. These courts also likely tried the slave conspirators discovered in the open fields in South Carolina in 1740 and Jamaica in 1745.[27] The fast pace of trials and executions in the field suggests that justices of the peace and freeholders, probably militia men, did the sentencing. Justices of the peace and the assembled freeholders ordered brutal executions, but they were quick and dirty, designed for "speedy prosecution of slaves." Fearing imminent rebellion, the planters sought to make an example of the accused men they had found in an open meeting.

With two established systems for prosecuting slaves, governors and their officials had to make a choice concerning the methods they would use to determine the extent of a conspiracy. In Antigua, at the special request of Arbuthnot, Mathew ordered a special investigative committee of judges to exhort confessions and determine the extent of a plot.

The judges produced a report on the conspiracy nearly three months after the first trials that concluded Court had led a conspiracy to blow up the leading planters on the island at a ball to commemorate the king. Their findings were based on the confessions they had secured from slaves under duress and torture.[28]

Although the evidence from the trial has not survived, it seems unlikely that Court formed a gunpowder plot as the judges claimed. Despite numerous searches of slave quarters all over the island and many confessions, white authorities never found the gunpowder required for such an explosion.[29] Gunpowder was notoriously difficult to acquire in any large amount on Antigua, so much so that the assembly required ship duties to be paid in gunpowder.[30] Even one attempt by a slave to purchase powder on 12 October 1736 had immediately created suspicion among white colonists.[31] The activities of slaves, the midnight meetings with weapons, and the ennobling ceremony helped convince white Antiguans of the far-reaching plot. For their part, Court and Tomboy insisted on their innocence until the moment of their execution.

We can be certain, however, that Court's dance was very real. On a Sunday afternoon before a group of Coromantee and Creoles slaves, Takyi had stepped out before his people and pledged himself in their defense. He had turned to Tomboy, a Creole and respected master carpenter, and before all the slaves of the island pressed his shield between their bodies and his blade against the face of his "Braffo." He had danced the motions of the sword and moved to the beat of drum. The people had chanted his name. In that moment, he had brought a long-suffering people together behind his leadership. His was a promise made to a divided people, an offer of protection and an acceptance of his pledge.

On 20 October, "King Court was brought to the Place of Execution," wrote an anonymous white witness. "There [he] was laid extended on a wheel, seiz'd by the Wrists and Ancles, and so laid basking in the Sun for the full Space of an Hour and a Quarter . . . when he begg'd Leave to plead." When the justices gave their assent, he "acknowledged every Thing that was alledged against him." At noon, the British executed Takyi in the marketplace. After he died, the authorities ordered that his head be severed and placed on a pole and that his body be burned. Although he was brutalized and harmed, one account noted that a slave preserved his green cap.[32]

Court's execution was but the first of many more. For four months, white authorities exhorted confessions and killed slaves by breaking on the wheel, gibbeting, or burning people alive. The Britons eventually executed eighty-eight people and banished forty-seven others.[33]

Then there were rumors of a new conspiracy, one in which slaves had met in anger over the killing of their king. According to the report by the judges, the enslaved men and women promised to "to stand by, and be true to each other."[34] But the threat of executions and the promise of a painful death encouraged more confessions. The British continued in their methods of interrogation, and slaves confessed or died.

In their promise to "to stand by, and be true to each other," the Black people of Antigua tried to follow in the path of the Coromantee leader who wore the green hat and carried the shield. This was the great meaning of Takyi's dance in September 1736. We can see in his execution the challenges confronted by slave leaders who sought to unify Black people in the British colonies in the 1730s. In the first half of the eighteenth century, the massive influx of forced migrants from Africa created profound tensions in the communities of the enslaved. The painful process of creating one people around a shared African ancestry and in opposition to their enslavement was a long historical struggle that spanned centuries. In Court's dance and in the conspiracies and insurrections of the 1730s we can see a formative moment in this story.

CHAPTER TEN

The Diaspora Imagined

December 1744
Kingston, Jamaica

FOR A BRIEF MOMENT IN 1744, Hector's life hung precariously in the balance. White Jamaican militiamen surrounded him on all sides, their eyes focused on a forest clearing where Hector had promised that rebel slaves would soon meet to launch an insurrection. He first warned his white mistress of the imminent slave uprising, and she had alerted her neighbors and raised the alarm. Governor Edward Trelawny ordered the Jamaican cavalry to set a trap.

The first Black men who stepped into the clearing saved Hector's life. The cavalry waited until a "great many negroes" assembled and then attacked, riding down "12 or 14 of them" and pursuing the rest of the men through the tall cane.[1] By the end of the week, Hector stood before the Jamaican assembly to receive his freedom for loyalty to mistress and Crown. As a special request, he asked the assembly to pay his transport to England, a place he imagined safe from the Black plantation slaves he had betrayed. As British officials burned the convicted conspirators alive, Hector sailed for England and a new life across the western ocean.[2]

Hector soon learned he could not so easily escape the Black men and women of the early eighteenth-century Atlantic world. On the streets of London, they sought him out. In a petition Hector submitted to the British king in 1746, he complained that both Black freedmen and slaves beat him so that he could not conduct his business. Black Londoners had heard news of his betrayal and taken up cause with slaves in far-off

Jamaica. In his petition, Hector asked the king to help him return to the island for "at least he might be with his wife and in a safer place."[3]

Like Hector in London, historians are only beginning to understand how stories of rebellion and conspiracy influenced the Black diaspora of the early eighteenth-century Atlantic. In the second quarter of the eighteenth century, white Britons described at least thirty-one slave plots and open insurrections in seventeen provinces.[4] Many of these episodes involved conspiracy trials that may have been fabricated by white officials or exaggerated by accused slaves caught up in the vengeful courts of British planters.[5] Yet even these events became news in the wider Atlantic world, passed by white mariners and slaves through routes of commerce and communication. Large-scale conflicts between colonists and slaves, such as the First Jamaican Maroon War (1729–1739) or the slave insurrection on the Danish Island of St. John (1733), became stories of general unrest in the West Indies and mainland North America.

For the Black slaves of the British Atlantic, the most provocative rumors involved opportunities for freedom. Stories of emancipation were common in the second quarter of the eighteenth century and inspired slave meetings and open challenges to planter authority. On the American mainland, Black men and women spread the rumor that King George II had freed slaves baptized by the Church of England. A thousand miles to the south, news of the St. John insurrection of 1733 circulated quickly through the slave quarters of the islands, transcending imperial boundaries with the urgency of rumor and the possibility of freedom. By the late 1730s, word that the Spanish would offer emancipation to British slaves who might escape to Florida had become an inspiration for flight and rebellion. In South Carolina and as far north as Boston, enslaved Black people sought to escape to the southern edge of empire. British authorities attempted to control slave populations with conspiracy trials, but the practice of banishing convicted slaves led to the transport of nearly two hundred witnesses into the wider Atlantic world. These "outcasts" became yet another source of news to slave communities in far-off lands. In the port towns of the West Indies and the

North American mainland, Black communities were ever more aware of the rebellious activities of other enslaved peoples.[6]

The year 1746 was an eventful one across the British Atlantic. In Boston, white Britons gathered in their churches to celebrate King George II's most recent victory over his Catholic enemies. The news of the Duke of Cumberland's defeat of Charles Stuart at the battle of Culloden, Scotland, assured the townspeople that the British Protestant interest would survive the great war which had slowly enveloped both Europe and the Americas. In his Thanksgiving Day sermon to a large congregation at South Church, Pastor Thomas Prince chose to begin with a passage from the book of Ezra. "And after all that is come upon us for our evil Deeds, and for our great Trespass," he read aloud, "seeing that Thou our God has punished us less than our Iniquities deserve, and has given us such Deliverance as this . . . should we again brake thy Commandments?" Prince explained that like the ancient Israelites, the Lord had "righteously chastised" the British people with "various Judgments." Although their "inveterate and Popish enemies both without and within the Kingdom" had been "restless to enslave and ruin us," the Britons had survived through God's "most undeserved and inexpressibly Great Deliverance." The pastor exhorted his congregation to remember the Lord's mercy and to forego their breaking of his commandments lest they "justly move Him to display his Anger in their utter Ruin."[7]

Prince was warning his parishioners not to be self-satisfied, a condition to which they might have thought themselves entitled. After all, challenges to their colonial project had been defeated at every turn. While the Spanish had managed to stymie invasions in the Caribbean and St. Augustine, British victories at Puerto Bello (1739) and French Louisburg (1745) had expanded the Protestant empire.[8] In the British Isles, loyalists to King George II sang "Rule Britannia" in their theaters, and London economists authored new broadsides arguing for expansion of plantation trade. The empire seemed poised for a new burst of economic growth.

It was in that same year that Malachy Postlethwayt authored *The National and Private Advantages of the African Trade Considered,* in which he advocated for renewed British support for the Royal African Company. In his pamphlet, he insisted that the "Trade to Africa is the Branch which renders our American Colonies and Plantations so advantagious to Great Britain."[9] British colonists shared with Postlethwayt a renewed fervor for enslaving Africans after 1746. In what was perhaps the surest sign of a return to business as usual, the South Carolina Assembly allowed the prohibitive duties on the slave trade to expire in 1744. In that year, four slave vessels arrived in Charles Town. By 1754, the governor of South Carolina reported to the Board of Trade that slave ships were delivering "upwards of 2000 negroes" to the colony a year.[10]

This new support for the African trade represented a broad consensus among Britons that the threat of general rebellion had subsided. Slave restiveness and accusations of conspiracy dropped off sharply in the British provinces after 1746. "There was a marked decline of organized rebellious activity on the part of Negro slaves," noted Herbert Aptheker of this period. "Precisely why this is so the present writer is not certain."[11] But after examining the causes of unrest in this era, the quiet that descended on most of the slave societies of the American and West Indian provinces seems far less mysterious.

In the West Indies, divisions within slave communities proved to be too much for any rebels to overcome. The African trade had built a plantation complex capable of widespread rebellion by the second quarter of the eighteenth century, but Black communities were contentious and divided. African nations and Creoles often struggled against each other in this era. In Jamaica, the success of the Maroons after the outbreak of war in 1729 and the rising proportion of slaves in the population represented a real opportunity for an alliance of Black people against planters. Yet rivalries within the Black ranks prevented the general rebellion white Britons feared. The Maroon Treaty of 1739 enshrined these differences into law, creating an alliance between planters and Maroons against the general slave population. In the 1740s, Maroons revealed slave conspiracies to planters and crushed the insurrections of 1740 and 1746. In the decades that followed and especially during Tacky's Revolt during the Seven Years' War, Maroons continued to play a decisive role in suppressing slave unrest on the island.[12] British planters allied themselves with the most formidable fighters in Jamaica and used them against African nations of slaves.

In the eastern Caribbean, on the island of St. John, the inability of rebels to unite large communities of Black people ruined any hope for victory. The Danish and British slave trade introduced new waves of Akwamu warriors onto St. John, many of whom attempted to wage war rather than accept slavery. However, their movement was in vain. Despite a shared language with many of their fellow "Aminas" from the Gold Coast, the aggressive Akwamu were unable to unite Black people on the island or inspire general unrest in the neighboring Leewards. The combined onslaught of Danish, British, and French forces beat back the efforts of the Akwamu and their allies who did rise, ending the only island-wide rebellion in the Caribbean up to that time. The Europeans' extirpation of the rebels quelled slave unrest in the Virgin Islands for a generation.[13]

The rumors of freedom that inspired slaves in colonial America had also run their course by 1746. Slave mobility and communication in the British Atlantic had developed to the extent that Black people could pass rumors of freedom among provinces. In the early 1730s, slaves in Virginia and later New Jersey shared news that King George II had freed all enslaved Christians. The rumor proved false, and planters attacked or arrested those slaves who had tried to organize open protests and challenge colonial authorities. The British debate over slave baptism—the underlying cause of the story of royal emancipation—also became less contentious. The bishop of London and his Anglican missionaries, evangelicals, and Moravians were all actively spreading the gospel to slaves by the mid-1740s. Although planters resisted allowing their slaves to be baptized, and some Africans demonstrated little enthusiasm, by the end of the period slaves in many North American mainland colonies were attending Protestant services.[14] The rumor that King George would free baptized slaves had faded away by 1746 and would not emerge again in the British colonies before the American Revolution.[15]

There was also a notable decline in both insurrections and accusations of conspiracy in South Carolina in the early 1740s. The Spanish king's edict of liberty for runaway British slaves persisted as a rumor of freedom much longer than the baptism stories of Virginia and New Jersey. Even with the cessation of hostilities between Spain and Great Britain in 1748, the Spanish continued with their edict until the end of the Seven Years' War in 1763.[16] But British invasions of St. Augustine discouraged large groups of slaves from attempting the long trek through Georgia and Florida. General Edward Oglethorpe led sieges and invasions of the Spanish province in 1740, 1742, and 1743. "The Siege of Augustine, and the continual incursions since made by his Excellency," wrote British officer Edward Kimber in 1743, "[has] . . . spoil'd their usual Methods of decoying our Negroes from Carolina, and elsewhere; whence, in Numbers, they used to desert to them."[17] British and American Indian raids up to the castle of St. Augustine blocked the passage south for any army of rebel slaves. Still, hope for some Black bondsmen did not die away completely. As late as 1749, planters were complaining that Black runaways were fleeing to the Spanish, but there was nothing akin to another Stono Rebellion in the years that followed.[18]

Throughout the British Atlantic, white colonial officials accused fewer slaves of conspiracy after the mid-1740s. As argued in chapter 5, news of slave unrest had created among white colonists a pervasive climate of racial fear during this era. These anxieties explain the choices officials made to force confessions from slaves and to commit brutal executions on scant evidence. British conspiracy trials in Jamaica, Antigua, South Carolina, and New York produced hundreds of victims and banished many others. After 1746, British colonists demonstrated a clear unwillingness to prosecute conspiracy trials as they had just a few years previous. When rumors of unrest did arise, colonial authorities treated them with skepticism. "There has been a new rumor of the rising of the Negroes," wrote New York's Cadwallader Colden to his wife in 1747, "but upon enquiry no foundation can be found of it."[19] In

South Carolina, a supposed slave conspiracy was dismissed after white authorities decided a planter had sowed false rumors for his own ends.[20]

Part of the reason for the decline in conspiracy trials came from growing British condemnation of the mass executions ordered by colonial officials. As early as January 1737, at the height of the trials in Antigua, council members and assemblymen were contesting the findings of judges and attempting to halt the executions.[21] Contributors to *Fog's Weekly Journal* and the *Gentleman's Magazine* in London questioned the necessity of killing so many Black bondsmen instead of some more merciful (and economical) punishment.[22] In New York, Judge Daniel Horsmanden complained that people said of his key witness, Mary Burton, that she was the "Wickedest of Mortals, to bring so many Innocents to this shameful, miserable and untimely end."[23] John Ury's written defense against charges of conspiracy was published as a broadside by Benjamin Franklin in Philadelphia and many New England newspapers.[24] "Who alive can think yt reads his defence & dying Declaration," wrote Josiah Cotton after reading the broadside, "but yt he was as innocent as ye child unborn."[25] The growing skepticism in the north was on full display in 1742, less than a year after the trials, when constables arrested a slave named Tom for attempting to burn down a house. He promised the judges that he would reveal a broad slave conspiracy in return for clemency. Although Judge Horsmanden and Lieutenant Governor George Clarke were eager to begin interrogations, other colonists refused to believe the accused slave and eventually Tom confessed that he had acted alone.[26] In response to growing criticism, judges in both Antigua and New York authored and published defenses of their proceedings for dissemination in the British Atlantic.

But the most important reason for the declining number of conspiracy accusations was the victories of colonial forces both at home and abroad. After 1746, the climate of fear was receding before the onslaught of British arms. The much feared "general rebellion" of slaves had never emerged in the provinces.[27] Planters had defeated insurrections in Jamaica and South Carolina and violently suppressed every public protest led by people of African descent. Spanish and French invasions had failed on the southern mainland and never emerged in the West Indies. On a day of national thanksgiving in August 1746, Pastor Thomas Prince could only wonder at God's "most undeserved and inexpressibly Great Deliverance" of the British people.[28]

In the years that followed, white Britons looked back at this period of racial fear and treated it as strange and distant. "Sometime ago the People of this Province were Annually alarmed with accounts of intended Invasions," wrote South Carolinian James Glen in 1748. "Even in time of profound Peace they were made believe that the Spaniards had prepared Embarkations for that purpose. . . . Sometimes the Negroes were to rise & cut their Masters Throats at other times the Indians were confederating to destroy us."[29] Glen celebrated the newfound peace. "There was no resisting the torrent of jealousy," William Smith remembered from his childhood experience the New York conspiracy as a time "when every man thought himself in danger from a foe in his own house."[30]

For some, the memories of fear and violence lasted a lifetime. In 1813, an old engineer named David Grim presented to the New-York Historical Society a plan of the colonial city as he remembered it from the years "1742, 1743, & 1744."[31] He had lived to see the colony of New York declare its independence and witnessed the birth of a new republic. But he wanted the people of his young country to remember the city as it had been. In remarkable detail, the seventy-six-year old man depicted more than 1,100 houses and 60 landmarks.[32] In the center of the map, Grim drew a small image of several silhouetted figures atop a pyre. "Plot Negroes burnt here," he wrote into his legend. He had only been a child of four years old when he witnessed the execution of the slaves in New York, but he wrote on the back of the map that he had the "perfect idea of seeing the Negroes chained to a stake, and there burned to death."[33] Grim sought to help new generations of Americans remember a period of racial fear in the city that had been long forgotten.

Like the old engineer of New York, this book reveals a period of history that has been little understood. As the first full-length longitudinal study of these conflicts, it is an argument for an era of slave unrest within the British Atlantic Empire nearly sixty years before the Age of Revolution. It approaches the slave conspiracies and insurrections of the first half of the eighteenth century not as singular events in the histories of specific colonies but rather as a shared moment in the history of the British provinces, when slaves in the Caribbean and mainland North America threatened white authority with open rebellion, and in turn inspired heightened fears of insurrection among white Britons. This project demonstrates that a Black Atlantic existed and flourished in British colonial America and the West Indies in the second quarter of the eighteenth century. My findings reveal, first, the surprising numbers of enslaved mariners aboard British vessels in colonial America and the West Indies, and second, that a communication network among slave communities was well developed by the 1730s. The rumors of freedom that inspired several episodes of unrest in this period were spread along these routes of communication. This discovery will contribute a great deal to the new history of a Black Atlantic. In his influential *The Black Atlantic* (1993), Paul Gilroy reconceptualized the cultural history of this diaspora by arguing that the Black experience was uniquely transnational. Gilroy explained that Black people in Europe and the Americas had developed a "double consciousness," an identity in which they were part of a political nation but also separated by an African ancestry, and this shared consciousness created the Black Atlantic.[34] This book reveals an important step in this historical process. Gilroy focused most of his attention on the centuries after the Age of Revolution, but the evidence suggests that Black people in the British provinces were communicating rumors of freedom and demonstrating a shared sense of purpose against slavery generations earlier than previously understood. The "double consciousness" that defined the Black Atlantic was taking shape in the early eighteenth century.

My research into the British slave trade has also revealed the deeply unsettling effect of this human trade on colonial America in this period. Ira Berlin referred to the influence of the slave trade on the North American colonies in the eighteenth century as "Africanization," a process by which the British introduced large numbers of enslaved migrants from Africa into communities of American-born slaves.[35] This process was far more painful and contentious for Black people than historians have previously understood. The African trade created rivalries and conflicts in these communities that played a violent role in the unrest of the era. It also created a paradox for white planters. Even as they imported more African people, the gentry expressed a growing anxiety that the proportions of slaves in their colonies were untenable. Insurrections and accusations of conspiracy were the result.

Behind revolts and conspiracies were a dynamic politics of African- and American-born slaves struggling to act together against the oppression of white authorities. Word of an opportunity for freedom allowed both African-born slaves and Creoles to articulate a shared plight. By following slave rumors of freedom across the British Atlantic of the second quarter of the eighteenth century, we can rediscover this process of political reinvention. There was not one revolutionary movement of slaves but there were rumors and many episodes of unrest. There was a call and a response, down the rivers and across the wide waters of the ocean, and in these actions the Black Atlantic took a great step forward.

ACKNOWLEDGMENTS

IT IS A GREAT PLEASURE to look back and remember the many people who helped me write this book. I see them as they were: colleagues and mentors, good friends and family who were kind enough to encourage me and to listen. I am surprised by the memories. One would think this tremendous project would leave impressions of long hours of study. Instead, I recall laughter and fellowship. I owe them all a debt of gratitude.

I am grateful to David Silverman, my graduate advisor at the George Washington University, for his generosity of heart and mind. His fascination with early American history is matched only by his patience in mentoring graduate students. Silverman always made himself available to encourage my Ph.D. dissertation research and read early drafts. He celebrated my discoveries and shrugged off my dead ends. Silverman guided me toward fellowships to support my research in the archives of North America, Europe, and the West Indies and wrote scores of letters supporting my grant applications. When they were rejected, he laughed and said he could wallpaper his walls with his own rejection letters. When they were accepted, he offered joyful congratulations and food and drink. Whenever I sit down to write, I remember his advice to "do good work." I have tried to emulate his generosity as I work with students of my own, seeing in their eyes the excitement I felt when Silverman first welcomed me into his office to study the history of early America and the Atlantic World.

The considerable research for this book would not have been possible without the assistance of many organizations. The earliest stages of this project began as a dissertation. Like so many graduate students in early American history, I owe a special thanks to the McNeil Center for Early American Studies at the University of Pennsylvania for a Barra Dissertation Fellowship. Dan Richter and the staff at the McNeil Center welcomed me into the academy at that remarkable gathering place for scholars of early American studies. The Andrew W. Mellon Foundation/American Council of Learned Societies Dissertation Completion Fellowship provided a year of invaluable funding to help me finish my graduate work on this project. I would like to thank the members of my Dissertation Committee, Denver Brunsman, Greg Childs, Nemata Blyden, and the late Ira Berlin for their guidance.

I am tremendously grateful for a joint postdoctoral fellowship at Brown University's Center for the Study of Slavery and Justice (CSSJ) and the John Carter Brown (JCB) Library. The daily encounters with scholars from around the world and the regular research presentations at the JCB and CSSJ introduced me to cutting-edge scholarship that made this book better. I would like to thank Anthony Bogues, Roquinaldo Ferreira, Linford Fisher, Seth Rockman, and Vincent Brown for gathering at the CSSJ to offer their insightful comments on an early draft of this book manuscript.

While a visiting professor at Beloit College, Beatrice McKenzie, Daniel Bruckenhaus, Ellen Joyce and Robert Andre LaFleur welcomed me into the Department of History and helped me secure funding for my research trip to the archives of Jamaica. They introduced me to teaching at a fine liberal arts college even as they encouraged my scholarship, an act of kindness that I have not forgotten.

The book took shape during my assistant professorship at Missouri University of Science and Technology. I am grateful for the encouragement of my department colleagues: Larry Gragg, Mike Bruening, Andrew Behrendt, Petra Dewitt, Kathleen Shephard, Michael Meagher, Tseggai Isaac, Jeff Schramm, Chris Ketcherside, John McManus, and Shannon Fogg. Critical final stages of research were funded by a 2018 University of Missouri Research Board Grant, which supported my archival work in Antigua and Seville, Spain. Benjamin Brown provided invaluable research assistance at the end of this project.

I owe special thanks to Andrew Davidson, editor at University of Missouri Press, for his support of this book. He calmly shepherded the manuscript through peer review. He provided insights and suggestions that made every revision better. Margaret Hogan's tireless copyediting improved the book's prose and caught my many errors. Chris Robinson created beautifully drawn maps from the limited information in the text, a testament to his talent. Drew Griffith, the project manager, somehow brought the entire book together with expertise and speed.

Many great friends have passed through my life as I wrote this book. For so much love and laughter, I must thank Nancy Campbell, Tatiana Seijas, Mattias Wiklund, Matthew Geheran, Berenice Gaillemin, Shaadi Khoury, Dan Berkhout, Chris Hickman, Michael Landis, Zach Stevenson, Appleton Scutchfield, Lucas Ellis, and always, the great Jeffrey Wisnoski.

Finally, I am grateful for the support of my family. Thank you to Joshua Seabolt and Claire Pope, Emden and Willa Seabolt, James Pope and Deborah Larkin for believing in me. Alanna Krolikowski, my love, has served as my greatest companion and confidante through every stage of the writing process. She has listened patiently to my ideas, sometimes late into the night, always challenging me and always encouraging me. Teddy Pope, my little son, is my greatest inspiration. I hope they know how much I love them all.

Justin Pope
Rolla, Missouri

NOTES

Introduction: The Dance

1. *A Genuine Narrative of the Intended Conspiracy*, 4; Antigua, Council Minutes, Arbuthnot Report, 8 January 1736/37, CO 9/10, National Archives of the United Kingdom (hereafter TNA).

2. *A Genuine Narrative of the Intended Conspiracy*, 8.

3. The Commissioners' Report states only that Court dressed in "royal habit." *Abirempon* dress is well-described and depicted in an engraving by Pieter de Marees. Marees, *Description and Historical Account of the Gold Kingdom of Guinea*, ed. and trans. Albert van Dantzig and Adam Jones (1602; Oxford: Oxford University Press, 1987), 34–39, 51, 55. For the 1602 engraving of an *abirempon* dressed in "royal habit," complete with cap, see 51.

4. DuPleiss, *The Material Atlantic*, 36–38.

5. "He had often worn it before, but without the feathers." *A Genuine Narrative of the Intended Conspiracy*, 8.

6. References to the use of the canopy appeared in newspaper accounts of the dance. The commissioners who wrote *A Genuine Narrative of the Intended Conspiracy* reported that Emanuel, a "faithful slave," refused to make the canopy, but this was contradicted by Emanuel's testimony to Justice of the Peace Arbuthnot. Court took the unfinished canopy from Emanuel and finished it himself. *Boston Weekly News-Letter*, 25 November 1736; Antigua, Council Minutes, Arbuthnot Report, TNA.

7. *A Genuine Narrative of the Intended Conspiracy*, 4.

8. "Braffo through whole Ceremony hath his face whitened over to prevent being known." Gift was designated as the *braffo*. The commissioners referred to the "Braffo" as an "officer." In Akan political culture, *obrafoos* were charged with enforcing the laws and will of the *ohene* (king). Within the Fante Confederacy, the *obrafo* was a head of state. *A Genuine Narrative of the Intended Conspiracy*, 8; T. C. McCaskie, *State and Society in Pre-Colonial Asante* (Cambridge: Cambridge University Press, 1995), 277.

9. The commissioners who wrote *A Genuine Narrative* described "Drums beating the Ikem beat" and musicians playing "the Musick of his Country" at the dance. The cowbell, or iron *dawuro*, was already popular on the Gold Coast at the time of Court's birth and in regular use by Africans on both sides of the Atlantic in the early eighteenth century. In seventeenth-century Jamaica, slaves used iron hoe blades for a similar

purpose. Bosman, *A New and Accurate Description*, 139; Richard Cullen Rath, "African Music in Seventeenth-Century Jamaica: Cultural Transit and Transition," *William and Mary Quarterly*, 3rd series, 50, no. 4 (October 1993): 700.

10. "Then the Drums beating the Ikem beat, he with an ikem . . . upon his left Arm, and a Lance in his right hand, begins the Dance." *A Genuine Narrative of the Intended Conspiracy*, 7.

11. Traditional Akan dances involve the crowd shouting encouragement to the dancer or singing in praise. In their description of the dance, the commissioners wrote that the Big Men shouted "Tackey, Tackey, Tackey" at the end of Court's dance, but they also would have shouted encouragement as he performed the movements. *A Genuine Narrative of the Intended Conspiracy*, 8.

12. "Leaping up at the same time, from one Horn or Point of the Semi-circle quite to the other." *A Genuine Narrative of the Intended Conspiracy*, 7.

13. Slave Voyages: The Trans-Atlantic Slave Trade Database.

14. C. G. A. Oldendorp, *History of the Mission of the Evangelical Brethren on the Caribbean Islands of St. Thomas, St. Croix, and St. John* (Ann Arbor, MI: Karoma, 1987).

15. J. L. Carstens, *St. Thomas in Early Danish Times: A General Description of All the Danish, American or West Indian Islands*, ed. and trans. Arnold R. Highfield (1740; St. Thomas: Virgin Islands Humanities Council, 1997).

16. William Mathew to the Board of Trade, 19 March 1733, Montserrat, Leeward Islands, Original Correspondence, CO 152/20, TNA.

17. "Begins the Dance, representing the defensive Motions of the Shield." *A Genuine Narrative of the Intended Conspiracy*, 7.

18. "Extract of Letters from Two Gentlemen in Antigua: One Dated Aug. 4 [1736]," *Virginia Gazette*, 17–24 September 1736; "Extract of Two Letters from Two Gentlemen," *South-Carolina Gazette*, 30 October 1736.

19. Josiah Martin to "Bayard," New York City, 16 December 1736, Josiah Martin Letterbook, part 1, f. 113, Martin Papers, Add. MSS 41,352, British Library, as cited in Gaspar, *Bondmen and Rebels*, 318n19.

20. Matthew Mulcahy and Stuart Schwartz, "Nature's Battalions: Insects as Agricultural Pests in the Early Modern Caribbean," *William and Mary Quarterly*, 3rd series, 75, no. 3 (July 2018): 453, 455–457; "Extract of a Letter from Antigua Dated Jan. 11, 1733, 4," *Pennsylvania Gazette*, 28 March–4 April 1734.

21. "Rhode Island, Aug. 27, We are informed by Mr. Isaac Martindale, who arrived here last week from Antigua, that the Distemper, which has prov'd so mortal to Children and young people in these Parts, is now in Antigua, and proves mortal; many Children and young people died of it every day while he was there." *London Daily Post and General Advertiser*, 8 October 1736.

22. "When the Prince begins to be fatigued, the Guards run in and support him, he delivers the Ikem and Lance to the Person who next dances, then is lead supported to the Chair, and is seated again in state." *A Genuine Narrative of the Intended Conspiracy*, 7.

23. *A Genuine Narrative of the Intended Conspiracy*, 7.

24. "And then returning to the Center of the Semi-circle with his General, makes several Flourishes with the Cutlass, gently touching with the General's Forehead." *A Genuine Narrative of the Intended Conspiracy*, 7.

25. I chose Willem Bosman's description of the Ikem oath, which he witnessed in person in the mid-1690s and translated in his memoir, over the more convoluted oath related secondhand to the commissioners. The commissioners' version of the oath: "He swears to the General, that where he falls, he will drop by his side rather than forsake or desert him in Battle; and that he will behave as a brave Prince ought." *A Genuine Narrative of the Intended Conspiracy*, 7; Bosman, *A New and Accurate Description*, 136.

26. The commissioners' *A Genuine Narrative* states, "Braffo standing behind Court with a wooden Cutlass cryed Tackey, Tackey, Tackey, Coquo Tackey which signifies King, King, King, great King." *A Genuine Narrative of the Intended Conspiracy*, 8. While there are many possible interpretations of "coquo," historian Kwasi Konadu's most recent interpretation, that "Coquo" was probably the Twi "Kokuroo" [great], is the most convincing. Konadu, "Lost at Sea: Black Atlantic History Off Africa's Gold Coast," Kwasi.Konadu, 30 June 2017, https://kwasikonadu.info/blog/2017/6/30/lost-at-sea-black-atlantic-history-off-africas-gold-coast.

27. For examples of localized studies, see Gaspar, *Bondmen and Rebels*; Wood, *Black Majority*; Lepore, *New York Burning*; Smith, ed., *Stono*, xii; and Parent, *Foul Means*.

28. British vessels made 66 transatlantic slave voyages from 1701 to 1710 and 202 voyages from 1731 to 1740. See chapter 3, table 1, below. The demand created by the plantations in the Americas coincided with the discovery of Brazilian gold in Minas Gerais, so Portuguese ships competed with merchant vessels of Britain and other European powers hoping to provide human chattel to provinces in the western hemisphere. For references to this expansion in Africa, see Lovejoy, *Transformations in Slavery*, 48, and Thornton, *Africa and Africans in the Making of the Atlantic World*, 305–306. The demand for slaves created dramatic price increases that intensified slave trading in Africa. For the changing prices of slaves, see Law, *The Slave Coast of West Africa*, 168–179; Curtin, *Economic Change in Pre-Colonial Africa*, 156–160; Lovejoy, *Transformations in Slavery*, 52–53; Thornton, *Africa and Africans*, 119, 305; and Eltis, *The Rise of African Slavery in the Americas*, 296.

29. There were 11,460 transatlantic slave passengers shipped to the mainland in British vessels in 1710, increasing to 45,710 in 1740. See chapter 3, table 2, below.

30. *A Genuine Narrative of the Intended Conspiracy*, 6.

31. Taylor, *American Colonies*, 302.

32. Michael Kwass, *The Consumer Revolution, 1650–1800* (Cambridge: Cambridge University Press, 2022); Joanne Sear and Ken Sneath, *The Origins of the Consumer Revolution in England: From Brass Pots to Clocks* (Cambridge: Routledge, 2020); Steele, *The English Atlantic*, 17; Kenneth J. Banks, *Chasing Empire across the Sea: Communications and the State in the French Atlantic, 1713–1763* (Montreal: McGill-Queen's University Press, 2002); David Armitage, *The Ideological Origins of the British Empire* (Cambridge: Cambridge University Press, 2000), 173; Clark, *The Public Prints*, 7.

33. Bernard Bailyn, *The Origins of American Politics* (New York: Knopf, 1968).

34. Lieutenant Governor Edwyn Stede to the Earl of Shrewsbury, 16 July 1689, in *Calendar of State Papers*, 13:262.

35. Edward Rugemer, *Slave Law and the Politics of Resistance in the Atlantic World* (Cambridge, MA: Harvard University Press, 2018).

36. For communication in early America, see Dubcovsky, *Informed Power*. For studies of slave communication in the era of the Age of Revolution, see, for example, Scott, "The Common Wind"; Tessa Murphy, *The Creole Archipelago: Race and Borders in the Colonial Caribbean* (Philadelphia: University of Pennsylvania Press, 2021); John D. Garrigus, *A Secret among the Blacks: Slave Resistance before the Haitian Revolution* (Cambridge, MA: Harvard University Press, 2023); Cassandra Pybus, *Epic Journeys of Freedom: Runaway Slaves of the American Revolution and Their Global Quest for Liberty* (Boston: Beacon Press, 2006); Alexander Byrd, *Captives and Voyagers: Black Migrants across the Eighteenth-Century British Atlantic World* (Baton Rouge: Louisiana State University Press, 2008); Sara E. Johnson, *The Fear of French Negroes: Transcolonial Collaboration in the Revolutionary Americas* (Berkeley: University of California Press, 2012); and Peter Blanchard, *Under the Flags of Freedom: Slave Soldiers and the Wars of Independence in Spanish South America* (Pittsburgh: University of Pittsburgh Press, 2008), 10–11, 13. For the influences of the Haitian Revolution on Cuba, see Ada Ferrer,"Cuba en la Sombra de Haiti: Noticias, sociedad y esclavitud," in *El Rumor de Haiti en Cuba: Temor, raza y rebeldia, 1789–1844*, ed. Maria Dolores Gonzalez-Ripoll et al. (Madrid: CSIC, 2004), 202–214; Ada Ferrer,"Speaking of Haiti: Slavery, Revolution and Freedom in Cuban Slave Testimony," in *The World of the Haitian Revolution*, ed. David Geggus and Norman Fiering (Indianapolis: Indiana University Press, 2009), 223–284; and Matt Childs, *The 1812 Aponte Rebellion and the Struggle against Atlantic Slavery* (Chapel Hill: University of North Carolina Press, 2006), 3–4. For Dutch Curacao, see Linda Rupert,"Inter-Colonial Networks and Revolutionary Ferment in Eighteenth Century Curacao and Tierra Firme," in *Curacao in the Age of Revolutions, 1795–1800*, ed. Wim Klooster and Gert Oostindie (Leiden: KITLV Press, 2011), 75–96. For the influences of the Haitian Revolution on slaves in Brazil, see Joao Jose Reis and Flavio dos Santos Gomes,"Repercussions of the Haitian Revolution in Brazil, 1791–1850," in Geggus and Fiering, *World of the Haitian Revolution*, 284–313. For an example of the Haitian Revolution's influence on the Spanish Empire, see Jane Landers, "Rebellion and Royalism in Spanish Florida: The French Revolution on Spain's Northern Colonial Frontier," in *A Turbulent Time: The French Revolution and the Greater Caribbean*, ed. David Gaspar and David Geggus (Bloomington: Indiana University Press, 1997), 156–177.

37. For Black rebels' political vision for their rebellion in the second half of the eighteenth century, see Marjolene Kars, *Blood on the River: A Chronicle of Mutiny and Freedom on the Wild Coast* (New York: New Press, 2020), and Vincent Brown, *Tacky's Revolt: The Story of an Atlantic Slave War* (Cambridge, MA: Harvard University Press, 2020), 10.

38. For a discussion of Black political reinvention in colonial slavery, see Vincent Brown, "Social Death and Political Life in the Study of Slavery," *American Historical Review* 114, no. 5 (2009–2012): 1231–1249. Walter C. Rucker argues for a collective

"commoner consciousness" among enslaved Gold Coast peoples in the Americas, who shared egalitarian, nonhierarchical, and democratic worldviews. Rucker, *Gold Coast Diasporas: Identity, Culture, and Power* (Bloomington: Indiana University Press, 2015), 151. For an excellent study of nineteenth-century political struggles of the enslaved in Berbice, see Randy Browne, *Surviving Slavery in the British Caribbean* (Philadelphia: University of Pennsylvania Press, 2017), 157–183.

39. Far a detailed discussion of ethnic identity and its transfer from Africa to America, see Gomez, *Exchanging Our Country Marks*, 6–8, passim.

40. *Great Newes from the Barbadoes; or, A True and Faithful Acount of the Grand Conspiracy of the Negroes against the English* (London, 1676), 9–13.

41. Thomas Smith Deposition, 19 March 1687, Antigua, Council Minutes, 24 March 1687, CO 155/1, 62–64, TNA.

42. Historians cast doubt on previous methodologies of conspiracy scares in a forum published in the *William and Mary Quarterly* in 2002. See, for example, Morgan, "Conspiracy Scares."

43. Jason Sharples, *The World That Fear Made: Slave Revolts and Conspiracy Scares in Early America* (Philadelphia: University of Pennsylvania Press, 2020).

44. Marisa J. Fuentes, *Dispossessed Lives: Enslaved Women, Violence, and the Archive* (Philadelphia: University of Pennsylvania Press, 2016), 6–7.

Chapter One: The Investigation

1. Antigua, Council Minutes, Arbuthnot Report, 8 January 1736/37, CO 9/10, National Archives of the United Kingdom (hereafter TNA).

2. *A Genuine Narrative of the Intended Conspiracy*, 2.

3. William Mathew to Board of Trade, 17 January 1736/37, W88, CO 152/22, 302–303, TNA.

4. *Antigua and the Antiguans*, vol. 2, *A Full Account of the Colony and Its Inhabitants from the Time of the Caribs to the Present Day* (London: Saunders and Otley, 1844), chapter 31; Michael Craton, *Testing the Chains: Resistance to Slavery in the British West Indies* (Ithaca, NY: Cornell University Press, 1982), 335–339; Gaspar, *Bondmen and Rebels*; Linebaugh and Rediker, *The Many-Headed Hydra*, chapter 6.

5. Historians cast doubt on previous methodologies of conspiracy scares in a forum published in the *William and Mary Quarterly* in 2002. See, for example, Morgan, "Conspiracy Scares," and Jason Sharples, *The World That Fear Made: Slave Revolts and Conspiracy Scares in Early America* (Philadelphia: University of Pennsylvania Press, 2020). For an opposing methodology, see Ada Ferrer, *Freedom's Mirror: Cuba and Haiti in the Age of Revolution* (Cambridge: Cambridge University Press, 2014). For another study that treats conspiracy trials as accurate depictions of slave plotting in the eighteenth century, see Linebaugh and Rediker, *The Many-Headed Hydra*, chapter 6.

6. *A Genuine Narrative of the Intended Conspiracy*, 19.

7. Keith Thomas, *In Pursuit of Civility: Manners and Civilization in Early Modern England* (Waltham, MA: Brandeis University Press, 2018), 28, 50–52. For a contemporary manual, see Jonathan Swift, *A Proposal for Correcting, Improving and Ascertaining the English Tongue, etc.* (London, 1712).

8. Antigua, Council Minutes, Arbuthnot Report, TNA.

9. The location of Thomas Kerby's home is recorded in a petition he submitted to the Antigua Council in 1716. "Thomas Kerby, merchant, petitions that he owns lands . . . in St. John's Town, E. and W. 51 feet, and N. and S. 80 feet, bounded E. with the marketplace now being laid out, W. with the land and tenement of Richard Denbow, and other lands and houses of petitioner, bounded N. with Church Street, S. with Long Street, also a plot 83 feet E. and W." The plots were still owned by the Kerby family in 1788, as depicted by surveyor John Killian's map of St. John. Thomas Kerby, Petition, 13 March 1715/16, in Vere Langford Oliver, *The History of the Island of Antigua, One of the Leeward Caribbees in the West Indies, from the First Settlement in 1635 to the Present Time* (London: Mitchell and Hughes, 1894), 2:122; John Killian, "A Plan of the Town of St. John in the Island of Antigua," British Library.

10. Arbuthnot described Kerby's home as a front room, within which he held court, and a private back room. The best description of early eighteenth-century buildings in the Leeward Islands came from property holders in St. Christopher, neighboring island to Antigua, who submitted claims to the English government after the French attacked and burned property in 1706. Most merchant dwellings in early eighteen-century St. Kitts were built of timber in the "earthfast" style, referring to a house with posts in the ground. Earthfast homes were far more common in the Leeward Islands than the Jacobean stone-and-brick-style houses that survive in Barbados. I have described the "hall" of an "earthfast" timber home based on "the Hermitage," a contemporary dwelling house with front and back rooms that is still extant in Nevis. CO 243/2, f. 34, TNA, as quoted in Roger H. Leech, "Impermanent Architecture in the English Colonies of the Eastern Caribbean: New Contexts for Innovation in the Early Modern Atlantic World," *Perspectives in Vernacular Architecture* 10 (2005): 153–167.

11. In 1702, the assembly noted that the entire town of St. John consisted of timber buildings. "An Act for Regulating the Towns and Harbours Settling of Markets, and Encouraging the Wharfs of the Island," in *The Laws of the Island of Antigua, Consisting of the Acts of the Leeward Islands, Commencing 8th November 1690, Ending 21st April 1798; and the Acts of Antigua, Commencing 10th April 1668, Ending 7th May 1804* (London: Samuel, Bagster, Strand, 1805), 1:142.

12. Antigua, Council Minutes, Arbuthnot Report, TNA.

13. "An Act for Attaining Several Slaves Now Run Away from Their Master's Service, and for the Better Government of Slaves," in *Laws of the Island of Antigua,* 1:219: "That all Slaves triable by Virtue of this Act, shall be tried, adjudged, punished, and executed in like Manners as Slaves for other Crimes are tried and adjudged by the Laws and usages of this Island now in Force, and where condemned to Death, shall be appraised in like Manner; and if the two Justices before whom Negroes are tried cannot agree in their Judgement, then they may and shall immediately call a third Justice of the peace to their Assistance, and the case shall be determined by the Agreement of any two of them; and in all Trials of Slaves the Justice or Justices shall and may hear the Evidence of any other Slaves, and shall give such Credit thereto, as the Justice or Justices shall think it in Conscience deserves."

14. "An Act for the Better Government of Slaves, and Free Negreoes," in *Laws of the Island of Antigua,* 1:161: "And it is further enacted, by the Authority aforesaid, That on Complaint made to any Justice of any Crime done by any Slaves or Slaves, such Justice shall issue out his Warrant for apprehending the Offenders, and for all Evidences; if the said Justice find such Crime not Capital, he may appoint publick Correction of such Slave, according to Discretion, and award Satisfaction to the Parties injured, not exceeding six Pounds; but if the crime be heinous, or the Damage greater than six Pounds, then the said Justice shall commit the said Offender to Prison, or take Security, at his Discretion, and then appoint a Day for the Witness to appear, which Crime, Day, and Time such Justice is to certiy to the next Neighbouring Justice, who shall join with the aforesaid Justice at the Tiem and Day appointed, as aforesaid; which said two Justices (according to the Evidences that shall be given before them) shall give Sentence as the Crime deserveth, and the said Justices shall forthwith issue out their Warrant for executing the said Sentence, and such Justices, may, if they see fit, condemn any Slave to the Party injured, until the Owner pay such Damage, as shall be by them adjudged to be paid to any Person injured."

15. "An Act Against Deceitful, Excessive, and Disorderly Gaming," in *Laws of the Island of Antigua,* 1:210–214.

16. "An Act for Attaining Several Slaves Now Run Away," 1:227: "And the Constable, or upon any going to his Assistance, are hereby authorized and required, upon seeing any Number or Negroes assembled in a tumultuous Manner, or playing at Dice, or any Game, Play or Diversion, to make three Proclamations, requiring such Negroes to separate, and disperse, and to retire to their Homes, and, upon Contempt of the said Proclamation, or the Negroes not dispersing, may seize one or more of such Slaves, and carry him before a Magistrate, who shall order such Slave or Slaves to Gaol, and the same Slave or Slaves shall be whipped publickly by a Justice's Order, on any Day withing three Days after the Offence, with any Number of Stripes at the Justice's Discretion; but if the Constable or any in his Assistance shall apprehend it necessary, in Contempt and Disobedience of the Proclamation, he or they may fire upon, and kill any of the Slaves so contemning or disobeying, and not be liable to any Prosecution therefore, and any Slaves so killed shall pe paid for by the Publick, and the Value settled as in Case of killing a Runaway in Pursuit."

17. Antigua, Council Minutes, Arbuthnot Report, TNA.

18. Antigua, Council Minutes, Arbuthnot Report, TNA.

19. Justices of the Peace who neglected their duty to prosecute slaves accused of criminal acts were subject to a fine of twenty pounds. "An Act for the Better Government of Slaves, and Free Negreoes," 1:162: "And any Justice, who shall neglect his Duty herein enjoined, shall forfeit for each Time offending twenty Pounds; but in case more than one Slave be combined in a Crime, it is at the Discretion of such [Justices] to adjudge one to Death for Example's Sake, and save the Rest."

20. Antigua, Council Minutes, Arbuthnot Report, TNA; "An Act for Attaining Several Slaves Now Run Away," 1:222: "That if any Slave or Slaves shall be guilty of any enormous Crime, whereby the Life of any White Person shall be endangered, or

attempted, or any Dwelling-house or Out-house belonging to any White Person shall be burnt, or attempted to be burnt, that then in such Cases such Slave or Slaves, and all his accessories, Concealers, or Abettors (being Slaves), shall be adjudged, and are hereby made and declared felons, and shall suffer Death therefore; and if any other Slave shall know of any such Crime as last mentioned, intended to be done, and shall discover and give Notice thereof to any Justice of the Peace of this Island, such Justice shall cause the Slave or Slaves accused to be apprehended; and if he find Grounds of just Suspicion, then he shall commit the Slave or Slaves accused to the Common Gaol, and give Notice thereof immediately to the next Justice of the Peace, who shall take all proper Measures for bringing the Slaves accused to Trial, as in case of other Felonies."

21. Antigua, Council Minutes, Arbuthnot Report, TNA.

22. English legal precedents held conspiracy as an agreement among two or more people to commit a crime. In 1641, Massachusetts was the first English colony in the Americas to pass an act making conspiracy unlawful. Following the early example of Barbados, many British colonial legislatures created a legal category for slave conspiracies in the early eighteenth century, specifying punishments for Indians or Black slaves who plotted to escape or rebel. Virginia, for example, passed a law in 1723 that defined conspiracy as *six* or more slaves who "consult, advise, or conspire, to rebel or make insurrection, or . . . plot or conspire the murder of any person or persons." In practice, the British charged most slave conspirators with the old English crime of "petit treason," or an attempt by a servant to murder one's master or family. Because the colonial courts relied on interrogations and torture to produce confessions, historians have tried to create a definition of slave conspiracy that reflects the ambiguity of the actual existence of a plot. Thomas J. Davis closely follows the contemporary British definition of a slave conspiracy, defining it as a "completed crime; it is complete when two or more persons agree to do an illegal act or even to do a legal act by illegal means." Most recently, Jason Sharples defined the discovery of a conspiracy as the "creation of official knowledge about an alleged plan for insurrection." Hoffer, *The Great New York Conspiracy of 1741*, 24–25; "An Act for the Governing of Negroes," in Rawlin, *The Laws of Barbados*, 156; Gaspar, "With a Rod of Iron"; Nicholson, "Legal Borrowing and the Origins of Slave Law in the British Colonies," 52; "An Act Directing the Trial of Slaves," in Hening, *The Statutes at Large*, 4:126; Davis, "Conspiracy and Credibility," 168; Jason Sharples, "Discovering Slave Conspiracies: New Fears of Rebellion and Old Paradigms of Plotting in Seventeenth-Century Barbados," *American Historical Review* 120, no. 3 (June 2015): 811–843. The material in this and the next paragraph appeared originally in Justin Pope, "Inventing an Indian Slave Conspiracy on Nantucket, 1738," *Early American Studies* 15, no. 3 (Summer 2017): 510–12. *Early American Studies* (Summer 2017) Copyright © 2017. The McNeil Center for Early American Studies. All rights reserved.

23. For the colonists' fear of an oppressed population's hidden "transcripts," see Scott, *Domination and the Arts of Resistance*. For European colonial anxieties produced through the exploitation of Indians, see Inga Clendinnen, *Ambivalent Conquests: Maya and Spaniard in Yucatan, 1517–1570* (Cambridge: Cambridge University Press, 1987). On the master's anxieties produced through slavery, see Patterson, *Slavery and Social Death*, chapter 2; Maria Martinez, "The Black Blood of New Spain: Limpieza de

Sangre, Racial Violence, and Gendered Power in Early Colonial Mexico," *William and Mary Quarterly*, 3rd series, 61, no. 3 (July 2004): 479–520; and Jordan, *White over Black*, chapter 1.

24. For the necessary role of the informant in a conspiracy trial, see Scott, *Domination and the Arts of Resistance*, 134–151.

25. Slave conspiracy scares followed this distinctive pattern throughout the Americas from the early sixteenth century into the late nineteenth century. Bertram Wyatt-Brown noted the remarkable similarities between slave conspiracies in the United States South, but they unfolded in similar ways throughout the western hemisphere and began on the earliest plantations of New Spain and Brazil. For comparisons, see Ferrer, *Freedom's Mirror*; Sherwin K. Bryant, *Rivers of Gold, Lives of Bondage: Governing through Slavery in Colonial Quito* (Chapel Hill: University of North Carolina Press, 2014), chapter 4; Joao Jose Reis and Flavio dos Santos Gomes, "Repercussions of the Haitian Revolution in Brazil, 1791–1850," in *The World of the Haitian Revolution*, ed. David Patrick Geggus and Norman Fiering (Bloomington: Indiana University Press, 2009), 284–313; Michael Mullin, *Africa in America: Slave Acculturation and Resistance in the American South and the British Caribbean, 1736–1831* (Urbana: University of Illinois Press, 1992); Winthrop Jordan, *Tumult and Silence at Second Creek: An Inquiry into a Civil War Slave Conspiracy*, rev. ed. (1993; Baton Rouge: Louisiana State University Press1995); and Bertram Wyatt-Brown, *Southern Honor: Ethics and Behavior in the Old South* (New York: Oxford University Press, 1982), 406.

26. "Proceedings in an Investigation of an Insurrection of Negroes and Indians, Slaves, in Surry and Isle of Wight," 19 March 1709, Colonial Papers, folder 20, no. 11, Library of Virginia.

27. For slave conspiracy confessions as a product of the court, see Jason Sharples, "Hearing Whispers, Casting Shadows: Jailhouse Conversation and the Production of Knowledge during the Antigua Slave Conspiracy Investigation of 1736," in *Buried Lives: Incarcerated in Early America*, ed. Michele Lise Tarter and Richard J. Bell (Athens: University of Georgia Press, 2012), 35–59; Morgan, "Conspiracy Scares."

28. McIlwaine, *Executive Journals of the Council of Colonial Virginia*, 3:234–235, 242–243; Parent, *Foul Means*, 152–153.

29. Before the Antigua conspiracy of 1736, colonists relied on informants for the discovery of conspiracies in Nevis (1725), St. Christopher (1734), Antigua (1729, 1736), Bermuda (1730), and the Bahamas (1734). On the mainland, British officials relied on informants for the discovery of slave conspiracies in Virginia (1710, 1723), South Carolina (1730, 1736), East Jersey (1734), and Maryland (1738). For a list of these conspiracies in the Caribbean, see Craton, *Testing the Chains*, 335–339. For Bermuda, see Maxwell, "'The Horrid Villainy.'" For the mainland, see Aptheker, *American Negro Slave Revolts*, 168–187.

30. "The following to join Troop of Carbineers under Colonel Gunthorpe:—Robert Arbuthnot." Oliver, *The History of the Island of Antigua*, 1:52.

31. *Antigua and the Antiguans*, chapter 31, note 8.

32. Antigua, Council Minutes, Arbuthnot Report, TNA.

33. Antigua, Council Minutes, Arbuthnot Report, TNA.

34. Antigua, Council Minutes, Arbuthnot Report, TNA.
35. Antigua, Council Minutes, Arbuthnot Report, TNA.
36. Antigua, Council Minutes, Arbuthnot Report, TNA.
37. Antigua, Council Minutes, Arbuthnot Report, TNA.
38. Antigua, Council Minutes, Arbuthnot Report, TNA.
39. "An Act for Attaining Several Slaves Now Run Away," 1:226: "And whereas Slaves do frequently on Saturdays in the Afternoon, and Sundays, gather and assemble in great Numbers in an about the town of St. John's, and commit Riots, and sometimes kill one another, to the great Terror and actual endangering of the Inhabitants; be it therefore, and it is hereby enacted by the Authority aforesaid, That the Justices of the Peace residing in the said Town, or the most adjacent to it, shall be directed by the Commander in Chier, or in his Absence, by the Lieutenant General of these Islands, or, in his Absence, by the Lieutenant Governor of this Island, to nominate two Constables to go in two Companies, with a convenient Number, not less in all than in six of the Militia of the said Town, in each Company with the Constable (one of which to be an Officer) through the said Town of St. John's, and the Pastures adjacent, known by the Name of Otto's Pasture, and Long's, or Morgan's Pasture, to disperse Negroes got together in any Number exceeding ten."
40. Antigua, Council Minutes, Arbuthnot Report, TNA.
41. The Cross Road refers to Cross Street, on the eastern edge of eighteenth-century St. John's Town. Morgan's isolated location at the "upper end of town" suggests he lived close to the intersection of Newgate Street and Cross Street, perhaps on the High Road (today's Cemetery Road and Friar's Hill Road).
42. The Country Pond still exists today on the west side of Independence Avenue in the southeast corner of town.
43. Antigua, Council Minutes, Arbuthnot Report, TNA.
44. Antigua, Council Minutes, Arbuthnot Report, TNA.

Chapter Two: A Memory of Africa

1. Historians have interpreted Court's shield dance in several ways. Marion Johnson was the first to compare his Antigua dance to an ennobling ceremony witnessed by Willem Bosman on the Gold Coast in the 1690s. John Thornton drew a similar comparison in his analysis of the dance in his studies of the "Coromantee." More recently, Kwasi Konadu argues Court's dance may have been an Asante Odwira ceremony, though he notes evidence for the Odwira does not extend back to the seventeenth century. Still, the timing of the dance corresponds well with the yam harvests in September and October on the Gold Coast. The dance was probably syncretic, combining persons and symbols of state with an ennobling shield ceremony. Johnson, "Ekyem, the State Shield"; Thornton, "War, the State, and Religious Norms"; Thornton, "The Coromantees," 169–170; Kwasi Konadu, *The Akan Diaspora in the Americas* (New York: Oxford University Press, 2010), 136–137.
2. *A Genuine Narrative of the Intended Conspiracy*, 2–3; Konadu, *The Akan Diaspora*, 136–137.

3. Rucker, *Gold Coast Diasporas*, 153–155.

4. "Tryal of Quawcoo on Old Oby Man & Physician & Cormantine Belonging to Mr. William Hunt 11th December," 89, in Antigua, Council Minutes, "Tryals of Such Slaves as Are Marked Down for Banishment," 12 January 1736/37, CO 9/10, National Archives of the United Kingdom (hereafter TNA).

5. Antigua, Council Minutes, Arbuthnot Report, 8 January 1736/37, CO 9/10, TNA.

6. Court's age is based on the "General Report" in the Antigua Council Minutes, 24 January 1736/37, and appears to be a correction to the original. The commissioners' initial report stated that Court was thirty-five years old. This report was sent by William Mathew to the Board of Trade on 17 January 1736/37 and published in Ireland as *A Genuine Narrative of the Intended Conspiracy*. Thomas Kerby, Court's owner, was the official source for estimates of Court's age. David Barry Gaspar argues Court was probably forty-five years old based on Kerby's description of him as an "Elderly, Distemper'd Fellow." Antigua, Council Minutes, 24 January 1736/37, CO 9/10, TNA; William Mathew to Board of Trade, 17 January 1736/37, CO 152/22, TNA; *A Genuine Narrative of the Intended Conspiracy*, 4; Gaspar, *Bondmen and Rebels*, 320n14.

7. Antigua, Council Minutes, Arbuthnot Report, TNA.

8. *A Genuine Narrative of the Intended Conspiracy*, 3.

9. Thornton, *A Cultural History of the Atlantic World*, 74–75; Thornton, "The Coromantees"; Brown, *Tacky's Revolt*, 90; Rucker, *Gold Coast Diasporas*, 7; Konadu, *The Akan Diaspora*, 17.

10. The estimate of forty-eight polities is based on Jean Baptiste Bourguignon D'Anville's 1729 map of the Gold Coast. The map underestimates the number of polities because of the many towns that comprised the Fante Confederacy. "A Map of the Gold Coast, from Issini to Alampi by Jean Baptiste Bourguignon D'Anville," Rare Book Division, New York Public Library, New York Public Library Digital Collections, https://digitalcollections.nypl.org/items/510d47df-ffd3-a3d9-e040-e00a18064a99.

11. Albert Van Dantzig, "Willem Bosman's 'New and Accurate Description of the Coast of Guinea': How Accurate Is It?" *History in Africa* 1 (1974): 101.

12. In his mid-eighteenth-century interviews with enslaved Gold Coast men and women in the Danish Virgin Islands, C. G. A. Oldendorp related the distances of marches from the interior to the coast: "These prisoners who are seized in these wars by the Bombra are taken by them to the Amina who sell them as slaves to the Whites on the Gold Coast. It is said that these captured Kassenti are on the road for approximately half a year before they arrive at the Gold Coast from their homeland." Oldendorp, *History of the Mission of the Evangelical Brethren on the Caribbean Islands of St. Thomas, St. Croix, and St. John* (Ann Arbor, MI: Karoma, 1987), 164; Romer, *Reliable Account*, 28. For later in the eighteenth century, see Brown, *Tacky's Revolt*, 234.

13. Antigua, Council Minutes, Arbuthnot Report, TNA.

14. Marion Johnson first suggested Court's birthplace as Eguafo. Johnson, "Ekyem, the State Shield," 6–10; *A Genuine Narrative of the Intended Conspiracy*, 8; Kwasi Konadu, "Lost at Sea: Black Atlantic History Off Africa's Gold Coast," Kwasi.Konadu, 30 June 2017, https://kwasikonadu.info/blog/2017/6/30/lost-at-sea-black-atlantic-history-off-africas-gold-coast.

15. For honorific or title names in the Ghanaian language, see Kofi Agyekum, "The Sociolinguistic of Akan Personal Names," *Nordic Journal of African Studies* 15, no. 2 (2006): 206–235, 223 (quotations).

16. Bosman, *A New and Accurate Description*, 209.

17. Ghanaian scholar Kweku Darko Ankrah believes the name "Tecki" was originally prominent among mfantse speakers, later adopted broadly by Akan and Ga speakers. Ankrah, email to author and Rebecca Shumway, 12 December 2022; Robin Law, email to author, 12 December 2022.

18. Note that John Thornton, Walter C. Rucker, Justin James Pope, and Vincent Brown previously suggested that Tacky was a name associated with the Ga. This interpretation was based on the existence of a "Tacky" stool among the Ga in the nineteenth century. "Takyi" appears to have been a surname associated with the Fante and to have had a specific meaning long before the adoption of the Ga stool. Thornton, "The Coromantees," 169–170; Rucker, *Gold Coast Diasporas*, 173; Justin James Pope, "Dangerous Spirit of Liberty: Slave Rebellion, Conspiracy, and the First Great Awakening, 1729–1746" (Ph.D. diss., George Washington University, 2014), 41, 114; Brown, *Tacky's Revolt*, 90.

19. "The Tryal of Tilgarth Penezar Commonly Called Fargut a Crole Christian Slave Belonging to the Widow Roach," 73, in Antigua, Council Minutes, "Tryals of Such Slaves as Are Marked Down for Banishment."

20. Kea, *Settlements, Trade, and Polities*, 223; Robin Law, "The Komenda Wars, 1694–1700: A Revised Narrative," *History in Africa* 34 (2007): 139.

21. Bosman, *A New and Accurate Description*, 38.

22. Johnson, "Ekyem, the State Shield," 6–10. Kwasi Konadu notes the lack of mentions of Takyi in other European records; see Konadu, "Lost at Sea." The earliest known reference to a King Takyi's ruling Eguafo extends back to 1640. Kea, *Settlements, Trade, and Polities*, 13.

23. James H. Sweet, "Defying Social Death: The Multiple Configurations of African Slave Family in the Atlantic World," *William and Mary Quarterly*, 3rd series, 70, no. 2 (April 2013): 262.

24. While the Eguafo were Fante speakers, so were the villages of the Fante Confederacy to the east. Many Fante peoples maintain oral traditions of migration from "Takyimon" (modern-day Techiman), a kingdom founded by Takyi Firi, "the hunter." But in considering Court's birthplace in the confederacy, it should be noted that the Fante did not have kings (*ohene*) in the seventeenth century. As Maria Johnson observes, they were ruled by *braffo*, a role Takyi assigned to Gift at his shield ceremony. That the enslaved Twi/Fante translator interpreted Takyi as "king" suggests the name was closely associated with royalty in the mind of Court and the enslaved Antiguans. Shumway, *The Fante and the Transatlantic Slave Trade*, 28–32; Konadu, *Our Own Way in This Part of the World*; Johnson, "Ekyem, the State Shield," 6–10.

25. Bosman was stationed at Axim, sixty miles west of Little Komenda, in the early 1690s, Little Komenda and Elmina in the mid- to late 1690s, and the slave coast around 1699. While he specifically mentioned Axim as an example of government, it is not clear where he witnessed the shield ceremony. Dantzig, "Willem Bosman's 'New and Accurate Description,'" 103.

26. Court also was shipmates with a woman named Coobah, a Fante day name for a female born on Wednesday. "Tryal of Morgan's Newport, 9th November 1736," 56, in Antigua, Council Minutes, "Tryals of Such Slaves as Are Marked Down for Banishment." For references to the name "Quamina" in Komenda in 1694, see Robin Law, *The English in West Africa, 1685–1688: The Local Correspondence of the Royal African Company of England, 1681–1699,* 3 vols. (Oxford: Oxford University Press, 2001), 3:139, 141.

27. Law, *The English in West Africa,* 3:372.

28. Law, "The Komenda Wars," 133–168.

29. McCaskie, *State and Society in Pre-Colonial Asante,* 277–278; Spiers, "The Eguafo Kingdom," 4–5.

30. John Parker explains that ancient ones were treated differently by the Akan than maternal ancestors. One did not pray to ancient ones. Parker, *In My Time of Dying,* 18.

31. Romer, *Reliable Account,* 81. Bosman recounted a similar story of Ananse from his time on the Eguafo Coast in the 1690s. Bosman, *A New and Accurate Description,* 322.

32. Romer, *Reliable Account,* 81–82.

33. Romer, *Reliable Account,* 81–82.

34. J. K. Fynn, "The Political System of the Fante of Ghana during the Pre-Colonial Period," *Unwersitas* 9 (1987): 108.

35. Chouin, "Forests of Power," 273, 88.

36. Chouin, "Forests of Power," 2.

37. Spiers, "The Eguafo Kingdom," 93; Christopher R. Decourse and Samuel Spiers, "A Tale of Two Polities: Socio-Political Transformation on the Gold Coast in the Atlantic World," *Australasian Historical Archaeology* 27 (2009): 34.

38. Bosman, *A New and Accurate Description,* 156.

39. Christaller, *Dictionary of the Asante and Fante Language,* 423. For discussion of seventeenth-century Akan ideas concerning death, see Parker, *In My Time of Dying,* 40.

40. Decourse and Spiers, "A Tale of Two Polities," 32.

41. Hair, Jones, and Law, *Barbot on Guinea,* 349; Decourse and Spiers, "A Tale of Two Polities," 32.

42. Hair, Jones, and Law, *Barbot on Guinea,* 506. Twentieth-century Akan children also stayed with their mothers until about the age of eight years old. Jack Lord, "The History of Childhood in Colonial Ghana, c.1900–57" (Ph.D. diss., University of London, 2015), 34.

43. Hair, Jones, and Law, *Barbot on Guinea,* 505.

44. Kyei, *Our Days Dwindle,* 13; Lord, "The History of Childhood," 287.

45. Lord, "The History of Childhood," 33–34, 65–66.

46. Lord, "The History of Childhood," 14.

47. Willem Bosman noted the ceremonial practice of naming infants in his history of the Gold Coast, but the first specific reference to an "outdooring ceremony" that I have found is in Romer's history published in 1760. The practice of "outdooring" is still common among Akan and Ga peoples, as well as in northern Ghana. Bosman, *A New and Accurate Description,* 123; Romer, *Reliable Account,* appendix C, 264; Lord, "The History of Childhood," 33–34, 72.

48. *A Genuine Narrative of the Intended Conspiracy*, 3–4.

49. Lord, "The History of Childhood," 45, 52; Jane Guyer, "Wealth in People, Wealth in Things—Introduction," *Journal of African History* 36, no. 1 (1995): 84; Miller, *Way of Death*, 43.

50. Romer, *Reliable Account*, 114.

51. Lord, "The History of Childhood," 33; Romer, *Reliable Account*, 165; Paul Lovejoy, "The Children of Slavery—The Transatlantic Phase," *Slavery and Abolition* 27, no. 2 (2006): 197–217.

52. Hair, Jones, and Law, *Barbot on Guinea*, 511–512.

53. Decourse and Spiers, "A Tale of Two Polities," 32.

54. Lord, "The History of Childhood," 151, 157.

55. R. S. Rattray, "The African Child in Proverb, Folklore, and Fact," *Africa* 6, no. 4 (1933): 456–471.

56. I based my estimate on Gerard Chouin's conjecture concerning the boundaries of the seventeenth-century Eguafo kingdom. Chouin, "Forests of Power," 96.

57. Bosman, *A New and Accurate Description*, 135.

58. Bosman, *A New and Accurate Description*, 135–136.

59. Johanne Rask describes such a parade in detail in early eighteenth-century Accra on the Gold Coast: "Wherever any kabuseer [*caboceer*], and even the commoner, goes he has his dreng [boy] with him, who carries 2 stools; one for his master to sit on, and the other, as already described, when he wants to lie down and sleep. Whenever a prominent kabuseer comes in a lively procession he usually has a following of 20 to 40, even more, young men, some with guns and swords, others with lances and spears called hasagajer. One dreng, as noted above, with the stool; one with the tobacco pouch and pipes, which have very large heads and, stems at times 2, even 3 alen long. One has a bundle on his neck [comprising] his master's bed, made up of a tiger or buffalo skin, 3 or 4 small reed mats, and a couple of thin blankets." Rask, *Two Views from Christiansborg Castle*, 176.

60. Parker, *Making the Town*, 22.

61. Kea, *Settlements, Trade, and Polities*, 100–101.

62. Thornton, "The Demographic Effect of the Slave Trade on Western Africa"; Thornton, *Africa and Africans in the Making of the Atlantic World*, 72–73; Thornton, "War, the State, and Religious Norms," 185–187.

63. Kea, *Settlements, Trade, and Polities*, 97–104.

64. Bosman, *A New and Accurate Description*, 132, 133.

65. Bosman, *A New and Accurate Description*, 133.

66. Law, "The Komenda Wars," 139.

67. Bosman, *A New and Accurate Description*, 38.

68. Law, *The English in West Africa*, 2:270.

69. Law, "The Komenda Wars," 139.

70. Law, "The Komenda Wars," 138–139.

71. T. C. McCaskie, "Denkyira in the Making of Asante, c. 1660–1720," *Journal of African History* 48, no. 1 (2007): 1–25.

72. The English noted Eguafo's trade with Akanni merchant caravans at Little Komenda. Law, *The English in West Africa*, 2:226.

73. Bosman, *A New and Accurate Description*, 164.

74. "He is the master of a town, or Head of a clan, who in Military Affairs, acts as General, and in Civil as a Judge, making up all palavers, or deciding Controversies among the poorer Sort." Smith *A New Voyage to Guinea*, 116.

75. Kea, *Settlements, Trade, and Polities*, 100–101; Spiers, "The Eguafo Kingdom," 6; Rucker, *Gold Coast Diasporas*, 41–43.

76. Eguafo's relationship to coastal trade is well-examined through the archaeological excavations and research of Samuel Spiers. Spiers, "The Eguafo Kingdom," 55–56.

77. Law, "The Komenda Wars," 143–144.

78. Law, "The Komenda Wars," 145–146.

79. Law, "The Komenda Wars," 147.

80. Bosman, *A New and Accurate Description*, 32–33.

81. Law, "The Komenda Wars," 149.

82. Law, *The English in West Africa*, 3:380. See also Law, "The Komenda Wars," 150.

83. Law, "The Komenda Wars," 149–150.

84. Law, *The English in West Africa*, 3:365.

85. For references to the use of white clay, or *hyire*, in seventeenth- and eighteenth-century Gold Coast warfare, see Bosman, *A New and Accurate Description*, 157. For the use of white clay in sacred rituals of the Eguafo in 1922, see Spiers, "The Eguafo Kingdom," 82. For a discussion of the meaning of *hyire*, see Ama Mazama, "Clay," and Yaba Amgborale Blay, "Color Symbolism," in *Encyclopedia of African Religion*, edited by Molefi Kele Asante and Ama Mazama, 2 vols. (Thousand Oaks, CA: Sage, 2009), 1:171, 175.

86. Bosman, *A New and Accurate Description*, 18.

87. Bosman, *A New and Accurate Description*, 182, 33.

88. Law, "The Komenda Wars," 149–150.

Chapter Three: Passages into Slavery

1. Parker, *In My Time of Dying*, 43–44.

2. Kyei, *Our Days Dwindle*, 192–193.

3. Robin Law provides a historical narrative of these negotiations. Law, "The Komenda Wars, 1694–1700: A Revised Narrative," *History in Africa* 34 (2007): 163–164.

4. Bosman, *A New and Accurate Description*, 37.

5. Robin Law, *The English in West Africa, 1685–1688: The Local Correspondence of the Royal African Company of England, 1681–1699*, 3 vols. (Oxford: Oxford University Press, 2001), 3:1179.

6. Hair, Jones, and Law, *Barbot on Guinea*, 2:343.

7. Karl Marx, *The Karl Marx Library*, ed. Saul K. Padover, 7 vols. (New York: McGraw-Hill, 1972), 1:245.

8. Law, "The Komenda Wars," 164–165.

9. Bosman, *A New and Accurate Description*, 37, 38.

10. Law, "The Komenda Wars," 167.

11. T. C. McCaskie, "Denkyira in the Making of Asante, c. 1660–1720," *Journal of African History* 48, no. 1 (2007): 3.

12. Hair, Jones, and Law, *Barbot on Guinea*, 2:549.

13. *A Genuine Narrative of the Intended Conspiracy*, 2.

14. Christaller, *Dictionary of the Asante and Fante Language*, 234, 91; Patterson, *Slavery and Social Death*, 40.

15. Christaller, *Dictionary of the Asante and Fante Language*, 102, 54, 269.

16. Smallwood, *Saltwater Slavery*, 57, 60–61.

17. Hair, Jones, and Law, *Barbot on Guinea*, 2:549.

18. Spiers, "The Eguafo Kingdom," 258; Law, *The English in West Africa*, 3:460.

19. Hair, Jones, and Law, *Barbot on Guinea*, 2:549.

20. Kea, *Settlement, Trade, and Polities*, 31; Smallwood. *Saltwater Slavery*, 27.

21. Hair, Jones, and Law, *Barbot on Guinea*, 2:391–392.

22. Stephanie Smallwood write eloquently of the desperate conditions at Cape Coast Castle. Smallwood, *Saltwater Slavery*, 37–38.

23. Equiano, *Interesting Narrative*, 48–50.

24. Lovejoy, *Transformations in Slavery*, 48.

25. Slave Voyages: The Trans-Atlantic Slave Trade Database.

26. Eltis, *The Rise of African Slavery in the Americas*, 114; Thornton, *Africa and Africans in the Making of the Atlantic World*, 305–306.

27. Snelgrave, *A New Account of Guinea*, 1–2.

28. For slave price changes in Senegambia, see Curtin, *Economic Change in Pre-Colonial Africa*, 156–160. For the changing prices of European factors on the slave coast, see Law, *The Slave Coast of West Africa*, 168–179. For overall recognition of the price change, see Lovejoy, *Transformations in Slavery*, 52–53; Thornton, *Africa and Africans in the Making of the Atlantic World*, 119, 305; and Eltis, *The Rise of African Slavery in the Americas*, 296.

29. Donnan, *Documents Illustrative of the History of the Slave Trade*, 2:56.

30. Thornton, *Africa and Africans in the Making of the Atlantic World*, 74–75, 88–89.

31. Hair, Jones, and Law, *Barbot on Guinea*, 2:549.

32. Philip Curtin's study of the Senegambia slave trade in the mid-eighteenth century calculated that feeding a slave with millet for one year cost an African owner more than a quarter of the total price a European might pay on the coast, and during a time of famine the cost of feeding a slave doubled. Curtin, *Economic Change in Pre-Colonial Africa*, 169. See also Thornton, *African and Africans in the Making of the Atlantic World*, 120.

33. Miller, *Way of Death*, 130–131, passim.

34. Morgan, "The Cultural Implications of the Atlantic Slave Trade," 132.

35. Lovejoy, *Transformations in Slavery*, 114; Daaku, *Trade and Politics on the Gold Coast*, 31.

36. Kwasi Konadu suggests Court might have sailed on the *Fauconberg*. Konadu, *The Akan Diaspora in the Americas*, 139–140.

37. "Journal of the *Fauconberg*, 1699," Royal African Company: Committee of Shipping, T 70/134, National Archives of the United Kingdom (hereafter TNA).

38. Slave Voyages: The Trans-Atlantic Slave Trade Database.

39. "Journal of the *Fauconberg*, 1699."

40. "Tryal of Morgan's Newport, 9th November 1736," 56, in Antigua, Council Minutes, "Tryals of Such Slaves as Are Marked Down for Banishment," 12 January 1736/37, CO 9/10, TNA.

41. Slave Voyages: The Trans-Atlantic Slave Trade Database.

42. David Eltis, "Methodology: Coverage of the Slave Trade," Slave Voyages: The Trans-Atlantic Slave Trade Database.

43. Hayes, *The Importance of Effectually Supporting the Royal African Company,* B2.

44. The torchlight ceremony held by the South Sea Company is described briefly by both David Brion Davis and Hugh Thomas, but neither historian provides a citation for their evidence of the event. Davis, *The Problem of Slavery in Western Culture,* 131; Thomas, *The Slave Trade,* 236.

45. Postlethwayt, *The National and Private Advantages,* 1. The centrality of the slave trade to British commerce was widely promoted in the public prints of the era. For additional examples, see *The Case of the Royal African Company of England,* D5–D6, and Bennett, *Two Letters and Several Calculations,* passim.

46. In the *Oxford History of the British Empire,* for example, David Richardson's chapter on the history of the British slave trade placed little significance on the growth of the trade in the first half of the eighteenth century. He noted the greatest volume in slave trading took place in the late 1760s. Richardson, "The British Empire and the Atlantic Slave Trade," 442.

47. For the significance of slave imports into Virginia, see Kulikoff, "A 'Prolifick People.'" For South Carolina, see Wood, *Black Majority.*

48. K. G. Davies, The *Royal African Company* (New York: Longman, 1957), 312.

49. Rawley and Behrendt, *The Transatlantic Slave Trade,* 135.

50. Littleton, *The Groans of the Plantations,* 4–5.

51. Rawley and Behrendt, *The Transatlantic Slave Trade,* 140–141. For interlopers in the 1690s, see Davies, *Royal African Company,* 142–151.

52. Herbert Klein, "Slaves and Shipping in Eighteenth Century Virginia," *Journal of Interdisciplinary History* 5, no. 3 (Winter 1975): 384.

53. Wright, "William Byrd I and the Slave Trade," 379–380.

54. Taylor, *American Colonies,* 302.

55. Eltis, *The Rise of African Slavery in the Americas,* 115.

56. "Journal of the *Fauconberg,* 1699."

57. There were approximately thirty-six windmills in operation on Antigua in 1705. John Cherry and Miriam Rothenberg, "Costly Signaling and Windmill-Building: Inter-Island Technological Variability on Eighteenth-Century Sugar Estates in the Lesser Antilles," *International Journal of Historical Archaeology* 26 (2021): 762.

58. Harms, *The Diligent,* 317.

59. Marcus Rediker, *The Slave Ship: A Human History* (New York: Penguin, 2007), 274–276.

60. "Journal of the *Fauconberg,* 1699."

61. Smallwood, *Saltwater Slavery,* 160–161.

62. For this and the next paragraph, see "Journal of the *Fauconberg,* 1699."

63. Harms, *The Diligent*, 254.

64. "Journal of the *Fauconberg*, 1699."

65. The trial minutes record that Court visited Coobah because they were shipmates. "Tryal of Morgan's Newport, 9th November 1736," 56.

66. Harms, *The Diligent*, 333–334; Smallwood, *Saltwater Slavery*, 160–163.

67. "Journal of the *Fauconberg*, 1699."

68. Gaspar, *Bondmen and Rebels*, 73.

69. J. R. Ward, "The Profitability of Sugar Planting in the British West Indies, 1650–1834," *Economic History Review* 31, no. 2 (1978): 199n1.

70. "Journal of the *Fauconberg*, 1699."

71. Richard Ligon, *A True and Exact History of the Island of Barbadoes* (London, 1673), 46.

72. Smallwood, *Saltwater Slavery*, 159–161; Harms, *The Diligent*, 333–334.

73. Journal of the *Fauconberg*, 1699."

74. Ligon, *A True and Exact History*, 46.

75. Smallwood, *Saltwater Slavery*, 176.

76. Cherry and Rothenberg, "Costly Signaling and Windmill-Building," 762.

77. "Tryal of Morgan's Newport, 9th November 1736," 56.

78. William Mathew to the Board of Trade, 31 August 1734, CO 152/20, f. 146, TNA.

79. Sheridan, *Sugar and Slavery*, 242–243.

80. Brown, *Reaper's Garden*, 52.

81. Leslie, *A New and Exact Account of Jamaica*, 238.

82. Robertson, *A Detection of the State*, 42–43.

83. Sheridan, *Sugar and Slavery*, 244–248.

84. David Hume, "Of the Populousness of Ancient Nations (1752)," as quoted in Sheridan, *Sugar and Slavery*, 244.

85. Morgan, *Slave Counterpoint*, 561.

86. Snelgrave, *A New Account of Guinea*, 179.

87. Gibson, *Two Letters of the Lord Bishop*, 15–16; Alexander Garden to the Society for the Preservation of the Gospel, 6 May 1740, as quoted in Morgan, *Slave Counterpoint*, 457.

88. Berlin, *Many Thousands Gone*, 112–115.

89. Bluett, *Some Memoirs of the Life of Job*, 20.

90. Long, *The History of Jamaica*, 397–398.

Chapter Four: The Waiting Man

1. Antigua, Council Minutes, Arbuthnot Report, 8 January 1736/37, CO 9/10, National Archives of the United Kingdom (hereafter TNA).

2. Gaspar, *Bondmen and Rebels*, 31.

3. Antigua, Council Minutes, Arbuthnot Report, TNA.

4. British American colonies did not permit slaves a peculium, or legal property of their own, though many masters permitted slaves to earn money. Jonathan A. Bush, "Free to Enslave: The Foundations of Colonial American Slave Law," *Yale Journal of*

Law and the Humanities 5, no. 2 (1993): 428; Alan Watson, *Slave Law in the Americas* (Athens: University of Georgia Press, 1989), 72.

5. Antigua, Council Minutes, Arbuthnot Report, TNA.

6. British crowns were worth five shillings a piece. Pistoles, or Spanish gold coins, were worth about eighteen shillings a piece. John McCusker, *Money and Exchange in Europe and America, 1600–1775:A Handbook* (Chapel Hill: University of North Carolina Press, 1978), 11.

7. Antigua, Council Minutes, Arbuthnot Report, TNA.

8. Antigua, Council Minutes, Arbuthnot Report, TNA

9. Robert Delap Esq. was compensated for his 1736 work as deputy provost marshal in 1738. The only known Robert Delap on Antigua was baptized in St. John's Parish in January 1719. Vere Langford Oliver, *The History of the Island of Antigua, One of the Leeward Caribbees in the West Indies, from the First Settlement in 1635 to the Present Time* (London: Mitchell and Hughes, 1894), 1:196.

10. The material for this and the next four paragraphs comes from Antigua, Council Minutes, Arbuthnot Report, TNA.

11. *A Genuine Narrative of the Intended Conspiracy*, 4.

12. For the translation of Plato, see William G. Thalman, "Despotic Authority, Fear and Ideology of Slavery," in *Fear of Slaves—Fear of Enslavement in the Ancient Mediterranean*, ed. Anastasia Serghidou (Besançon, France: Presses Universitaires de Franche-Comté, 2007), 193.

13. Patterson, *Slavery and Social Death*, 35; Thalman, "Despotic Authority," 193–194.

14. *A Genuine Narrative of the Intended Conspiracy*, 17–18.

15. Morgan, *Slave Counterpoint*, 258–259.

16. Thomas Kerby wrote a report to the Antigua Council in 1724 as RAC agent: "Reasons Offered to Prove That It Is More for the Advantage of the Sugar Colonys to Have the Trade to That Coast of Africa for Slaves Managed by a Joint Stock under the Direction of an United Company Than by Separate Adventurers," Minutes of Council in Assembly, 23 December 1724, CO 9/5, TNA.

17. Many of Kerby's genealogical records are transcribed in Oliver, *History of the Island of Antigua*, 1:196.

18. "Deposition of Thomas Kerby," 24 May 1735, 1, Antigua Collection, Clements Library, University of Michigan, Ann Arbor.

19. "Thomas Kerby, Dept. Secretary & Clerk Council," in "Kirby, Thomas, [Certificate to the Effect That John Yeomans, Lieut. Governor of Antigua Has Received No Salary from the Council or Assembly of the Island]," 5 February 1704/5, box 7, William Blathwayt Papers, Huntington Library.

20. Oliver, *History of the Island of Antiqua*, 1:103. Kerby's grandson would marry a Byam.

21. I have not identified the parents of Jane Gamble nor George Gamble's children. Because so few Gambles lived on Antigua, they were very likely related. For Kerby's marriage, see Oliver, *History of the Island of Antiqua*, 2:122.

22. In 1736, Kerby told Arbuthnot that he had owned Court for "about 30 years," indicating he had purchased Court around 1706. The close timing of the wedding in

1705 makes it possible that Jane Gamble brought Court to Kerby as part of her dowery. Antigua, Council Minutes, Arbuthnot Report, TNA.

23. See, for example, the inventory of Jamaican Thomas Gregory in the late seventeenth century. Robert DuPlessis, *The Material Atlantic: Clothing, Commerce and Colonization in the Atlantic World, 1650–1800* (Cambridge: Cambridge University Press, 2016), 168–169.

24. DuPlessis, *The Material Atlantic*, 131.

25. Gaspar, *Bondmen and Rebels*, 231–232.

26. The slaves accused in the Antigua Conspiracy of 1736 were mostly Creoles and skilled artisans in St. John's. Gaspar, *Bondmen and Rebels*, 30–34, 231–233.

27. Bosman, *A New and Accurate Description*, 125–126, 158.

28. See Oliver, *History of the Island of Antiqua*, 2:120.

29. *A Genuine Narrative of the Intended Conspiracy*, A2–4.

30. Oliver, *History of the Island of Antiqua*, 1:lxxxi; George French, *The History of Col. Parke's Administration Whilst He Was Captain-General and Chief Governor of the Leeward Islands; with an Account of the Rebellion in Antegoa* (London, 1717), 53.

31. *Some Instances of the Oppression and Male Administration of Col. Parke, Late Governor of the Leeward Islands, with an Account of the Rise and Progress of the Insurrection at Antegoa, and Remarks on a Paper Intituled, Truth Brought to Light, or Murder Will Out* (London?, 1713), 2.

32. Thomas Morris to the Council of Trade and Plantations, 26 February 1710/11, in *Calendar of State Papers*, 25:683.

33. Thomas Morris to the Council of Trade and Plantations, 26 February 1710/11, in *Calendar of State Papers*, 25:683.

34. *Some Instances of the Oppression*, 2.

35. Thomas Morris to the Council of Trade and Plantations, 26 February 1710/11, in *Calendar of State Papers*, 25:683.

36. *Some Instances of the Oppression*, 2.

37. "Seven or eight soldiers." Thomas Morris to the Council of Trade and Plantations, 26 February 1710/11, in *Calendar of State Papers*, 25:683.

38. *Some Instances of the Oppression*, 2.

39. *Some Instances of the Oppression*, 2.

40. Thomas Morris to the Council of Trade and Plantations, 26 February 1710/11, in *Calendar of State Papers*, 25:683.

41. *Truth Brought to Light; or, Murder Will Out; Being a Short, but True, Account of the Most Horrid, Barbarous, and Bloody Murther and Rebellion Committed at Antego in the West Indies, against Her Majesty and Her Government. Designed to Show That the Murder Was the Result of a Conspiracy* (London, 1713), 3.

42. Oliver, *History of the Island of Antiqua*, 1:lxxiii.

43. Helen Hill Miller, *Colonel Parke of Virginia: The Greatest Hector in the Town: A Biography* (Chapel Hill, NC: Algonquin Books, 1989), 8–10.

44. Miller, *Colonel Parke of Virginia*, 44.

45. Steven Saunders Webb, *Marlborough's America* (New Haven, CT: Yale University Press, 2013), 67–68.

46. These battles are remarkably well narrated in Webb, *Marlborough's America*, 71.

47. Webb, *Marlborough's America*, 92.

48. Oliver, *History of the Island of Antiqua*, 1:lxxviii; French, *History of Col. Parke's Administration*, 91.

49. Oliver, *History of the Island of Antiqua*, 1:lxxvi; French, *History of Col. Parke's Administration*, 91, 99, 102.

50. Edward Perrie to Rowland and William Tryon, 6 November 1712, in *Calendar of State Papers*, 27:129.

51. French, *History of Col. Parke's Administration*, 101.

52. The articles, along with Parke's detailed attempts to refute them, are transcribed in French, *History of Col. Parke's Administration*, 90.

53. Lieutenant Governor and Council of Antigua to the Council of Trade and Plantations, 20 June 1709, in *Calendar of State Papers*, 24:589.

54. French, *History of Col. Parke's Administration*, 106.

55. French, *History of Col. Parke's Administration*, 37–38.

56. French, *History of Col. Parke's Administration*, 52.

57. *Truth Brought to Light*, 3.

58. Oliver, *History of the Island of Antiqua*, 2:122.

59. *Truth Brought to Light*, 3.

60. Webb, *Marlborough's America*, 282.

61. French, *History of Col. Parke's Administration*, 56.

62. *Truth Brought to Light*, 3.

63. French, *History of Col. Parke's Administration*, 57.

64. Thomas Morris to the Council of Trade and Plantations, 26 February 1710/11, in *Calendar of State Papers*, 25:683.

65. Thomas Morris to the Council of Trade and Plantations, 26 February 1710/11, in *Calendar of State Papers*, 25:683.

66. Webb, *Marlborough's America*, 283.

67. *Truth Brought to Light*, 4, 5; Thomas Morris to the Council of Trade and Plantations, 26 February 1710/11, in *Calendar of State Papers*, 25:683.

68. *Truth Brought to Light*, 5–6.

69. *Truth Brought to Light*, 5–6.

70. *Some Instances of the Oppression*, 3.

71. French, *History of Col. Parke's Administration*, 65.

72. Webb, *Marlborough's America*, 288.

73. Governor Robert Lowther to the Council of Trade and Plantations, 30 March 1713, in *Calendar of State Papers*, 27:306.

74. Governor Walter Douglas to the Council of Trade and Plantations, 1 November 1712, in *Calendar of State Papers*, 27:126.

75. Oliver, *History of the Island of Antiqua*, 2:122.

76. Sir William Young, *A Tour through the Several Islands of Barbados, St. Vincent, Antigua, Tobago, and Grenada in the Years 1791 and 1792* (London: John Stockdale, 1801), 248.

77. The quotations for the remainder of this section come from Antigua, Council Minutes, Arbuthnot Report, TNA.

Chapter Five: The Ambassador

1. William Gooch to the Board of Trade, 14 September 1730, CO 5/1322, 156, William Gooch, Official Correspondence, John D. Rockefeller Library.

2. *Evening Post*, 17 September 1730.

3. James Blair to the Bishop of London, 28 June 1729, Fulham Palace Papers (hereafter FPP)/15, 109, Virginia Colonial Records Project (hereafter VCRP), John D. Rockefeller Library.

4. James Blair to the Bishop of London, 20 July 1730, FPP/13, 131, VCRP.

5. *Evening Post*, 15 September 1730.

6. William Gooch to the Board of Trade, 23 July 1730, CO 5/1322, ff. 68–74, National Archives of the United Kingdom (hereafter TNA).

7. Gooch referred to the meetings in a September letter. He did not mention any meetings in his correspondence on 23 July, so I assume the many gatherings took place sometime in late July or August. William Gooch to the Board of Trade, 14 September 1730, CO 5/1322, 156, William Gooch, Official Correspondence.

8. William Gooch to the Board of Trade, 14 September 1730, CO 5/1322, 156, William Gooch, Official Correspondence.

9. William Gooch to the Bishop of London, 28 May 1731, FPP/15, 111, as cited in Parent, *Foul Means*, 161; James Blair to the Bishop of London, 20 July 1730, FPP/13, 131, VCRP.

10. William Gooch to the Board of Trade, 12 February 1730/31, CO 5/1322, ff. 161–163, William Gooch, Official Correspondence.

11. William Gooch to the Board of Trade, 12 February 1730/31, CO 5/1322, ff. 161–163, William Gooch, Official Correspondence.

12. Brickell, *The Natural History of North Carolina*, 357.

13. Parent, *Foul Means*, 159.

14. James Blair to the Bishop of London, Williamsburg, 14 May 1731, FPP/15, 110, VCRP.

15. I rely heavily on Charles Tillly and Lesley J. Wood's definition of a social movement in describing the actions of slaves in the Chesapeake Rebellion. Tilly and Wood, "Contentious Connections in Great Britain: 1828–1834," in *Social Movements and Networks: Relational Approaches to Collective Action*, ed. Mario Diani and Doug McAdam (Oxford: Oxford University Press, 2003), 147–148. For an excellent summary, see also Rudbeck, "Popular Sovereignty and the Historical Origin of the Social Movement."

16. Tilly and Wood, "Contentious Connections in Great Britain," 147–148.

17. Jens Rudbeck, "Popular Sovereignty and the Historical Origin of the Social Movement," *Theory and Society* 41, no. 6 (2012): 581–601.

18. *North Briton*, 16 July 1768.

19. Humphreys, *An Account of the Endeavours*, 3–5; An American Pastor, *Two Sermons*, iii–vi.

20. Benjamin Dennis to the Secretary, Goose Creek, 3 September 1711, Society for the Propagation of the Gospel Archives, 143, VCRP; Edmund Gibson *Two Letters of the Lord Bishop*, 22–26.

21. Gibson, *Two Letters of the Lord Bishop*, 22–26; Humphreys, *An Account of the Endeavours*, 3–5; An American Pastor, *Two Sermons*, iii–vi; Ingersoll, "'Release Us Out of This Cruell Bondegg.'"

22. Travis Glasson, "'Baptism Doth Not Bestow Freedom': Missionary Anglicanism, Slavery, and the Yorke-Talbot Opinion, 1701–30," *William and Mary Quarterly*, 3rd series, 67, no. 2 (April 2010): 280.

23. *Boston Gazette*, 7 September 1730.

24. *Pennsylvania Gazette*, 12 November 1730.

25. Wim Klooster has examined royal emancipation rumors across empires, noting that slaves looked to monarchs for protection and to dispense justice. Monarchial emancipation rumors were not ubiquitous in the British Empire in the seventeenth or eighteenth centuries, however, and the Chesapeake emancipation rumor was very specific to its time and place. It was the direct result of the controversy concerning slave baptism that erupted in the first quarter of the eighteenth century. Klooster, "Slave Revolts, Royal Justice, and a Ubiquitous Rumor in the Age of Revolutions," *William and Mary Quarterly*, 3rd series, 71, no. 3 (2014): 401–424.

26. *London Evening Post*, 15 September 1730.

27. Parent, *Foul Means*, 160.

28. William Gooch to the Board of Trade, 23 July 1730, CO 5/1322, ff. 68–74, TNA.

29. Brickell, *The Natural History of North Carolina*, 260–261.

30. William Gooch to the Board of Trade, 23 July 1730, CO 5/1322, ff. 68–74, TNA.

31. "List of All Ships and Vessels Belonging to Antigua Including the Number of Seamen Belonging to Each Respective Vessel Together with the Built and Burthen of Each of Them Commencing the Eight Day of August 1718 and Ending the Eighth May 1720," John Hamilton to the Board of Trade, 22 August 1720, encl. 62, CO 152/13, Q51, TNA. For Jamaica, see Edward Trelawny to the Lords of Admiralty, 21 December 1743, ADM 1/3817, TNA. For Bermuda, see "Answers to Queries," John Pitt to the Board of Trade, 25 May 1733, CO 37/12, TNA.

32. Byrd, *Histories of the Dividing Line*, 36.

33. For enslaved sailors, see "Answers to Queries."

34. Morgan, "Maritime Slavery," 316; Berkeley, *A Proposal for the Better Supplying of Churches*, 6–8.

35. *Virginia Gazette*, 17 December 1736.

36. Benjamin Franklin described the meetings beginning around Williamsburg, Virginia. *Pennsylvania Gazette*, 15 December 1730.

37. *Evening Post*, 15 September 1730.

38. Gooch to the Bishop of London, 28 May 1731, FPP/15, 111, VCRP.

39. *New York Gazette*, 18 March 1734.

40. *American Weekly Mercury*, 5 March 1734; McConville, *The King's Three Faces*, 177–178.

41. John Adams, *The Diary and Autobiography of John Adams*, vol. 2, *1771–1781*, ed. L. H. Butterfield (Cambridge, MA: Harvard University Press, 1961), 181–183.

42. Morgan, *Slave Counterpoint*, 61.
43. Morgan, *Slave Counterpoint*, 63, table 11.
44. Voyages: The Trans-Atlantic Slave Trade Database.
45. Kulikoff, *Tobacco and Slaves*, 330; Morgan, *Slave Counterpoint*, 41.
46. Gomez, *Exchanging Our Country Marks*, 175–176.
47. Gibson, *Two Letters of the Lord Bishop*, 15–16.
48. Robert Carter to Unknown, 1728, Robert Carter Letterbook, 1728–1750, Virginia Historical Society, as cited in Morgan, *Slave Counterpoint*, 459.
49. *Evening Post*, 17 September 1730.

Chapter Six: News of St. John

1. *New York Gazette*, 4 February 1734.
2. *New York Gazette*, 18 March 1734.
3. Wilks, "Akwamu," 48.
4. Romer, *Reliable Account*, 128–129.
5. Kea, "'When I Die, I Shall Return to My Own Land,'" 168–169.
6. Westergaard, *The Danish West Indies under Company Rule*, 130, 124–125.
7. Westergaard, *The Danish West Indies under Company Rule*, 168.
8. Pannet, *Report on the Execrable Conspiracy*, 12.
9. Sensbach, *Rebecca's Revival*, 3.
10. Pannet, *Report on the Execrable Conspiracy*, 12.
11. Westergaard, *The Danish West Indies under Company Rule*, 168–169.
12. Steele, *The English Atlantic*, 17.
13. Bolster, *Black Jacks*, 21.
14. The literature on slave unrest during the Age of Revolution is vast. See, for example, Dubois, *Avengers of the New World*; Davis, *The Problem of Slavery in the Age of Revolution*; and Berlin, *Slavery and Freedom in the Era of the American Revolution*. For a discussion of the influence of republican ideology in the wider Atlantic, see Scott, "The Common Wind," and for a contrarian view, Geggus, "Slavery, War, and Revolution in the Greater Caribbean."
15. William Stephens, "A Journal of the Proceedings in Georgia," in *The Colonial Records of the State of Georgia*, vol. 4, ed. Alan D. Candler (Atlanta, GA: Franklin Printing, 1906), 247–248.
16. Salley, *Journal of the Commons House of Assembly of South Carolina*, 1741–1742, 83.
17. For studies of Black mariners in this period, see Bolster, *Black Jacks*; Foy, "Ports of Slavery, Ports of Freedom"; and Scott, "The Common Wind."
18. Gaspar, *Bondmen and Rebels*, 110.
19. British authorities did not differentiate in these documents between free Black and slave mariners, making it difficult to determine the status of those people described simply as "negro." However, the very small numbers of free Black men in the Caribbean during the 1730s suggest that they would have been quite outnumbered by slave crews aboard most vessels. In Antigua in 1707, for example, there were only 18 free Blacks

in the colony as compared to a population of 12,892 slaves. Perhaps most telling, the fact that white authorities grouped both free and slave together as "negroes" reveals the shared racial status of these laborers. "List of All Ships and Vessels Belonging to Antigua Including the Number of Seamen Belonging to Each Respective Vessel Together with the Built and Burthen of Each of Them Commencing the Eight Day of August 1718 and Ending the Eighth May 1720," Walter Hamilton to the Board of Trade, 22 August 1720, encl. 62, CO 152/13, Q51, National Archives of the United Kingdom (hereafter TNA).

20. Edward Trelawny to the Lords of Admiralty, 21 December 1743, ADM 1/3817, TNA.

21. "Answers to Queries," John Pitt to the Board of Trade, 25 May 1733, CO 37/12, TNA.

22. Jarvis, "Maritime Masters and Seafaring Slaves in Bermuda," 593–594.

23. Morgan, "Maritime Slavery," 316.

24. See for example, two white and two Black sailors rescued from a Bermuda schooner off the coast of New York. *American Weekly Mercury*, 12 September 1734.

25. Steele, *The English Atlantic*, 34, 33.

26. Morgan, "Slave Sales in Colonial Charleston," 909.

27. Steele, *The English Atlantic*, 33–34.

28. Bolster, *Black Jacks*, 21–22.

29. Morgan, *Slave Counterpoint*, 337–338.

30. *South-Carolina Gazette*, 5 November 1737, as quoted in Morgan, *Slave Counterpoint*, 339.

31. Bolster, *Black Jacks*, 22.

32. Robert Pringle to Richard Partridge, Charles Town, 29 January 1742/43, in Pringle, *Letterbook*, 489. For slaves in North Carolina, see Celeski, *The Waterman's Song*.

33. Pringle to Partridge, Charles Town, 29 January 1742/43, in Pringle, *Letterbook*, 489.

34. Morgan, *Slave Counterpoint*, 339–340.

35. William Gooch to the Board of Trade, 23 July 1730, CO 5/1322, ff. 68–74, TNA.

36. Brickell, *The Natural History of North Carolina*, 260–261.

37. Byrd, *Histories of the Dividing Line*, 36.

38. "An Act for Amending the Staples of Tobacco," in Hening, *The Statutes at Large*, 4:247.

39. Bolster, *Black Jacks*, 24.

40. Foy, "Ports of Slavery, Ports of Freedom," 388.

41. Bolster, *Black Jacks*, 242n1.

42. *Boston Gazette*, 18 March 1734.

43. Bolster, *Black Jacks*, 32.

44. Antigua, Council Minutes, Arbuthnot Report, 8 January 1736/37, CO 9/10, TNA.

45. Council Minutes of Bermuda, 4 August 1741, *Bermuda Historical Quarterly* 27, no. 1 (Spring 1970): 2–3.

46. Council Minutes of Bermuda, 1 September 1741, *Bermuda Historical Quarterly* 27, no. 1 (Spring 1970): 3–4; Council Minutes of Bermuda, 6 April 1742, *Bermuda Historical Quarterly* 28, no. 2 (Summer 1971): 35–36.

47. Scott, "Sufferers in the Charleston Fire of 1740."

48. Lorenzo Johnston Greene mistakenly described this conviction for arson as taking place in Charlestown, Massachusetts, instead of Charles Town, South Carolina. Greene, *The Negro in Colonial New England*, 161–162; *Boston Gazette*, 5 October 1741.

49. Wood, *Black Majority*, 296–297.

50. Genovese, *From Rebellion to Revolution*, 24.

51. *Boston Weekly News-Letter*, 7 March 1734.

52. Antigua, Minutes of Council, 4 April 1734, CO 241/3, TNA.

53. William Mathew to the Board of Trade, 17 January 1736/37, CO 152/22, W88, TNA.

54. The affidavit of John Hanson was sent as an attachment to Mathew's letter and is available in the record. William Mathew to the Board of Trade, 17 January 1736/37, CO 152/22, W88, TNA.

55. William Mathew to the Board of Trade, 17 January 1736/37, CO 152/22, W88, TNA.

56. Robert Paquette, "Introduction," in Paquette and Engerman, *The Lesser Antilles in the Age of European Expansion*, 4–6.

57. James Knight, "The Natural, Moral, and Political History of Jamaica," 2:79, British Library.

58. Gaspar, *Bondmen and Rebels*, 183, 205, 201.

59. Petersen, Watters, and Nicholson, "Continuity and Syncretism in Afro-Caribbean Ceramics," 179–183.

60. "Answers to Queries."

61. Gaspar, *Bondmen and Rebels*, 110.

62. Governor Philip Gardelin to Vestindisk-Guinesk Kompagni (VGK), 1 January 1734, 99 Breve og Dokumenter for Vestindien, Danish National Archives.

63. Kea, "'When I Die, I Shall Return to My Own Land,'" 168–170, 176–179.

64. Pannet, *Report on the Execrable Conspiracy*, 13–14.

65. Pannet, *Report on the Execrable Conspiracy*, 17.

66. Pannet, *Report on the Execrable Conspiracy*, 18.

67. Westergaard, *The Danish West Indies under Company Rule*, 174–176.

68. *Weekly Rehearsal*, 21 January 1734.

69. Westergaard, *The Danish West Indies under Company Rule*, 174–175.

70. *Weekly Rehearsal*, 21 January 1734.

71. Kea, "'When I Die, I Shall Return to My Own Land,'" 159–161.

72. Genovese, *From Rebellion to Revolution*.

Chapter Seven: The Jamaican War

1. Sheridan, "Caribbean Plantation Society," 401.

2. "America and West Indies: December 1730, 24–31," in *Calendar of State Papers*, 37:410–424; Campbell, *The Maroons of Jamaica*, 101.

3. Patterson, "Slavery and Slave Revolts," 250.

4. Patterson, "Slavery and Slave Revolts," 253–254.

5. Long, *The History of Jamaica*, 345.

6. Dallas, *The History of the Maroons*, 1:82–87.

7. Robert Hunter to the Board of Trade, 12 March 1729/30, CO 137/18, S82, National Archives of the United Kingdom (hereafter TNA).

8. Robert Hunter to the Board of Trade, 12 March 1729/30, CO 137/18, S82, TNA.

9. Robert Hunter to the Board of Trade, 7 November 1730; Council of Trade and Plantations to the Duke of Newcastle, 29 September 1730, in *Calendar of State Papers*, 25:519, 457.

10. Campbell, *The Maroons of Jamaica*, 58–59, 66–67.

11. Swanton Report, 4 September 1733, in Robert Hunter to the Board of Trade, 8 September 1733, CO 137/20, TNA.

12. Carey, *The Maroon Story*, 285.

13. "America and West Indies: December 1730, 24–31."

14. Quoted in Campbell, *The Maroons of Jamaica*, 77.

15. Campbell, *The Maroons of Jamaica*, 45–46.

16. John Ayscough to the Board of Trade, 27 February 1735, CO 137/21, TNA.

17. Patterson, "Slavery and Slave Revolts," 269.

18. Patterson, "Slavery and Slave Revolts," 268–269; Campbell, *The Maroons of Jamaica*, 80–81.

19. Robert Hunter to the Duke of Newcastle, 1 June 1732, CO 137/20, TNA.

20. *New York Weekly Journal*, 20 January 1734.

21. "America and West Indies: December 1730, 24–31."

22. John Ayscough to the Board of Trade, 27 February 1735, CO 137/21, TNA.

23. John Gregory to the Board of Trade, 20 February 1734, CO 137/21, TNA, as quoted in Campbell, *The Maroons of Jamaica*, 80.

24. Patterson, "Slavery and Slave Revolts," 269.

25. "Examination of Sarra," 1 October 1733, CO 137/21, TNA.

26. Campbell, *The Maroons of Jamaica*, 80–81.

27. Patterson, "Slavery and Slave Revolts," 266.

28. Robert Hunter to the Board of Trade, 13 November 1731, CO 137/19, TNA.

29. Patterson, "Slavery and Slave Revolts," 261–262.

30. Patterson, "Slavery and Slave Revolts," 263n10.

31. Campbell, *The Maroons of Jamaica*, 82, 83.

32. Dallas, *The History of the Maroons*, 1:59–60.

33. Campbell, *The Maroons of Jamaica*, 135.

34. Long, *The History of Jamaica*, 348.

35. Long, *The History of Jamaica*, 348.

36. Assembly Minutes, 1 May 1742, in Jamaica, Assembly, *Journals of the Assembly of Jamaica*, 3:594.

37. Campbell, *The Maroons of Jamaica*, 148.

38. The newspaper reports did not name the location, but they do mention council member "Simon Clark," almost certainly Simon Clarke the baronet who was born and buried in St. Catherine Parish, Middlesex, Jamaica. The location in Middlesex also corresponds well with the story that the planter was in town playing cards and received a note from his wife warning of the conspiracy. Spanish Town was located in St. Catherine Parish and would have been quickly accessible with such a message. The slave informant Hector was said to be owned by Thomas Fuller, who appears in the acts of Jamaica applying for improvements for his property in St. John. For this reason, I assume the conspiracy took place in St. John. "13. An Act for . . . Repairing, the Road from Spring Garden . . . to Thomas Fuller's Plantation in Saint John, Anno 13—Georgio II, 1740," in *The Laws of Jamaica, 1681–1759* (St. Jago de la Vega, Jamaica: Alexander Aikman, 1802), 1:12, 290.

39. *Boston Evening Post*, 1 April 1745; *Pennsylvania Gazette*, 12 April 1745.

40. *American Weekly Mercury*, 21 January 1746.

41. *American Weekly Mercury*, 21 January 1746.

42. "Extract of a Private Letter from a Gentleman in Jamaica, Dated in St David's Parish, Nov. 18 1745," *American Weekly Mercury*, 21 January 1746.

43. "Extract of a Private Letter from a Gentleman in Jamaica, Dated in St David's Parish, Nov. 18 1745," *American Weekly Mercury*, 21 January 1746.

44. Hauser, *An Archaeology of Black Markets*, 72.

45. Long, *The History of Jamaica*, 348.

46. Hauser, *An Archaeology of Black Markets*, 72.

47. Hauser, *An Archaeology of Black Markets*, 44–46.

48. Campbell, *The Maroons of Jamaica*, 59–60.

49. "Sabbati, 28 die Martii," in Jamaica, Assembly, *Journals of the Assembly of Jamaica*, 2:707.

50. "Martis, 23 die Junii," in Jamaica, Assembly, *Journals of the Assembly of Jamaica*, 2:712.

51. "America and West Indies: December 1730, 24–31."

52. Campbell, *The Maroons of Jamaica*, 148.

53. This is my interpretation of Ian K. Steele's table of entries and clearances in 1687. Steele, *The English Atlantic*, 287.

54. Edward Trelawny to the Lords of Admiralty, 21 December 1743, ADM 1/3817, TNA; Foy, "Seeking Freedom in the Atlantic World," 54.

55. Campbell, *The Maroons of Jamaica*, 54.

56. I base this statement on Jack's descriptions of his interactions with the slaves Ben and Jamaica and many others. Given the willingness of his fellow white artisans to translate for Jack and because "they had a desire of being by when he was examined," it appears that Jack had a strong working relationship with his fellow coopers. By all accounts, he did a great deal of visiting and hosting of Black people who attended the well. Horsmanden, *Journal of the Proceedings*, 63–65.

57. Horsmanden, *Journal of the Proceedings*, 63.
58. Horsmanden, *Journal of the Proceedings*, 63.
59. Lepore, *New York Burning*, 110–111.
60. Horsmanden, *Journal of the Proceedings*, 63.
61. Lepore, *New York Burning*, 111.
62. Horsmanden, *Journal of the Proceedings*, 63.
63. Horsmanden, *Journal of the Proceedings*, 63–64.
64. Jill Lepore makes this astute point concerning the role of Jack in conveying news in Manhattan. Lepore, *New York Burning*, 148.
65. Horsmanden, *Journal of the Proceedings*, 63.
66. Koeppel, *Water for Gotham*, 26–27; Lepore, *New York Burning*, 135–136.
67. Lepore, *New York Burning*, 133–135. Charles Foy lists these slaves as participating in gathering tea water. Foy, "Ports of Slavery, Ports of Freedom," 96–98.
68. The count of conspirators mentioning tea water is my own. Lepore, *New York Burning*, 144.
69. Lepore, *New York Burning*, 142.
70. Horsmanden, *Journal of the Proceedings*, 62.
71. Daniel Horsmanden, "A List of Negroes Committed on Account of the Conspiracy," in Horsmanden, *Journal of the Proceedings*, 11–16.
72. *American Weekly Mercury*, 20–26 February 1744.
73. Jamaica Legislative Council Minutes, 21 December 1744, CO 140/31, TNA.
74. "An Act for the Banishment of Several Negroe Slaves Concern'd in the Late Conspiracy," 8 March 1728/29, CO 8/6, TNA; Council Minutes, 24 January 1728/29, CO 9/6, TNA; Council Minutes, 28 January 1728/29, CO 9/6, TNA; Council Minutes, 28 February 1728/29, CO 9/6, TNA; Gaspar, *Bondmen and Rebels*, 210.
75. Minutes of the Provincial Council, Pennsylvania, 12 December 1737, in *Minutes of the Provincial Council of Philadelphia*, 4:259.
76. *Pennsylvania Gazette*, 26 February 1745. The story was first printed in Philadelphia's *American Weekly Mercury*, 20 February 1745, and then in the *Boston Evening Post*, 4 March 1745.
77. The term "twice condemned" is taken from Schwarz, *Twice Condemned*.

Chapter Eight: Organizing the Islands

1. The narrative of this section all comes from Antigua, Council Minutes, Arbuthnot Report, 8 January 1736/37, CO 9/10, National Archives of the United Kingdom (hereafter TNA).
2. "Trial of Quawcoo, an Old Coromantee, Belonging to Mr. John Pare, Dec. 9th, 1736," in Antigua, Council Minutes, "Tryals of Such Slaves as Are Marked Down for Banishment," 12 January 1736/37, CO 9/10, TNA.
3. *A Genuine Narrative of the Intended Conspiracy*, 5.
4. Zacek, *Settler Society in the English Leeward Islands*, 213.
5. Samuel Martin, *An Essay upon Plantership* (London, 1765), ix.
6. Rhys Isaac, *The Transformation of Virginia* (Chapel Hill: University of North Carolina Press, 1982), 113.

7. Isaac, *The Transformation of Virginia*, 111.

8. "The Tryal of Tilgarth Penezar Commonly Called Fargut a Crole Christian Slave belonging to the Widow Roach," 73, in Antigua, Council Minutes, "Tryals of Such Slaves as Are Marked Down for Banishment."

9. The material in this next section comes from "Tryal of Tom Hanson's Quashee, his Mother a Cormantee 24th November," 67, in Antigua, Council Minutes, "Tryals of Such Slaves as Are Marked Down for Banishment."

10. "The Tryal of Tilgarth Penezar Commonly Called Fargut," 73.

11. Here and below, Jemmy is quoted in "The Tryal of Tilgarth Penezar Commonly Called Fargut," 73.

12. Jemmy quoted Tomboy in his testimony. "The Tryal of Tilgarth Penezar Commonly Called Fargut," 73.

13. Treblin acted as a witness against Fargut in the trial. "The Tryal of Tilgarth Penezar Commonly Called Fargut," 73.

14. "The Examination of Emanuel, a Portuguese Negro Slave Belonging to Mr. Edward Gregory a Cooper in the Town of St John's Taken on Tuesday the 12th of October 1736," in Antigua, Council Minutes, Arbuthnot Report, TNA.

15. For the quotations in the remainder of this section, see Antigua, Council Minutes, Arbuthnot Report, TNA.

16. Kofi Agyekum, "The Sociolinguistic of Akan Personal Names," *Nordic Journal of African Studies* 15, no. 2 (2006): 214; Joseph Farquharson, *The African Lexis in Jamaican: Its Linguistic and Sociohistorical Significance* (Mona, Jamaica: University of the West Indies, 2012), 24–25.

17. "Tryal of Morgan's Newport, 9th November 1736," 56, in Antigua, Council Minutes, "Tryals of Such Slaves as Are Marked Down for Banishment."

18. Smallwood, *Saltwater Slavery*, 196.

19. Tryal of Mr. Langford's Robin a Coromantee the 13th of November," 57, in Antigua, Council Minutes, "Tryals of Such Slaves as Are Marked Down for Banishment."

20. "Tryal of Quawcoo an Old Oby Man and Physician and Cormantine Belonging to Mr. William Hunt 11th December," 89, in Antigua, Council Minutes, "Tryals of Such Slaves as Are Marked Down for Banishment."

21. The location of Hunt's estate is indicated in Robert Baker, "A New and Exact Map of the Island of Antigua in America According to an Actual and Accurate Survey Made in the Years 1746, 1747 and 1748" (London, 1749).

22. "Tryal of Quawcoo an Old Oby Man," 89.

23. For this section, see Antigua, Council Minutes, Arbuthnot Report, TNA.

Chapter Nine: Trials

1. For the location of Governor Mathew's plantation, see Robert Baker, "A New and Exact Map of the Island of Antigua in America," 1749, John Carter Brown Library, Providence, Rhode Island. For slaves executed on 15 March 1736/37, see "A List of the Names of Negroes That Were Executed for the Late Conspiracy, Their Trades, To Whom They Belonged, the Day and Manner of their Respective Execution," in Mathew to the Board of Trade, 26 May 1737, CO 152/53, X7, and Mathew to the

Board of Trade, 17 January 1736/37, CO 152/22, W88, National Archives of the United Kingdom (hereafter TNA).

2. *A Genuine Narrative of the Intended Conspiracy*, 11.

3. Gaspar, *Bondmen and Rebels*, 21–22.

4. Martyn, *An Impartial Inquiry in the State and Utility of Colony of Georgia*, 38.

5. *Boston Evening Post*, 1 April 1745.

6. Gaspar, *Bondmen and Rebels*, 21–22, 34–36.

7. Hoffer, *The Great New York Conspiracy of 1741*, 78.

8. Horsmanden, *Journal of the Proceedings*, appendix; Lepore, *New York Burning*, xii.

9. "An Act for the Governing of Negroes," in Rawlin, *The Laws of Barbados*, 156.

10. This quote is taken from Peter Charles Hoffer. Hoffer, *The Great New York Conspiracy of 1741*, 24. I was not able to locate the text of the 1661 law as it was replaced with the new "Act for the Governing of Negroes" in 1688 and so not included in Rawlin's *Laws of Barbados* (1699). My reading of the 1688 law does not make this definition as clear as Hoffer implies. The law equates conspiracy with insurrection and sets out special martial laws for either crime. Conspiracy of slaves is not specifically defined within the 1688 act. For a discussion of the implications of the Barbados slave code on slave conspiracy, see Hoffer, *The Great New York Conspiracy of 1741*, 24–25.

11. Gaspar, "With a Rod of Iron"; Nicholson, "Legal Borrowing and the Origins of Slave Law in the British Colonies," 52; Hoffer, *The Great New York Conspiracy of 1741*, 18, 24.

12. Hoffer, *The Great New York Conspiracy of 1741*, 24–25.

13. "An Act Directing the Trial of Slaves, Committing Capital Crimes; and for the More Effectual Punishing Conspiracies and Insurrections of Them; and for the Better Government of Negros, Mulattos, and Indians, Bond or Free," in Hening, *The Statutes at Large*, 4:126; Schwarz, *Twice Condemned*, 88; Parent, *Foul Means*, 129.

14. "An Act for the Governing of Negroes," 162.

15. Jerome Handler and Hilary Beckles described the conspiracies as intended insurrections. Handler, "Slave Revolts and Conspiracies," 23; Beckles, *Black Rebellion*, 44–46.

16. Beckles, *Black Rebellion*, 44.

17. Handler, "Slave Revolts and Conspiracies," 24–25.

18. Handler, "Slave Revolts and Conspiracies," 23–24.

19. Colden, *Letters and Papers*, 3:272–273.

20. "An Act for the Governing of Negroes," 160–161.

21. In Virginia, freeholder's courts were referred to as courts of oyer and terminer for slaves. They were enacted in 1692 as part of the "Act for the More Speedy Prosecution of Slaves Committing Capital Crimes," in Hening, *The Statutes at Large*, 2:270, 481–482, as quoted in Schwarz, *Twice Condemned*, 17.

22. For Pennsylvania, see Eastman, *Courts and Lawyers of Pennsylvania*, 173–175. For the creation of freeholder's courts in New York and New Jersey, see Hoffer, *The Great New York Conspiracy of 1741*, 18, 25.

23. Maryland did allow a version of the freeholder system by permitting a magistrate or any justice of the peace to give a slave forty lashes for theft or burglary. "A

Supplementary Act to the Act Relating to Servants and Slaves," in Browne et al., *Archives of Maryland*, 75:18–20. This series is ongoing and available online at http://archive sofmaryland.net.

24. "An Act for the Governing of Negroes," 160–161.

25. "Act for the More Speedy Prosecution of Slaves Committing Capital Crimes," in Hening, *The Statutes at Large*, 2:270, 481–482, as quoted in Schwarz, *Twice Condemned*, 17.

26. Schwarz, *Twice Condemned*, 48–49, 45–46.

27. I am making this assumption because no trial record exists in either case. The minutes of the South Carolina Common Council and the South Carolina Assembly do not show the creation of any special committees.

28. *A Genuine Narrative of the Intended Conspiracy*, 19–20.

29. Sharples, "The Flames of Insurrection," 265–267.

30. Antigua, Assembly Minutes, 5 July 1735, CO 9/9, TNA.

31. Antigua, Council Minutes, Arbuthnot Report, 8 January 1736/37, CO 9/10, TNA.

32. *Virginia Gazette*, 15 January 1737; Gaspar, *Bondmen and Rebels*, 22–23.

33. Gaspar, *Bondmen and Rebels*, 29–37.

34. *A Genuine Narrative of the Intended Conspiracy*, 13.

Chapter Ten: The Diaspora Imagined

1. *American Weekly Mercury*, 20 February 1744/45.

2. Jamaica, Council Minutes, 21 December 1744, CO 140/31, National Archives of the United Kingdom (hereafter TNA).

3. Hector renamed himself Thomas Edwards. "Petition of Thomas Edwards, Late Slave to Thomas Fuller Esquire of Jamaica," 1744, f. 92, CO 137/48, TNA.

4. The period began with the escalation of the first Jamaican Maroon War and the Antigua Conspiracy in 1729. Virginia authorities also mounted an attempt to destroy Maroons in the Blue Mountains in the same year. I have ended the era with the debunked slave conspiracies in New York and South Carolina between 1747 and 1748.

5. I have found slave testimony concerning conspiracy plots too problematic to trust. For the debate of the use of conspiracy trials as evidence, see Johnson, "Denmark Vesey and His Co-Conspirators." The New York City slave conspiracy has consistently been viewed as a kind of judicial farce by scholars. See "Preface to the Second Edition," in Daniel Horsmanden, *The New York Conspiracy* (New York: Southwick and Pelsue, 1810), and, more recently, Plaag, "'Greater Guilt Than Theirs'"; Hoffer, *The Great New York Conspiracy of 1741*; Zabin, *The New York Conspiracy Trials of 1741*, 1–33; and Lepore, *New York Burning*. John Thornton has also described the Antigua Conspiracy as a product of planter fear. Thornton, "The Coromantees."

6. Many scholars have commented on the extensive number of conspiracies and insurrections in this era. See, for example, Davis, *The Problem of Slavery in Western Culture*, 138–139, and Aptheker, *American Negro Slave Revolts*, 196. For unrest in the West Indies, see Gaspar, "A Dangerous Spirit of Liberty." The most well-known discussion of this era is Linebaugh and Rediker, *The Many-Headed Hydra*, 193.

7. Thomas Prince, *A Sermon Delivered at the South Church in Boston* (Boston, 1746), 5–6, 12.

8. *An Impartial Representation of the Conduct of the Several Powers of Europe Engaged in the Late War*, 4 vols. (London, 1749), 1:47–65.

9. Postlethwayt, *The National and Private Advantages*, 1.

10. James Glen to the Board of Trade, 26 August 1754, as quoted in Darold D. Wax, "'The Great Risque We Run': The Aftermath of Slave Rebellion at Stono, South Carolina, 1739–1745," *Journal of Negro History* 67, no. 2 (Summer 1982): 144.

11. Aptheker, *American Negro Slave Revolts*, 196.

12. Trevor Burnard, *Mastery, Tyranny and Desire: Thomas Thistlewood and His Slaves in the Anglo-Jamaican World* (Chapel Hill: University of North Carolina Press, 2004), 170–172.

13. Westergaard, "Account of the Negro Rebellion on St. Croix."

14. Sylvia R. Frey and Betty Wood, *Come Shouting to Zion: African American Protestantism in the American South and British Caribbean to 1830* (Chapel Hill: University of North Carolina Press, 1998), 80–117; Sensbach, *Rebecca's Revival*.

15. McConville, *The King's Three Faces*, 176–178.

16. Landers, *Black Society in Spanish Florida*, 39–46.

17. Edward Kimber, *A Relation; or, Journal, of a Late Expedition* (London, 1744), 30.

18. Landers, *Black Society in Spanish Florida*, 46.

19. Cadwallader Colden to Alice Colden, New York, 18 April 1747, in Colden, *Letters and Papers*, 3:345.

20. Jordan, *White over Black*, 122; Morgan and Terry, "Slavery in Microcosm," 142–143.

21. Antigua, Council Minutes, 31 January 1736/37, CO 9/10, TNA.

22. The reference to *Fog's Weekly Journal*, 26 February 1736/37, was made in the rebuttal to *Gentleman's Magazine*, 1 March 1737, 187–188.

23. Horsmanden, *Journal of the Proceedings*, 200.

24. John Ury, "The Dying Speech of John Ury, Who Was Executed the 29th of August, 1741" (Philadelphia, 1741).

25. Josiah Cotton, Memoirs, 8 January 1741/42, Massachusetts Historical Society.

26. Lepore, *New York Burning*, 212–213.

27. The Jamaican assembly warned the governor of the island of a "General Rebellion" of slaves in 1734. "America and West Indies: March 1734, 1–15," in *Calendar of State Papers*, 41:45–55.

28. Prince, *A Sermon Delivered at the South Church*, 12.

29. James Glen to the Board of Trade, 3 February 1748, CO 5/372, TNA.

30. William Smith, "Continuation of the History of New York," in *Collections of the New York Historical Society* (New York: New-York Historical Society, 1826), 4:60–61.

31. David Grim, "A Plan of the City and Environs of New York as They Were in the Years 1742, 1743, & 1744" (New York: New-York Historical Society Library, 1813).

32. Lepore, *New York Burning*, 2.

33. I. N. Phelps Stokes, *The Iconography of Manhattan Island, 1498–1909* (New York: Arno Press, 1967), 270–271.

34. Paul Gilroy, *The Black Atlantic: Modernity and Double Consciousness* (Cambridge, MA: Harvard University Press, 1993), 4, 15–16, 1, 30, 114–127.

35. Berlin, *Many Thousands Gone*, 97, 102, especially 107.

BIBLIOGRAPHY

Manuscript Collections

Bermuda Archives (Hamilton)

Book of Assizes, 1726–1735.

British Library (London)

"Copy of Correspondence of Archibald Hutcheson, of the Middle Temple, with William Mathews, Governor of the Leeward Islands, and Others, Relative to the Claims of Robert Cunningham upon Property Bequeathed to Him in Montserrat and St. Christopher's." 28 September 1733–22 May 1734.

Killian, John. "A Plan of the Town of St. John in the Island of Antigua." London, 1788.

Knight, James. "The Natural, Moral, and Political History of Jamaica, and the Territories Thereon Depending, in America, from the First Discovery of the Island by Christopher Columbus to the Year 1746. By a Gentle-Man, Who Resided Above 20 Years in Jamaica." 2 vols.

Danish National Archives (Copenhagen)

99 Breve og Dokumenter for Vestindien.

George Historical Society (Savannah)

Hamilton, Marmaduke, and D. B. Floyd Papers.

Historical Society of Pennsylvania (Philadelphia)

Board of Trade Papers. The Proprietaries, 1697–1776, volume 14, 1737–1740.

Logan, James. Letter Books. 1734–1748.

Huntington Library (San Marino, CA)

Blathwayt, William. Papers.

John D. Rockefeller Library,
Colonial Williamsburg Foundation (Williamsburg, Virginia)

Gooch, William. Official Correspondence (transcripts).

Virginia Colonial Records Project. Fulham Papers. Papers of the Bishops of London, 1–40. Colonial 13, volume 13, General Correspondence.

Massachusetts Historical Society (Boston)

Cotton, Josiah. Memoirs. 1726–1756.
Hall, David. Diaries. 1740–1789.
Letters Written to Hugh Hall. 1719–1765.
Notes on Sermons Delivered at Boston's Old South Church. 1738–1740.

Maryland Historical Society (Baltimore)

Bordley, Stephen. Letter Books. 1727–1759.

Maryland State Archives (Annapolis)

Governor and Council Records. Commission Record. 1726–1826.
Prerogative Court. Wills.
Prince George's County. Accounts.
Prince George's County. Wills.
Prince George's County Court. Land Records.
Prince George's County Court Records.

Nantucket Historical Society (Nantucket, Massachusetts)

"Personal Reminiscences of Mrs. Eliza W. Mitchell." 1895.

National Archives of the United Kingdom (Kew, England)

Admiralty Papers.

ADM 1/3817. Admiralty. Jamaica. Letters from Governors of Plantations, Colonies, and Channel Islands. 1 January 1728–31 December 1745.

Antigua

CO 8/6. Colonial Office and Predecessors: Antigua, Acts. Antigua, Acts. 1728–1737.
CO 8/8. Colonial Office and Predecessors: Antigua, Acts. Antigua, Acts. 1 January 1740–31 December 1742.
CO 9/5. Colonial Office and Predecessors: Antigua, Sessional Papers. Antigua, Sessional Papers. Council; Assembly; Council in Assembly. 1722–1724.
CO 9/6. Colonial Office and Predecessors: Antigua, Sessional Papers. Council; Assembly; Council in Assembly. 1 January 1726–31 December 1729.
CO 9/9. Colonial Office and Predecessors: Antigua, Sessional Papers. Council; Assembly; Council in Assembly. 1 January 1735–31 December 1736.
CO 9/10. Colonial Office and Predecessors: Antigua, Sessional Papers. Council. 1 January 1736–31 December 1737.
CO 9/11. Colonial Office and Predecessors: Antigua, Sessional Papers. Council. 1 January 1737–31 December 1738.

Bahamas

CO 23/3. Colonial Office and Predecessors: Bahamas, Original Correspondence. Correspondence, Original—Board of Trade. B. Nos. 90–158. 1 January 1731–31 December 1737.

CO 23/14. Colonial Office and Predecessors: Bahamas, Original Correspondence. Correspondence, Original—Secretary of State. Despatches. Letters from Phenney, Fitzwilliam, and Tinker. 1 January 1728–31 December 1746.

CO 26/2A. Colonial Office and Predecessors: Bahamas, Sessional Papers. Council. Assembly. Council in Assembly. 1 January 1729–31 December 1738.

Bermuda

CO 37/12. Colonial Office and Predecessors: Bermuda, Original Correspondence. Correspondence, Original—Board of Trade. L. Nos. 51–113. 1 January 1727–31 December 1737.

HM Treasury

T 70/134. Company of Royal Adventurers of England Trading with Africa and Successors, Records. Minutes Books. Royal African Company: Committee of Shipping. 1715–1718.

Jamaica

CO 137/18. Colonial Office and Predecessors: Jamaica, Original Correspondence. Correspondence, Original—Board of Trade. S. Nos. 51–108. 1 January 1729–31 December 1730.

CO 137/19. Colonial Office and Predecessors: Jamaica, Original Correspondence. Correspondence, Original—Board of Trade. S. Nos. 109–154. 1 January 1730–31 December 1732.

CO 137/20. Colonial Office and Predecessors: Jamaica, Original Correspondence. Correspondence, Original—Board of Trade. S. Nos. 155–231. 1 January 1732–31 December 1733.

CO 137/21. Colonial Office and Predecessors: Jamaica, Original Correspondence. Correspondence, Original—Board of Trade. T. 1 January 1733–31 December 1735.

CO 137/47. Colonial Office and Predecessors: Jamaica, Original Correspondence. Correspondence, Original—Secretary of State. 1 January 1729–31 December 1734.

CO 140/31. Colonial Office and Predecessors: Jamaica, Sessional Papers. Council; Council in Assembly, Council. 1742–1746.

Leeward Islands

CO 152/13. Colonial Office and Predecessors: Leeward Islands, Original Correspondence. Correspondence, Original—Board of Trade. Q. 1 January 1719–31 December 1720.

CO 152/20. Colonial Office and Predecessors: Leeward Islands, Original Correspondence. Correspondence, Original—Board of Trade. V. No. 1–51. 1733–1734.

CO 152/22. Colonial Office and Predecessors: Leeward Islands, Original Correspondence. Correspondence, Original—Board of Trade. W. 1 January 1735–31 December 1737.

CO 155/1. Colonial Office and Predecessors: Leeward Islands, Sessional Papers. Council; Assembly, Council in Assembly. 1680–1695.

CO 241/3. Colonial Office and Predecessors: St. Christopher (St. Kitts), Nevis and Anguilla, Sessional Papers. Council; Assembly; Council in Assembly. 1729–1737.

South Carolina

CO 5/388. Board of Trade and Secretaries of State: America and West Indies, Original Correspondence. Carolina, South. Correspondence, Original—Secretary of State. 1 January 1730–31 December 1746.

Virginia

CO 5/1322. Board of Trade and Secretaries of State: America and West Indies, Original Correspondence. Virginia. Correspondence, Original—Board of Trade. R. Nos. 119–178. 1 January 1729–31 December 1732.

Library of Virginia (Richmond)

Colonial Papers.

Virginia Historical Society (Richmond)

Virginia House of Burgesses, Committee of Propositions and Grievances. Papers. 1711–1730.

William L. Clements Library, University of Michigan (Ann Arbor)

Antigua Collection. "Depositions of Thomas Kerby, about the Secretary's Office." 1735.

Historical Periodicals

Colonial Newspapers

American Weekly Mercury (Philadelphia)
Boston Evening Post
Boston Gazette
Boston Post Boy
Boston Weekly News-Letter
New England Weekly Journal (Boston)
New York Gazette (New York City)
New York Weekly Journal (New York City)
Pennsylvania Gazette (Philadelphia)
South-Carolina Gazette (Charles Town)
Virginia Gazette (Richmond)
Weekly Jamaica Courant (Kingston)
Weekly Rehearsal (Boston)

<b>Periodicals from the British Isles</b>
British Journal (London)
British Mercury (London)
Common Sense; or, The Englishman's Journal (London)
Daily Courant (London)
Daily Journal (London)
Echo; or, Edinburgh Weekly Journal
Evening Post (London)

Flying Post; or, The Post-Master (London)
Gentleman's Magazine (London)
London Daily Post and General Advertiser
London Evening Post
London Journal
London Magazine
North Briton (London)
Read's Weekly Journal; or, British Gazetteer (London)
Universal Spectator and Weekly Journal (London)

Printed Primary Sources

An American Pastor. *Two Sermons, Preached to the Congregation of Black Slaves, at the Parish Church of S.P. in the Province of Maryland.* London, 1749.

Atkins, John. *A Voyage to Guinea, Brasil, and the West-Indies.* London, 1735.

Barham, Henry. *Account of Jamaica.* London, 1722.

Bennett, John. *Two Letters and Several Calculations on the Sugar Colonies and Trade.* London, 1738.

Berkeley, George. *A Proposal for the Better Supplying of Churches in Our Foreign Plantations.* London, 1725.

Bermuda, Council. "Minutes of His Majesty's Council, 1741 (King George II)." *Bermuda Historical Quarterly* 25–28, no. 1 (1970–1971): 1–6.

Bluett, Thomas. *Some Memoirs of the Life of Job.* London, 1734.

Bosman, Willem. *A New and Accurate Description of the Coast of Guinea.* London, 1705.

Brickell, John. *The Natural History of North Carolina; with an Account of the Trade, Manners, and Customs of the Christian and Indian Inhabitants.* Dublin, 1737.

Browne, William Hand, et al., eds. *The Archives of Maryland.* 215 vols. to date. Baltimore and Annapolis: Maryland Historical Society, 1883–. This series is ongoing and available online at http://archivesofmaryland.net.

Bryan, Hugh. *Living Christianity Delineated, in the Diaries and Letters of Two Eminently Pious Persons Lately Deceased; viz. Mr. Hugh Bryan, and Mrs. Mary Hutson, Both of South-Carolina.* London, 1760.

Bureau of the Census. *Historical Statistics of the United States, Colonial Times to 1790.* Part 2. Washington, DC: U.S. Government Printing Office, 1976.

Byrd, William. *Histories of the Dividing Line betwixt Virginia and North Carolina.* Edited by William K. Boyd. New York: Dover, 1967.

Byrd, William. *The Secret Diary of William Byrd of Westover, 1709–1712.* Edited by Louis B. Wright and Marion Tinling. Richmond, VA: Dietz Press, 1941.

Calendar of Maryland State Papers: The Black Books. Annapolis, MD: Hall of Records Commission, 1943.

Calendar of State Papers, Colonial Series, America and West Indies, 1574–1739. 41 vols. London: Longman, Green, Longman and Roberts, 1860–1994.

The Case of the Coffee-Men of London and Westminster. London, 1726.

The Case of the Royal African Company of England. London, 1730.

Catterall, Helen Tunnicliff, ed. *Judicial Cases Concerning American Slavery and the Negro*. Washington, DC: Carnegie Institution of Washington, 1926–1933.

Christaller, J. G. *A Dictionary of the Asante and Fante language Called Tshi (Chwee, Twi) with a Grammatical Introduction and Appendices on the Geography of the Gold Coast and Other Subjects*. London: Trübner, 1881.

Colden, Cadwallader. *Letters and Papers of Cadwallader Colden*, vol. 2, *1730–1742*. New York: New-York Historical Society, 1919.

Colden, Cadwallader. *Letters and Papers of Cadwallader Colden*, vol. 3, *Additional Letters and Papers, 1715–1748*. New York: New-York Historical Society, 1937.

Coleman, Kenneth, and Milton Ready, eds. *The Colonial Records of the State of Georgia: Original Papers, Correspondence to the Trustees, James Oglethorpe, and Others, 1732–1735*. Vol. 20. Athens: University of Georgia Press, 1982.

Collections of the Georgia Historical Society. 9 vols. Savannah: Georgia Historical Society, 1840–1859.

A Critical History of the Administration of Sr Robert Walpole. London, 1743.

Dallas, R. C. *The History of the Maroons*. 2 vols. London: A. Strahan, 1803.

Dexter, Samuel. "The Diary of Samuel Dexter." *New England Historical and Genealogical Register* 14, no. 1 (January 1860): 36–37.

Donnan, Elizabeth, ed. *Documents Illustrative of the History of the Slave Trade to America*. 4 vols. Washington, DC: Carnegie Institution of Washington, 1932.

Easterby, J. H. *The Journal of the Commons House of Assembly, 1736–1739*. Columbia: Historical Commission of South Carolina, 1951.

Edwards, Jonathan. *A Faithful Narrative of the Surprising Work of God in the Conversion of Many Hundred Souls in Northampton, and the Neighbouring Towns and Villages of the County of Hampshire, in the Province of the Massachusetts-Bay in New-England*. 3rd edition. Boston, 1738.

Edwards, Jonathan. *Sinners in the Hands of an Angry God*. Boston, 1741.

Equiano, Olaudah. *The Interesting Narrative of the Life of Olaudah Equiano or Gustavus Vassa, the African*. London, 1794.

An Essay Concerning Slavery, and the Danger Jamaica Is Expos'd to from the Too Great Number of Slaves. London, [1747].

Evans, John. *National Ingratitude Lamented: Being the Substance of a Sermon Preach'd at the Old Meeting House in Charles-Town in South-Carolina, September 14th, 1744, A Day of Publick Fast*. Charles-Town, SC, 1745.

Gardern, Alexander. *Six Letters to the Rev. George Whitefield*. Boston, 1740.

A Genuine Narrative of the Intended Conspiracy of the Negroes at Antigua; Extracted from an Authentic Copy of a Report, Made to the Chief Governor of the Carabee Islands by the Commissioners, or Judges Appointed to Try the Conspirators. Dublin, 1737.

Gibson, Edmund. *Two Letters of the Lord Bishop of London*. London, 1729.

Hair, P. E. H., Adam Jones, and Robin Law, eds. *Barbot on Guinea: The Writings of Jean Barbot on West Africa, 1678–1712*. 2 vols. London: Hakluyt Society, 1972.

Hamilton, Alexander. *Gentleman's Progress: The Itinerarium of Dr. Alexander Hamilton*. Edited by Carl Bridenbaugh. Chapel Hill: University of North Carolina Press, 1948.

Hayes, Charles. *The Importance of Effectually Supporting the Royal African Company of England, Impartially Consider'd*. London, 1744.

Hening, William Waller, comp. *The Statutes at Large; Being a Collection of All the Laws of Virginia, from the First Session of the Legislature in the Year 1619*. 13 vols. New York: R. and W. and G. Bartow, 1819–1823. Reprint Charlottesville: University Press of Virginia, 1969.

Hoffer, Peter Charles, and William B. Scott, eds. *Criminal Proceedings in Colonial Virginia*. Athens: University of Georgia Press, 1984.

Horsmanden, Daniel. *History of the Negro Plot, with the Journal of the Proceedings*. New York: Southwick and Pelsue, 1810.

Horsmanden, Daniel. *Journal of the Proceedings in the Detection of the Conspiracy FORMED BY Some White People, in Conjunction with Negro and Other Slaves, FOR Burning the City of NEW-YORK in AMERICA, and Murdering the Inhabitants*. New York, 1744.

Humphreys, David. *An Account of the Endeavours Used by the Society for the Propagation of the Gospel in Foreign Parts, to Instruct the Negroes Slaves in New York*. London, 1730; reprint Philadelphia, 1768.

Ingersoll, Thomas. "'Release Us Out of This Cruell Bondegg': An Appeal from Virginia in 1723." *William and Mary Quarterly*, 3rd series, 51, no 4 (October 1994): 777–782.

Jamaica, Assembly. *Journals of the Assembly of Jamaica*. 14 vols. Jamaica, 1664–1826.

Kyei, T. E. *Our Days Dwindle: Memories of My Childhood Days in Asante*. Edited by Jean Allman. Portsmouth, NH: ABC-CLIO, 2001.

Lemay, J. A. Leo, and P. M. Zall, eds. *Benjamin Franklin's Autobiography: An Authoritative Text, Backgrounds, Criticism*. New York: Norton, 1986.

Leslie, Charles. *A New and Exact Account of Jamaica*. Edinburgh, 1739.

Littleton, Edward. *The Groans of the Plantations; or, A True Account of Their Grievous and Extreme Sufferings by the Heavy Impositions upon Sugar*. London, 1689; reprint London, 1698.

Logan, James. *Memoirs of James Logan; a Distinguished Scholar and Christian Legislator*. Edited by Wilson Armistead. London: Charles Gilpin, 1851.

Long, Edward. *The History of Jamaica: Reflections on its Situation, Settlements, Inhabitants, Climate, Products, Commerce, Laws, and Government*. Vol. 2. London, 1774; reprint Montreal and Kingston: McGill-Queen's University Press, 2002.

Marsden, R. G., ed. *Documents Relating to Law and Custom of the Sea*. 2 vols. Union, NJ: Lawbook Exchange, 1999.

Martyn, Benjamin. *An Impartial Inquiry in the State and Utility of Colony of Georgia*. London, 1741.

McIlwaine, H. R., ed. *Executive Journals of the Council of Colonial Virginia*. 6 vols. Richmond: Virginia State Library, 1925–1966.

McIlwaine, H. R., ed. *Journals of the House of Burgesses, 1619–1776*. 13 vols. Richmond: Colonial Press, 1905–1915.

Minutes of the Provincial Council of Pennsylvania. 16 vols. Harrisburg, PA: J. Severns, 1840.

Minutes of the Provincial Council of Philadelphia, from the Organization to the Termination of the Proprietary Government. Vol. 4. Harrisburg, PA: J. Severns, 1851.

Morgan, Kenneth, ed. *The British Transatlantic Slave Trade*, vol. 2, *The Royal African Company*. London: Pickering and Chatto, 2003.

O'Callaghan, E. B., ed. *Documents Relative to the Colonial History of the State of New York; Procured in Holland, England, and France.* 7 vols. Albany, NY: J. Severns, 1854.

Oglethorpe, James Edward. *Some Account of the Design of the Trustees for Establishing Colonys in America.* Edited by Rodney Baine and Phinizy Spalding. Athens: University of Georgia Press, 1990.

Pannet, Pierre J. *Report on the Execrable Conspiracy Carried Out by the Amina Negroes on the Danish Island of St. Jan in America 1733.* Edited by Aimery P. Caron and Arnold R. Highfield. Christiansted, St. Croix, U.S. Virgin Islands: Antilles Press, 1984.

Penney, Norman, ed. *Correspondence of James Logan and Thomas Story, 1724–1741.* Philadelphia: Friends Historical Association, 1927.

Pennsylvania, Assembly. *The Pennsylvania Archives.* Compiled by Samuel Hazard. 1st series, vol. 1. Philadelphia: J. Severns, 1852.

Poole, Christian. *The Beneficient Bee; or, Traveller's Companion.* London, 1753.

Postlethwayt, Malachy. *The African Trade, the Great Pillar and Support of the British Plantation Trade in North America.* London, 1745.

Postlethwayt, Malachy. *The National and Private Advantages of the African Trade Considered.* London, 1746.

Pringle, Robert. *Letterbook of Robert Pringle*, vol. 1, *April 2, 1737–September 25, 1742.* Edited by Walter B. Edgar. Columbia: University of South Carolina Press, 1972.

"Proclamation of Governor Drummer." *New England Historical and Genealogical Register* 14, no. 1 (January 1860): 36.

Rask, Johannes. *Two Views from Christiansborg Castle: A Description of the Guinea Coast and Its Inhabitants.* Vol. 1. Accra, Ghana: Sub-Saharan Publishers, 2010.

Rawlin, William, comp. *The Laws of Barbados Collected in One Volume by William Rawlin, of the Middle-Temple, London, Esquire, and Now Clerk of the Assembly of the Said Island.* London, 1699.

Robertson, Rev. Robert. *A Detection of the State and Situation of the Present Sugar Planters.* London, 1732.

Robison, Jeannie Floyd Jones, and Henrietta Collins Bartlett. *Genealogical Records: Manuscript Entries of Births, Deaths and Marriages Taken from Family Bibles, 1581–1917.* New York, NY: Colonial Dames of the State of New York, 1917.

Romer, Ludewig. *A Reliable Account of the Coast of Guinea (1760).* Translated by Selena Axelrod Winsnes. Oxford: Oxford University Press, 2000.

Salley, A. S., ed. *Journal of the Commons House of Assembly of South Carolina.* 22 vols. Columbia: Historical Commission of South Carolina, 1907–1949.

Slave Voyages: The Trans-Atlantic Slave Trade Database. 2019. http://www.slavevoyages.org.

Smith, Josiah. *The Burning of Sodom. With Its Moral Causes.* Boston, 1741.

Smith, Mark, ed. *Stono: Documenting and Interpreting a Southern Slave Revolt.* Columbia: University of South Carolina Press, 2005.

Smith, William. *The History of the Province of New York, from the First Discovery of the Year MDCCXXXII.* London, 1757.

Smith, William. *A Natural History of Nevis.* Cambridge, 1745.

Smith, William. *A New Voyage to Guinea.* London, 1744.

Snelgrave, William. *A New Account of Guinea.* London, 1754.

Tarter, Brent, ed. *The Order Book and Related Papers of the Common Hall of the Borough of Norfolk, Virginia, 1736–1798.* Richmond: Virginia State Library, 1979.

Thomson, James. *Works of James Thomson: With His Last Corrections and Improvements.* Vol. 2. N.p., 1763.

Tinling, Marion, ed. *The Correspondence of the Three William Byrds of Westover, Virginia, 1684–1776.* Charlottesville: University Press of Virginia, 1977.

Westergaard, Waldemar. "Account of the Negro Rebellion on St. Croix, Danish West Indies, 1759." *Journal of Negro History* 11, no. 1 (January 1926): 50–61.

Whitefield, George. *A Continuation of the Reverend Whitefield's Journal.* London, 1740.

Whitefield, George. *George Whitefield's Journals: A New Edition Containing Fuller Material Than Any Hitherto Published.* London: Banner of Truth Trust, 1960.

Whitefield, George. *Letters of George Whitefield, for the Period 1734–1742.* Edinburgh: Banner of Truth Trust, 1976.

Whitefield, George. *Letter to the Inhabitants of Maryland, Virginia, and North and South Carolina.* Philadelphia, 1740.

Wigglesworth, Samuel. *An Essay for Reviving Religion.* Boston, [1733].

Zabin, Serena R. *The New York Conspiracy Trials of 1741: Daniel Horsmanden's Journal of the Proceedings with Related Documents.* Boston: Bedford/St. Martin's, 2004.

Secondary Sources

Aptheker, Herbert. *American Negro Slave Revolts.* New York: International, 1987.

Aptheker, Herbert. *A Documentary History of the Negro People in the United States.* New York: Citadel Press, 1951.

Armor, William C. *Lives of the Governors of Pennsylvania, with the Incidental History of the State, From 1609 to 1872.* Philadelphia: James K. Simon, 1872.

Beasley, Nicholas M. "Ritual Time in British Plantation Colonies, 1650–1780." *Church History* 76, no. 3 (September 2007): 541–568.

Beckles, Hilary. *Black Rebellion in Barbados: The Struggle against Slavery, 1627–1838.* Bridgetown, Barbados: Carib Research, 1987.

Beckles, Hilary. *A History of Barbados: From Amerindian Settlement to Caribbean Single Market.* Cambridge: Cambridge University Press, 2006.

Beckles, Hilary. "A 'Rioutous and Unruly Lot': Irish Indentured Servants and Freemen in the English West Indies, 1644–1713." *William and Mary Quarterly*, 3rd series, 47, no. 4 (October 1990): 503–522.

Berlin, Ira. *Many Thousands Gone: The First Two Centuries of Slavery in North America.* Cambridge, MA: Belknap Press of Harvard University Press, 1998.

Berlin, Ira. *Slavery and Freedom in the Era of the American Revolution.* Charlottesville: University Press of Virginia, 1983.

Berlin, Ira. "Time, Space, and the Evolution of Afro-American Society on British Mainland North America." *American Historical Review* 85, no. 1 (February 1980): 44–78.

Black, Jeremy, ed. *Britain in the Age of Walpole.* London: Macmillan, 1984.

Blackburn, Robin. "The Old World Background to European Colonial Slavery." *William and Mary Quarterly,* 3rd series, 54, no. 1 (January 1997): 65–102.

Blake, John B. *Public Health in the Town of Boston, 1630–1822.* Cambridge, MA: Harvard University Press, 1959.

Bloch, Marc. *The Historian's Craft.* New York: Knopf, 1953.

Bolster, W. Jeffrey. *Black Jacks: African-American Sailors in the Age of Sail.* Cambridge, MA: Harvard University Press, 1997.

Bonomi, Patricia. *Under the Cope of Heaven: Religion, Society, and Politics in Colonial America.* Updated edition. 1986; New York: Oxford University Press, 2003.

Botein, Stephen. "'Mere Mechanics' and an Open Press." In *The Press and the American Revolution,* edited by Bernard Bailyn and John B. Hench, 11–58. Worcester, MA: American Antiquarian Society, 1980.

Brown, Vincent. *The Reaper's Garden: Death and Power in the World of Atlantic Slavery.* Cambridge, MA: Harvard University Press, 2008.

Brown, Vincent. *Tacky's Revolt: The Story of an Atlantic Slave War.* Cambridge, MA: Harvard University Press, 2020.

Burnard, Trevor. "'The Countrie Continues Sicklie': White Mortality in Jamaica, 1655–1780." *Social History of Medicine* 12 (1999): 45–72.

Burnard, Trevor, and Emma Hart. "Kingston, Jamaica, and Charleston, South Carolina: A New Look at Comparative Urbanization in Plantation Colonial British America." *Journal of Urban History* 39 (2013): 214–234.

Butler, Jon. *Awash in a Sea of Faith: Christianizing the American People.* Cambridge, MA: Harvard University Press, 1990.

Byers, Edward. *The Nation of Nantucket: Society and Politics in an Early American Commercial Center, 1660–1820.* Boston: Northeastern University Press, 1987.

Campbell, Mavis. *The Maroons of Jamaica, 1655–1796: A History of Resistance, Collaboration, and Betrayal.* South Hadley, MA: Bergin and Garvey, 1988.

Carey, Bev. *The Maroon Story: The Authentic and Original History of the Maroons in the History of Jamaica, 1490–1880.* Kingston, Jamaica: Agouti Press, 1997.

Celeski, David S. *The Waterman's Song: Slavery and Freedom in Maritime North Carolina.* Chapel Hill: University of North Carolina Press, 2001.

Christaller, J. G. *Dictionary of the Asante and Fante Language Called Tshi (Twi).* 2nd edition. Basel, Switzerland: Basel Evangelical Missionary Society, 1933.

Clark, Charles E. *The Public Prints: The Newspaper in Anglo-American Culture, 1665–1740.* New York: Oxford University Press, 1994.

Clifton, Robin. "Fear of Popery." In *The Origins of the English Civil War,* edited by Conrad Russell, 144–167. London: Red Globe Press, 1973.

Clifton, Robin. "The Popular Fear of Catholics during the English Revolution." *Past and Present*, no. 52 (August 1971): 23–55.

Clowse, Converse D. *Measuring Charleston's Overseas Commerce, 1717–1767, Statistics from the Ports Naval Lists*. Washington, DC: University Press of America, 1981.

Coclanis, Peter A. "Death in Early Charleston: An Estimate of the Crude Death Rate for the White Population of Charleston, 1722–1732." *South Carolina Historical Magazine* 85, no. 4 (October 1984): 280–291.

Copeland, David A. *Colonial American Newspapers: Character and Content*. Newark: University of Delaware Press, 1997.

Cowan, Brian. "Mr. Spectator and the Coffeehouse Public Sphere." *Eighteenth-Century Studies* 37, no. 3 (Spring 2004): 345–366.

Craton, Michael, and Gail Saunders. *Islanders in the Stream: A History of the Bahamian People*, vol. 1, *From Aboriginal Times to the End of Slavery*. Athens: University of Georgia Press, 1992.

Curtin, Philip D. *The Atlantic Slave Trade: A Census*. Madison: University of Wisconsin Press, 1969.

Curtin, Philip D. *Economic Change in Pre-Colonial Africa*. Madison: University of Wisconsin Press, 1975.

Daaku, Kwame. *Trade and Politics on the Gold Coast, 1600–1720*. Oxford: Clarendon Press, 1970.

Davis, David Brion. "Constructing Race: A Reflection." *William and Mary Quarterly*, 3rd series, 54, no. 1 (January 1997): 7–18.

Davis, David Brian. *The Problem of Slavery in the Age of Revolution, 1770–1823*. Ithaca, NY: Cornell University Press, 1975.

Davis, David Brion. *The Problem of Slavery in Western Culture*. Ithaca, NY: Cornell University Press, 1966.

Davis, Thomas J. "Conspiracy and Credibility: Look Who's Talking, about What: Law Talk and Loose Talk." *William and Mary Quarterly*, 3rd series, 59, no. 1 (January 2002): 167–174.

Davis, Thomas J. *A Rumor of Revolt: The Great Negro Plot in Colonial New York*. New York: Free Press, 1985.

Desrochers, Robert E., Jr. "Slave-for-Sale Advertisements and Slavery in Massachusetts, 1704–1781." *William and Mary Quarterly*, 3rd series, 59, no. 3 (July 2002): 623–664.

Dubcovsky, Alejandra. *Informed Power: Communication in the Early American South*. Cambridge, MA: Harvard University Press, 2016.

Dubois, Laurent. *Avengers of the New World: The Story of the Haitian Revolution*. Cambridge, MA: Belknap Press of Harvard University Press, 2004.

DuPleiss, Robert S. *The Material Atlantic: Clothing, Commerce, and Colonization in the Atlantic World, 1650–1800*. Cambridge: Cambridge University Press, 2016.

Dunn, Richard. *Sugar and Slaves: The Rise of the Planter Class in the English West Indies, 1624–1713*. Chapel Hill: University of North Carolina Press, 1972.

Eastman, Frank M. *Courts and Lawyers of Pennsylvania: A History, 1623–1923*. Vol. 1. New York: American Historical Society, 1922.

Eltis, David. *The Rise of African Slavery in the Americas*. Cambridge: Cambridge University Press, 2000.

Eltis, David, and David Richardson. "Productivity in the Transatlantic Slave Trade." *Explorations in Economic History* 32, no. 4 (October 1995): 465–484.

Fitts, Robert K. *Inventing New England's Slave Paradise: Master/Slave Relations in Eighteenth-Century Narragansett, Rhode Island*. New York: Garland, 1998.

Fogleman, Aaron S. "From Slaves, Convicts, and Servants to Free Passengers: The Transformation of Immigration in the Era of the American Revolution." *Journal of American History* 85, no. 1 (June 1998): 43–76.

Foy, Charles R. "Seeking Freedom in the Atlantic World, 1713–1783." *Early American Studies: An Interdisciplinary Journal* 4, no. 1 (2006): 46–77.

Gallay, Alan. "The Origins of Slaveholders' Paternalism, George Whitefield, the Bryan Family, and the Great Awakening in the South." *Journal of Southern History* 53 (August 1987): 369–394.

Gaspar, David Barry. "The Antiguan Slave Conspiracy of 1736: A Case Study of the Origins of Collective Resistance." *William and Mary Quarterly*, 3rd series, 35, no. 2 (April 1978): 308–323.

Gaspar, David Barry. *Bondmen and Rebels: A Study of Master-Slave Relations in Antigua, with Implications for Colonial British America*. Baltimore: Johns Hopkins University Press, 1985.

Gaspar, David Barry. "A Dangerous Spirit of Liberty: Slave Rebellion in the West Indies during the 1730s." *Cimarrons* 1 (1981): 79–91.

Gaspar, David Barry. "With a Rod of Iron: Barbados Slave Laws as a Model for Jamaica, South Carolina, and Antigua, 1661–1697." In *Crossing Boundaries: A Comparative History of Black People in the Diaspora*, edited by Darlene Clark Hine and Bradley J. Nicholson, 335–346. Bloomington: Indiana University Press, 1999.

Geggus, David. "Slavery, War, and Revolution in the Greater Caribbean, 1789–1815." In *A Turbulent Time: The French Revolution and the Greater Caribbean*, edited by David Gaspar and David Geggus, 1–50. Bloomington: University of Indiana Press, 1997.

Genovese, Eugene. *From Rebellion to Revolution: Afro-American Slave Revolts in the Making of the Modern World*. Baton Rouge: Louisiana State University Press, 1979.

Genovese, Eugene. *Roll, Jordan, Roll: The World the Slaves Made*. New York: Pantheon, 1974.

Gomez, Michael. *Exchanging Our Country Marks: The Transformation of African Identities in the Colonial and Antebellum South*. Chapel Hill: University of North Carolina Press, 1998.

Greene, Jack P. "Changing Identity in the British Caribbean: Barbados as a Case Study." In *Colonial Identity in the Atlantic World*, edited by John Elliot, 213–266. Princeton, NJ: Princeton University Press, 1987.

Greene, Lorenzo B. *The Negro in Colonial New England*. New York: Atheneum, 1968.

Guitar, Lynne. "Boiling It Down: Slavery on the First Commercial Sugarcane Ingenios in the Americas (Hispaniola, 1530–45)." In *Slaves, Subjects and Subversives: Black in Colonial Latin America*, edited by Jane G. Landers and Barry Robinson, 39–72. Albuquerque: University of New Mexico Press, 2006.

Handler, Jerome S. "Slave Revolts and Conspiracies in Seventeenth-Century Barbados." *New West Indian Guide / Nieuwe West-Indische Gids* 56, nos. 1–2 (1982): 5–42.

Handler, Jerome S. *The Unappropriated People: Freedmen in the Slave Society of Barbados*. Baltimore: Johns Hopkins University Press, 1974.

Harms, Robert. *The Diligent: A Voyage through the Worlds of the Slave Trade*. New York: Basic Books, 2002.

Harris, Michael. *London Newspapers in the Age of Walpole: A Study of the Origins of the Modern English Press*. Cranbury, NJ: Associated University Press, 1987.

Hauser, Mark. *An Archaeology of Black Markets: Local Ceramics and Economies in Eighteenth-Century America*. Gainesville: University Press of Florida, 2008.

Haydon, Colin. *Anti-Catholicism in Eighteenth-Century England*. Manchester, UK: Manchester University Press, 1993.

Hodges, Graham Russell. *Root and Branch: African Americans in New York and East Jersey, 1613–1863*. Chapel Hill: University of North Carolina Press, 1999.

Hoffer, Peter Charles. *The Great New York Conspiracy of 1741: Slavery, Crime, and Colonial Law*. Lawrence: University Press of Kansas, 2003.

Hollowak, Thomas, ed. *Maryland Genealogies: A Consolidation of Articles from the Maryland Historical Magazine*. 2 vols. Baltimore: Genealogical Publishing, 1980.

Holton, Woody. *Forced Founders: Indians, Debtors, Slaves, and the Making of the American Revolution in Virginia*. Chapel Hill: University of North Carolina, 1999.

Howe, George. *History of the Presbyterian Church in South Carolina*. Columbia, SC: Duffie and Chapman, 1870.

Jackson, Harvey H. "Hugh Bryan and the Evangelical Movement in Colonial South Carolina." *William and Mary Quarterly*, 3rd series, 43, no. 4 (October 1986): 594–614.

Jackson, Harvey H., and Phinizy Spalding, eds. *Forty Years of Diversity: Essays on Colonial Georgia*. Athens: University of Georgia Press, 1984.

Jarvis, Michael T. "Maritime Masters and Seafaring Slaves in Bermuda, 1680–1783." *William and Mary Quarterly*, 3rd series, 59, no. 3 (July 2002): 585–622.

Johnson, Marion. "Ekyem, the State Shield," *Akan-Asante Studies* 3 (1979): 6–10.

Johnson, Michael P. "Denmark Vesey and His Co-Conspirators." *William and Mary Quarterly*, 3rd series, 58, no. 4 (October 2001): 915–976.

Jordan, Winthrop. *White over Black: American Attitudes toward the Negro, 1550–1812*. Chapel Hill: University of North Carolina Press, 1968.

Kea, Ray A. *Settlements, Trade, and Polities in the Seventeenth-Century Gold Coast*. Baltimore: Johns Hopkins University Press, 1982.

Kea, Ray A. "'When I Die, I Shall Return to My Own Land': An 'Amina' Slave Rebellion in the Danish West Indies, 1733–34." In *The Cloth of Many Colored Silks:*

Papers on History and Society, Ghanaian and Islamic in Honor of Ivor Wilks, edited by John Hunwick and Nancy Lawler, 159–193. Evanston, IL: Northwestern University Press, 1996.

Kenney, William Howland, III. "Alexander Garden and George Whitefield: The Significance of Revivalism in South Carolina 1738–1741." *South Carolina Historical Magazine* 71, no. 1 (January 1970): 1–16.

Kidd, Thomas S. *The Great Awakening: The Roots of Evangelical Christianity in Early America*. New Haven, CT: Yale University Press, 2007.

Kidd, Thomas S. *The Protestant Interest: New England after Puritanism*. New Haven, CT: Yale University Press, 2004.

Koeppel, Gerard T. *Water for Gotham: A History*. Princeton, NJ: Princeton University Press, 2000.

Konadu, Kwasi. *The Akan Diaspora in the Americas*. New York: Oxford University Press, 2010.

Konadu, Kwasi. *Our Own Way in This Part of the World: Biography of an African Community, Culture, and Nation*. Durham, NC: Duke University Press, 2019.

Kulikoff, Allan. "The Origins of Afro-American Society in Tidewater Maryland and Virginia, 1700 to 1790." *William and Mary Quarterly*, 3rd series, 35, no. 2 (April 1978): 226–259.

Kulikoff, Allan. "A 'Prolifick People': Black Population Growth in the Chesapeake Colonies, 1700–1790." *Southern Studies* 16, no. 4 (1997): 391–428.

Kulikoff, Allan. *Tobacco and Slaves: The Development of Southern Cultures in the Chesapeake, 1680–1800*. Chapel Hill: University of North Carolina Press, 1986.

Lambert, Frank. *Inventing the "Great Awakening."* Princeton, NJ: Princeton University Press, 1999.

Landers, Jane. *Black Society in Spanish Florida*. Urbana: University of Illinois Press, 1999.

Landers, Jane. "Gracia Real de Santa Teresa de Mose: A Free Black Town in Spanish Colonial Florida," *American Historical Review* 95, no. 1 (February 1990): 9–30.

Law, Robin. *The Slave Coast of West Africa, 1550–1750: The Impact of the Atlantic Slave Trade on an African Society*. New York: Oxford University Press, 1991.

Lepore, Jill. *New York Burning: Liberty, Slavery, and Conspiracy in Eighteenth Century Manhattan*. New York: Knopf, 2005.

Linebaugh, Peter, and Marcus Rediker. *The Many-Headed Hydra: Sailors, Slaves, Commoners, and the Hidden History of the Revolutionary Atlantic*. Boston: Beacon Press, 2000.

Lovejoy, Paul E. *Transformations in Slavery: A History of Slavery in Africa*. Cambridge: Cambridge University Press, 1983.

Maxwell, Clarence V. H. "'The Horrid Villainy': Sarah Bassett and the Poisoning Conspiracies in Bermuda, 1727–1730." *Slavery and Abolition* 21, no. 3 (December 2000): 48–74.

McCain, James Ross. *Georgia as a Proprietary Province: The Execution of a Trust*. Boston: Richard P. Badger, 1917.

McCaskie, T. C. *State and Society in Pre-Colonial Asante*. Cambridge: Cambridge University Press, 1995.

McConville, Brendan. *The King's Three Faces: The Rise and Fall of Royal America, 1688–1776*. Chapel Hill: University of North Carolina Press, 2006.

McConville, Brendan. "Of Slavery and Sources: *New York Burning: Liberty, Slavery, and Conspiracy in Eighteenth-Century Manhattan* by Jill Lepore." *Reviews in American History* 34, no. 3 (September 2006): 281–290.

McCusker, John J., and Russell R. Menard. *The Economy of British America*. 1985; reprint Chapel Hill: University of North Carolina Press, 1991.

Menard, Russell R. "From Servants to Slaves: The Transformation of the Chesapeake Labor System." In *Migrants, Servants, and Slaves: Unfree Labor in Colonial British America*, edited by Russell R. Menard, 366–382. Burlington, VT: Ashgate, 2001.

Miller, Joseph C. "Central Africa during the Era of the Slave Trade, c1490s–1850." In *Central Africans and Cultural Transformations in the American Diaspora*, edited by Linda M. Heywood, 21–70. Cambridge: Cambridge University Press, 2003.

Miller, Joseph C. *Way of Death: Merchant Capitalism and the Angolan Slave Trade, 1730–1830*. Madison: University of Wisconsin Press, 1988.

Miller, Perry. *The New England Mind: From Colony to Province*. Cambridge, MA: Harvard University Press, 1953.

Morgan, Edmund S. "Slavery and Freedom: The American Paradox." *Journal of American History* 59, no. 1 (June 1972): 5–29.

Morgan, Kenneth. "Slave Sales in Colonial Charleston." *English Historical Review* 113, no. 453 (September 1998): 905–927.

Morgan, Kenneth. "Trelawny, Edward (bap. 1699, d. 1754)." In *Oxford Dictionary of National Biography*, https://www.oxforddnb.com/.

Morgan, Philip D. "African Americans." In *A Companion to Colonial America*, edited by Daniel Vickers, 138–171. Malden, MA: Blackwell, 2006.

Morgan, Philip D. "Black Life in Eighteenth Century Charleston." *Perspective in American History* 1 (1984): 188–232.

Morgan, Philip D. "Conspiracy Scares." *William and Mary Quarterly*, 3rd series, 59, no. 1 (January 2002): 159–166.

Morgan, Philip D. "The Cultural Implications of the Atlantic Slave Trade: African Regional Origins, American Destinations, and New World Developments." *Slavery and Abolition* 18, no. 1 (1997): 122–145.

Morgan, Philip D. "Maritime Slavery." *Slavery and Abolition* 31, no. 3 (2010): 311–326.

Morgan, Philip D. *Slave Counterpoint: Black Culture in the Eighteenth-Century Chesapeake and Lowcountry*. Chapel Hill: University of North Carolina Press, 1998.

Morgan, Philip D., and George D. Terry, "Slavery in Microcosm: A Conspiracy Scare in Colonial South Carolina." *Southern Studies* 21 (1982): 121–45.

Mulcahy, Matthew. "The 'Great Fire' of 1740 and the Politics of Disaster Relief in Colonial Charleston." *South Carolina Historical Magazine* 99, no. 2 (April 1998): 135–157.

Nash, Gary B. "The New York Census of 1737: A Critical Note on the Integration of Statistical and Literary Sources." *William and Mary Quarterly*, 3rd series, 36, no. 3 (July 1979): 428–435.

Nash, Gary B., et al. "Notes and Documents: The Population of Eighteenth Century Philadelphia." *Pennsylvania Magazine of History and Biography* 99, no. 3 (July 1975): 362–375.

Nicholson, Bradley. "Legal Borrowing and the Origins of Slave Law in the British Colonies." *American Journal of Legal History* 38, no. 1 (January 1994): 38–54.

Norris, Walter B. *Annapolis: Its Colonial and Naval Story*. New York: Thomas Crowell, 1925.

Oberholtzer, Ellis Paxson. *Philadelphia: A History of the City and Its People: A Record of 225 Years*. Vol. 1. Philadelphia: S. J. Clarke, 1912.

Olson, Alison. "The Zenger Case Revisited: Satire, Sedition and Political Debate in Eighteenth Century New York." *Early American Literature* 35, no. 3 (2000): 223–245.

O'Mally, Gregory. "Beyond the Middle Passage: Slave Migration from the Caribbean to North America, 1619–1807." *William and Mary Quarterly*, 3rd series, 66, no. 1 (January 2009): 125–172.

Overton, J. H. *The NonJurors: Their Lives, Principles, and Writings*. New York: Smith Elder, 1903.

Paquette, Robert L., and Stanley L. Engerman, eds. *The Lesser Antilles in the Age of European Expansion*. Gainesville: University Press of Florida, 1996.

Parent, Anthony S., Jr. *Foul Means: The Formation of a Slave Society in Virginia, 1660–1740*. Chapel Hill: University of North Carolina Press, 2003.

Pares, Richard. *War and Trade in the West Indies, 1739–1748*. London: F. Cass, 1963.

Parker, John. *In My Time of Dying: A History of Death and the Dead in West Africa*. Princeton, NJ: Princeton University Press, 2021.

Parker, John. *Making the Town: Ga State and Society in Early Colonial Accra*. Oxford: Oxford University Press, 2000.

Patterson, Orlando. "Slavery and Slave Revolts: A Sociohistorical Analysis of the First Maroon War, 1665–1740." In *Maroon Societies: Rebel Slave Communities in the Americas*, edited by Richard Price, 246–297. Baltimore: Johns Hopkins University Press, 1979.

Patterson, Orlando. *Slavery and Social Death*. Cambridge, MA: Harvard University Press, 1982.

Petersen, James, David Watters, and Desmond Nicholson. "Continuity and Syncretism in Afro-Caribbean Ceramics from the Northern Lesser Antilles." In *African Sites Archaeology in the Caribbean*, edited by Jay B. Haviser, 157–220. Princeton, NJ: Markus Wiener, 1999.

Philbrick, Nathaniel. *Abram's Eyes: The Native American Legacy of Nantucket Island*. Nantucket, MA: Mill Hill Press, 1998.

Plaag, Eric W. "'Greater Guilt Than Theirs': New York's 1741 Slave Conspiracy in a Climate of Fear and Anxiety." *New York Historical Quarterly* 84 (2003): 275–299.

Price, Jacob. "Economic Function and the Growth of American Port Towns in the Eighteenth Century." *Perspective in American History* 8 (1974): 123–186.

Ramsey, William L. "'Something Cloudy in Their Looks': The Origins of the Yamasee War Reconsidered." *Journal of American History* 90, no. 1 (June 2003): 44–75.

Rawley, James A., and Stephen D. Behrendt. *The Transatlantic Slave Trade: A History*. Revised edition. 1981; Lincoln: University of Nebraska Press, 2005.

Richardson, David. "The British Empire and the Atlantic Slave Trade." In *The Oxford History of the British Empire*, vol. 2, *The Eighteenth Century*, edited by P. J. Marshall, 440–464. Oxford: Oxford University Press, 1998.

Roosevelt, Theodore. *New York*. New York, 1903.

Rucker, Walter C. *Gold Coast Diasporas: Identity, Culture, and Power*. Bloomington: Indiana University Press, 2015.

Schlenther, Boyd Stanley. "Religious Faith and Commercial Empire." In *The Oxford History of the British Empire*, vol. 2, *The Eighteenth Century*, edited by P. J Marshall, 128–150. Oxford: Oxford University Press, 1998.

Schmidt, Leigh Eric. "'The Grand Prophet,' Hugh Bryan: Early Evangelicalism's Challenge to the Establishment and Slavery in the Colonial South." *South Carolina Historical Magazine* 87, no. 4 (October 1986): 238–250.

Schwarz, Philip J. *Twice Condemned: Slaves and the Criminal Laws of Virginia, 1705–1865*. Baton Rouge: Louisiana State University Press, 1988.

Scott, James C. *Domination and the Arts of Resistance: Hidden Transcripts*. New Haven, CT: Yale University Press, 1990.

Scott, Kenneth. "The Slave Insurrection in New York in 1712." *New-York Historical Society Quarterly* 415, no. 1 (1961): 43–74.

Scott, Kenneth. "Sufferers in the Charleston Fire of 1740." *South Carolina Historical Magazine* 64, no. 4 (October 1963): 203–211.

Sensbach, Jon. *Rebecca's Revival: Creating Black Christianity in the Atlantic World*. Cambridge, MA: Harvard University Press, 2005.

Sheridan, Richard B. "Caribbean Plantation Society, 1689–1748." In *The Oxford History of the British Empire*, vol. 1, *The Eighteenth Century*, edited by P. J. Marshall, 366–382. New York: Oxford University Press, 1998.

Sheridan, Richard B. *Sugar and Slavery: An Economic History of the British West Indies, 1623–1775*. Kingston, Jamaica: Canoe Press, 1994.

Shumway, Rebecca. *The Fante and the Transatlantic Slave Trade*. Rochester, NY: University of Rochester Press, 2011.

Smallwood, Stephanie E. *Saltwater Slavery: A Middle Passage from Africa to American Diaspora*. Cambridge, MA: Harvard University Press, 2007.

Smith, Billy G., and Richard Wojtowicz. *Blacks Who Stole Themselves: Advertisements for Runaways in the Pennsylvania Gazette, 1728–1790*. Philadelphia: University of Pennsylvania Press, 1989.

Smith, Jeffery A. "Impartiality and Revolutionary Ideology: Editorial Policies of the *South-Carolina Gazette*, 1732–1745." *Journal of Southern History* 49, no. 4. (November 1983): 511–526.

Smith, Lisa. *The First Great Awakening in Colonial American Newspapers: A Shifting Story*. Lanham, MD: Lexington, 2012.

Steele, Ian K. *The English Atlantic, 1675–1740: An Exploration of Communication and Community*. New York: Oxford University Press, 1986.

Taylor, Alan. *American Colonies: The Settling of North America*. New York: Penguin, 2001.

Thomas, Hugh. *The Slave Trade: The Story of the Atlantic Slave Trade, 1440–1870.* New York: Simon and Schuster, 1997.

Thomas, Keith. *Religion and the Decline of Magic.* New York: Scribner, 1971.

Thornton, John K. *Africa and Africans in the Making of the Atlantic World, 1400–1680.* Cambridge: Cambridge University Press, 1992.

Thornton, John K. "The African Dimensions of the Stono Rebellion." *American Historical Review* 96, no. 4 (October 1991): 1101–1113.

Thornton, John K. "The Coromantees: An African Cultural Group in Colonial North America and the Caribbean." *Journal of Caribbean History* 32, nos. 1–2 (1998): 161–178.

Thornton, John K. *A Cultural History of the Atlantic World, 1250-1820.* Cambridge: Cambridge University Press, 2012.

Thornton, John K. "The Demographic Effect of the Slave Trade on Western Africa, 1500–1850." In *African Historical Demography,* vol. 2, edited by C. Fyfe and D. McMaster, 691–720. Edinburgh: Centre of African Studies, 1981.

Thornton, John K. "I Am the Subject of the King of Congo." *Journal of World History* 4 (1993): 181–214.

Thornton, John K. "War, the State, and Religious Norms in 'Coromantee' Thought: The Ideology of an African Nation." In *Possible Pasts: Becoming Colonial in Early America,* edited by Robert Blair St. George, 181–200. Ithaca, NY: Cornell University Press, 2000.

Tindol, Robert. "Getting the Pox Off All Their Houses: Cotton Mather and the Rhetoric of Puritan Science." *Early American Literature* 46, no. 1 (2011): 2–8.

Warner-Lewis, Maureen. *Central Africa in the Caribbean: Transcending Time, Transforming Cultures.* Barbados: University of the West Indies Press, 2003.

Wax, Darold D. "Negro Import Duties in Colonial Virginia: A Study of British Commercial Policy and Local Public Policy." *Virginia Magazine of History and Biography* 79, no. 1, part 1 (January 1971): 29–44.

Wax, Darold D. "Negro Imports into Pennsylvania, 1720–1766." *Pennsylvania History* 32 (1965): 254–287.

Wax, Darold D. "'New Negroes Are Always in Demand': The Slave Trade in Eighteenth-Century Georgia." *Georgia Historical Quarterly* 68, no. 2 (Summer 1984): 193–220.

Wax, Darold D. "Preferences for Slaves in Colonial America." *Journal of Negro History* 58, no. 4 (October 1973): 371–401.

Weir, Robert M. *Colonial South Carolina: A History.* 1983; reprint Columbia: University of South Carolina Press, 1997.

Wells, Robert V. *The Population of the British Colonies in America before 1776.* Princeton, NJ: Princeton University Press, 1975.

Westergaard, Waldemar. *The Danish West Indies under Company Rule (1671–1754).* New York: Macmillan, 1917.

Whitford, David M. *The Curse of Ham in the Early Modern Era: The Bible and the Justifications for Slavery.* Burlington, VT: Ashgate, 2009.

Williams, Eric. *Capitalism and Slavery.* Chapel Hill: University of North Carolina Press, 1944.

Winiarski, Douglas L. "'Pale Blewish Lights' and a Dead Man's Groan: Tales of the Supernatural from Eighteenth-Century Plymouth, Massachusetts." *William and Mary Quarterly*, 3rd series, 55, no. 4 (October 1998): 3–46.

Wood, Betty. *Slavery in Colonial Georgia, 1730–1775*. Athens: University of Georgia Press, 1984.

Wood, Peter H. *Black Majority: Negroes in Colonial South Carolina from 1670 through the Stono Rebellion*. New York: Knopf, 1974.

Wood, Peter H. "'I Did the Best I Could for My Day': The Study of Early Black History during the Second Reconstruction, 1960 to 1976." *William and Mary Quarterly*, 3rd series, 35, no. 2 (April 1978): 185–225.

Wright, Louis B. "William Byrd I and the Slave Trade." *Huntington Library Quarterly* 8, no. 4 (August 1945): 379–387.

Zacek, Natalie. *Settler Society in the English Leeward Islands, 1670–1776*. New York: Cambridge University Press, 2010.

Zuckerman, Michael. "William Byrd's Family." *Perspectives in American History* 12 (1979): 253–311.

Dissertations and Theses

Chouin, Gerard. "Forests of Power and Memory: An Archaeology of Sacred Groves in the Eguafo Polity (c. 500–1900 AD)." Ph.D. diss., Syracuse University, 2009.

Feight, Andrew Lee. "The Good and the Just: Slavery and the Development of Evangelical Protestantism in the American South, 1700–1830." Ph.D. diss., University of Kentucky, 2001.

Foy, Charles R. "Ports of Slavery, Ports of Freedom: How Slaves Used Northern Seaports' Maritime Industry to Escape and Create Trans-Atlantic Identities, 1713–1783." Ph.D. diss., Rutgers University, 2008.

McCusker, John J. "The Rum Trade and the Balance of Payments of the Thirteen Continental Colonies, 1650–1775." Ph.D. diss., University of Pittsburgh, 1970.

Scott, Julius Sherard, III. "The Common Wind: Currents of Afro-American Communication in the Era of the Haitian Revolution." Ph.D. diss., Duke University, 1986.

Sharples, Jason. "The Flames of Insurrection: Fearing Slave Conspiracy in Early America, 1670–1780." Ph.D. diss., Princeton University, 2010.

Spiers, Sam. "The Eguafo Kingdom: Investigating Complexity in Southern Ghana." Ph.D. diss., Syracuse University, 2003.

Wilks, Ivor. "Akwamu, 1650–1750: A Study of the Rise and Fall of a West African Empire." M.A. thesis, University of Wales, 1958.

INDEX

Note: page numbers followed by *f* and *t* refer to figures and tables respectively. Those followed by *m* refer to maps.